Adobe® Photoshop® CC

Digital Classroom®

Adobe® Photoshop® CC Digital Classroom®

Jennifer Smith and the AGI Creative Team

Adobe® Photoshop® CC Digital Classroom®

Published by
John Wiley & Sons, Inc.
10475 Crosspoint Blvd.
Indianapolis, IN 46256

Copyright © 2013 by John Wiley & Sons, Inc., Indianapolis, Indiana
Published simultaneously in Canada
ISBN: 978-1-118-63956-6
Manufactured in the United States of America
10 9 8 7 6 5 4 3 2 1

For general information on our other products and services or to obtain technical support, please contact our Customer Care Department within the U.S. at (877) 762-2974, outside the U.S. at (317) 572-3993 or fax (317) 572-4002.

Wiley publishes in a variety of print and electronic formats and by print-on-demand. Some material included with standard print versions of this book may not be included in e-books or in print-on-demand. If this book refers to media such as a CD or DVD that is not included in the version you purchased, you may download this material after registering your book at www.digitalclassroombooks.com/CS6/Photoshop. For more information about Wiley products, visit www.wiley.com.

Please report any errors by sending a message to errata@agitraining.com

Library of Congress Control Number: 2013936332

Credits

President, American Graphics Institute and Digital Classroom Series Publisher
Christopher Smith

Executive Editor
Jody Lefevere

Technical Editors
Haziel Olivera, Lauren Mickol

Editor
Karla E. Melendez

Editorial Director
Robyn Siesky

Business Manager
Amy Knies

Senior Marketing Manager
Sandy Smith

Vice President and Executive Group Publisher
Richard Swadley

Vice President and Executive Publisher
Barry Pruett

Senior Project Coordinator
Katherine Crocker

Project Manager
Cheri White

Graphics and Production Specialist
Jason Miranda, Spoke & Wheel

Media Development Project Supervisor
Chris Leavey

Proofreading
Karla E. Melendez

Indexing
Michael Ferreira

Stock Photography
iStockPhoto.com

About the Authors

Jennifer Smith is a designer, educator, and author. She has authored more than 20 books on digital design and creative software tools. She provides consulting and training services across a wide range of industries, including working with software developers, magazine publishers, catalog and online retailers, as well as some of the biggest names in fashion, apparel, and footwear design. When not writing and consulting you'll often find her delivering professional development workshops for colleges and universities.

Jennifer also works extensively in the field of web usability and user experience design. Jennifer works alongside application developers and web developers to create engaging and authentic experiences for users on mobile devices, tablets, and traditional computers. She has twice been named a Most Valuable Professional by Microsoft for her work in user experience (UX), user interface (UI) design fields, and her leadership in educating users on how to integrate design and development skills.

Jennifer Smith's books on Photoshop, Illustrator, and the Creative Suite tools include the *Photoshop Digital Classroom*, the *Illustrator Digital Classroom*, and the *Adobe Creative Suite for Dummies*, all published by Wiley. She has also authored *Wireframing and Prototyping with Expression Blend & Sketchflow*.

Jennifer is the cofounder of the American Graphics Institute (AGI). You can find her blog and contact her at *JenniferSmith.com* and follow her on Twitter @jsmithers.

The **AGI Creative Team** is composed of Adobe Certified Experts and Instructors from AGI. The AGI Creative Team has authored more than 25 Digital Classroom books and has created many of Adobe's official training guides. The AGI Creative Team works with many of the world's most prominent companies, helping them use creative software to communicate more effectively and creatively. They work with design, creative, and marketing teams around the world, delivering private customized training programs, while also teaching regularly scheduled classes at AGI's locations. The AGI Creative Team is available for professional development sessions at companies, schools, and universities. Get more information at *agitraining.com*.

Acknowledgments

Thanks to our many friends at Adobe Systems, Inc. who made this book possible and assisted with questions and feedback during the writing process. To the many clients of AGI who have helped us better understand how they use Photoshop and provided us with many of the tips and suggestions found in this book. A special thanks to the instructional team at AGI for their input and assistance in the review process and for making this book such a team effort.

Thanks iStockPhoto (*iStockPhoto.com*) for their permission to use exclusive photographers for images throughout the *Adobe Photoshop CC Digital Classroom* book.

Contents

Starting up

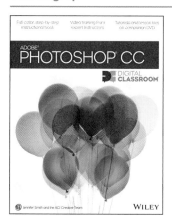

Lesson 1: Navigating Photoshop CC: Workspace, Tools, and Panels

Lesson 2: Introduction to Photoshop CC

Lesson 3: Organizing and Managing Your Files with Adobe Bridge

Lesson 4: Making Selective Changes in Photoshop CC

Lesson 5: Painting and Retouching

Lesson 6: Color Correcting an Image

Lesson 7: Using Content-Aware Tools in Photoshop

Lesson 8: Introduction to Photoshop Layers

Lesson 9: Removing Backgrounds to Create Layered Compositions

Lesson 10: Using Layer Styles and Adjustment Layers

Lesson 11: Working with the Pen Tool

Lesson 12: Using Smart Objects in Photoshop

Lesson 13: Creating Images for Web, Video, and Interactive Use

Lesson 14: New Features in Photoshop CC

Appendix A: Top Photoshop Keyboard Shortcuts

Starting up

About Photoshop Digital Classroom

The *Adobe® Photoshop® CC Digital Classroom* provides a broad foundation of essential Photoshop skills. It is the perfect way to learn Photoshop if you are just starting out with the software, upgrading from a previous version, or if you have never received formal training—even if you have been using Photoshop for years. The *Adobe Photoshop CC Digital Classroom* provides you with essential skills across a wide range of Photoshop's capabilities. Whether you plan to use Photoshop for color correction and retouching of images, creating digital artwork, designing web pages, or creating advertisements, the *Photoshop Digital Classroom* is your starting point for beginning to understand everything that Photoshop offers. It has been a best-selling Photoshop book for many versions, and is widely used by schools teaching Photoshop, digital imaging, and digital design.

The *Adobe Photoshop CC Digital Classroom* helps you get up-and-running right away. You can work through all the lessons in this book, or complete only specific lessons. Each lesson includes detailed, step-by-step instructions, along with lesson files, useful background information, and video tutorials on the included DVD–it is like having your own expert instructor guiding you through each lesson while you work at your own pace. This book includes 14 self-paced lessons that let you discover essential skills, explore new features, and understand capabilities that will save you time. You'll be productive right away with real-world exercises and simple explanations. The *Adobe Photoshop CC Digital Classroom* lessons are developed by the same team of Photoshop experts who have created many official training titles for Adobe Systems.

Prerequisites

Before you start the *Adobe Photoshop CC Digital Classroom* lessons, you should have a working knowledge of your computer and its operating system. You should know how to use the directory system of your computer so that you can navigate through folders. You also need to understand how to locate, save, and open files, and you should also know how to use your mouse to access menus and commands.

Before starting the lessons files in the *Adobe Photoshop CC Digital Classroom*, make sure that you have installed Adobe Photoshop CC. The software is sold as part of the Creative Cloud, and is not included with this book. Find more information about the Creative Cloud at *www.adobe.com/CreativeCloud*. You may use the free 30-day trial version of Adobe Photoshop CC available at the *adobe.com* website, subject to the terms of its license agreement.

System requirements

Before starting the lessons in the *Adobe Photoshop CC Digital Classroom*, make sure that your computer is equipped for running Adobe Photoshop CC. The minimum system requirements for your computer to effectively use the software

are listed below and you can find the most current system requirements at
http://www.adobe.com/products/photoshop/tech-specs.html.

Windows

- Intel® Pentium® 4 or AMD Athlon® 64 processor (2GHz or faster)
- Microsoft® Windows® 7 with Service Pack 1 or Windows 8 with Service Pack 1
- 1GB of RAM
- 2.5GB of available hard-disk space for installation; additional free space required during installation (cannot install on removable flash storage devices)
- 1024x768 display (1280x800 recommended) with 16-bit color and 256 MB of VRAM (512MB of VRAM recommended for 3D features)
- OpenGL 2.0–capable system
- Internet connection and registration are necessary for required software activation, membership validation, and access to online services.

Mac OS

- Multicore Intel processor with 64-bit support
- Mac OS X v10.7 (64 bit) or v10.8 (64 bit)
- 1GB of RAM
- 3.2GB of available hard-disk space for installation; additional free space required during installation (cannot install on a volume that uses a case-sensitive file system or on removable flash storage devices)
- 1024x768 display (1280x800 recommended) with 16-bit color and 256 MB of VRAM (512MB of VRAM recommended for 3D features)
- OpenGL 2.0–capable system
- Internet connection and registration are necessary for required software activation, membership validation, and access to online services.

Starting Adobe Photoshop CC

As with most software, Adobe Photoshop CC is launched by locating the application in your Programs folder (Windows) or Applications folder (Mac OS). If you are not familiar with starting the program, follow these steps to start the Adobe Photoshop CC application:

Windows

1   Choose Start > All Programs > Adobe Photoshop CC.

2   If a Welcome Screen appears, you can close it.

Mac OS

1   Open the Applications folder, and then open the Adobe Photoshop CC folder.

2   Double-click the Adobe Photoshop CC application icon.

3　　If a Welcome Screen appears, you can close it.

Menus and commands are identified throughout the book by using the greater-than symbol (>). For example, the command to print a document appears as File > Print.

Resetting Adobe Photoshop CC preferences

When you start Adobe Photoshop, it remembers certain settings along with the configuration of the workspace from the last time you used the application. It is important that you start each lesson using the default settings so that you do not see unexpected results when working with the lessons in this book. The method described in the following steps restores Photoshop back to the original setting. If you have made changes to your Colors Settings and want to maintain them, follow the steps in the section, "Steps to reset default settings, but keep color settings."

Steps to reset Adobe Photoshop CC preferences

1　　If Photoshop is open, choose File > Exit (Windows) or Photoshop > Quit (Mac OS).

2　　Press and hold the Ctrl+Alt+Shift keys (Windows) or Command+Option+Shift keys (Mac OS) simultaneously while launching Adobe Photoshop CC.

3　　A dialog box appears verifying that you want to delete the Adobe Photoshop settings file. Release the keys, and then click OK.

Steps to reset default settings, but keep color settings

As you reset your preferences to the default settings, you might want to keep your color settings. This is important if you have created specific color settings, or work in a color-calibrated environment.

Use the following steps to reset your Adobe Photoshop CC preferences and save your color settings.

1　　Launch Adobe Photoshop CC.

2　　Choose Edit > Color Settings, and then click the Save button. The Save dialog box opens. Enter an appropriate name for your color settings, such as the date. Leave the destination and format unchanged, then click the Save button. The Color Settings Comment dialog box opens.

3　　In the Color Settings Comment dialog box, enter a description for the color settings you are saving and then click OK. Click OK again in the Color Settings dialog box to close it. You have saved your color settings so they can be accessed again in the future.

4　　Choose File > Quit to exit Adobe Photoshop CC.

5   Press and hold the Ctrl+Alt+Shift keys (Windows) or Command+Option+Shift keys (Mac OS) simultaneously when launching Adobe Photoshop CC. A dialog box appears verifying that you want to delete the Adobe Photoshop settings file. Release the keys and then click OK.

6   After Adobe Photoshop CC launches, choose Edit > Color Settings. The Color Settings dialog box appears.

7   From the Settings drop-down menu, choose your saved color settings file. Click OK. Your color settings are restored.

A note about color warnings

Depending upon how your Color Settings are configured, there may be times when you will receive a Missing Profile or Embedded Profile Mismatch warning. If you do receive Missing Profile and Embedded Profile Mismatch warnings, choose the Assign working option, or Convert document's colors to the working space. What is determined to be your working space is what you have assigned in the Color Settings dialog box. Color Settings are discussed in more detail in Lesson 5, "Painting and Retouching" and in Lesson 6, "Color Correcting an Image."

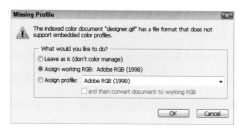

Missing color profile.

Mismatched color profile.

Access lesson files and videos any time

Register your book at *www.digitalclassroombooks.com/CC/Photoshop* to gain access to your lesson files on any computer you own, or to watch the videos on any Internet-connected computer, tablet, or smart phone. You'll be able to continue your learning anywhere you have an Internet connection. This provides you access to lesson files and videos even if you misplace your DVD.

Checking for updated lesson files

Make sure you have the most up-to-date lesson files and learn about any updates to your *Photoshop CC Digital Classroom* book by registering your book at *www.digitalclassroombooks.com/CC/Photoshop*.

Loading lesson files

The *Photoshop CC Digital Classroom* DVD includes files that accompany the exercises for each of the lessons. You can copy the entire lessons folder from the supplied DVD to your hard drive, or copy only the lesson folders for the individual lessons you want to complete.

For each lesson in the book, the files are referenced by file name. The exact location of each file on your computer is not used, as you might have placed the files in a unique location on your hard drive. We suggest placing the lesson files in the My Documents folder (Windows), at the top level of your hard drive (Mac OS), or on your desktop for easy access.

Copying the lesson files to your hard drive

1   Insert the *Photoshop CC Digital Classroom* DVD supplied with this book.

2   On your computer desktop, navigate to the DVD and locate the folder named pslessons.

3   You can install all the files, or just specific lesson files. Do one of the following:

  • Install all lesson files by dragging the pslessons folder to your hard drive.

  • Install only some of the files by creating a new folder on your hard drive named pslessons. Open the pslessons folder on the supplied DVD, select the lesson you want to complete, and drag the folder(s) to the pslessons folder you created on your hard drive.

Unlocking Mac OS files

Macintosh users might need to unlock the files after copying them from the accompanying disc. This only applies to Mac OS computers and is because the Mac OS may view files that are copied from a DVD or CD as being locked for writing.

If you are a Mac OS user and have difficulty saving over the existing files in this book, you can use these instructions so that you can update the lesson files as you work on them and also add new files to the lessons folder.

Note that you only need to follow these instructions if you are unable to save over the existing lesson files, or if you are unable to save files into the lesson folder.

1   After copying the files to your computer, click once to select the pslessons folder, then choose File > Get Info from within the Finder (not Photoshop).

2   In the pslessons info window, click the triangle to the left of Sharing and Permissions to reveal the details of this section.

3   In the Sharing and Permissions section, click the lock icon, if necessary, in the lower-right corner so that you can make changes to the permissions.

4   Click to select a specific user or select everyone, then change the Privileges section to Read & Write.

5   Click the lock icon to prevent further changes, and then close the window.

Working with the video tutorials

Your *Photoshop CC Digital Classroom* DVD comes with video tutorials developed by the authors to help you understand the concepts explored in each lesson. Each tutorial is approximately five minutes long and demonstrates and explains the concepts and features covered in the lesson.

The videos are designed to supplement your understanding of the material in the chapter. We have selected exercises and examples that we feel will be most useful to you. You may want to view the entire video for each lesson before you begin that lesson. Additionally, at certain points in a lesson, you will encounter the DVD icon. The icon, with appropriate lesson number, indicates that an overview of the exercise being described can be found in the accompanying video.

DVD video icon.

Setting up for viewing the video tutorials

The DVD included with this book includes video tutorials for each lesson. Although you can view the lessons on your computer directly from the DVD, we recommend copying the folder labeled videos from the *Photoshop CC Digital Classroom* DVD to your hard drive.

Copying the video tutorials to your hard drive

1   Insert the *Photoshop CC Digital Classroom* DVD supplied with this book.

2   On your computer desktop, navigate to the DVD and locate the folder named videos.

3   Drag the videos folder to a location on your hard drive.

Viewing the video tutorials with the Adobe Flash Player

The videos on the *Photoshop CC Digital Classroom* DVD are saved in the Flash projector format. A Flash projector file wraps the Digital Classroom video player and the Adobe Flash Player in an executable file (.exe for Windows or .app for Mac OS). Note that the extension (on both platforms) might not always be visible. Projector files allow the Flash content to be deployed on your system without the need for a browser or prior stand-alone player installation.

Playing the video tutorials

1   On your computer, navigate to the videos folder you copied to your hard drive from the DVD. Playing the videos directly from the DVD could result in poor quality playback.

2   Open the videos folder and double-click the Flash file named PLAY_PSCCvideos to view the video tutorials.

3   After the Flash player launches, click the Play button to view the videos.

The Flash Player has a simple user interface that allows you to control the viewing experience, including stopping, pausing, playing, and restarting the video. You can also rewind or fast-forward, and adjust the playback volume.

A. Go to beginning. B. Play/Pause. C. Fast-forward/rewind. D. Stop. E. Volume Off/On. F. Volume control.

Playback volume is also affected by the settings in your operating system. Be certain to adjust the sound volume for your computer, in addition to the sound controls in the Player window.

Additional resources

The Digital Classroom series goes beyond the training books. You can continue your learning online, with training videos, at seminars and conferences, and in-person training events.

On-demand video training from the authors

Comprehensive video training from the authors are available at *DigitalClassroom.com*. Find complete video training along with thousands of video tutorials covering Photoshop and related Creative Cloud apps along with digital versions of the Digital Classroom book series. Learn more at *DigitalClassroom.com*.

Training from the Authors

The authors are available for professional development training workshops for schools and companies. They also teach classes at American Graphics Institute, including training classes and online workshops. Visit *agitraining.com* for more information about Digital Classroom author-led training classes or workshops.

Additional Adobe Creative Cloud Books

Expand your knowledge of creative software applications with the Digital Classroom book series. Books are available for most creative software applications as well as web design and development tools and technologies. Learn more at *DigitalClassroomBooks.com*

Seminars and conferences

The authors of the Digital Classroom seminar series frequently conduct in-person seminars and speak at conferences, including the annual CRE8 Conference. Learn more at *agitraining.com* and *CRE8summit.com*.

Resources for educators

Visit *digitalclassroombooks.com* to access resources for educators, including instructors' guides for incorporating Digital Classroom into your curriculum.

What you'll learn in this lesson:

- Opening a file using Mini Bridge
- Using Photoshop tools
- Saving workspaces
- Navigating your image area

Navigating Photoshop CC: Workspace, Tools, and Panels

In this lesson, you'll learn how to use the Adobe Photoshop CC work area efficiently. You will also discover how to open a document using Adobe Bridge, use the Tools panel, and easily navigate through images.

Starting up

Before starting this lesson, make sure that your tools and panels are at the Photoshop CC default settings by resetting your preferences. See "Resetting Adobe Photoshop CC preferences" in the Starting up section of this book.

You will work with several files from the ps01lessons folder in this lesson. Make sure that you have loaded the pslessons folder onto your hard drive from the supplied DVD. See "Loading lesson files" in the Starting up section of this book.

Use the accompanying video to gain a better understanding of how to use some of the features shown in this lesson. You can find the video tutorial for this lesson on the included DVD.

Adobe Photoshop is an image-editing program that can open an image stored on your system, captured by a scanner, digital camera, phone, tablet device, or downloaded from the Web. It can also open captured video images and vector illustrations. In addition, you can create new documents in Photoshop. The documents that you create or edit in Photoshop are typically created from pixels, but can also include vector graphics. Vector graphics can be enlarged or reduced in size with no loss of clarity.

In this lesson, you will discover how to open existing files in Adobe Photoshop using a feature called Mini Bridge. In addition to many other helpful options, Mini Bridge allows you to see details about your file before opening it in Photoshop.

Although Adobe Bridge is available and works with all the applications in the Creative Cloud, it might not be installed on your system. Keep in mind that you must have Adobe Bridge installed to use both Adobe Bridge and Mini-Bridge. You can check your Programs folder (Windows) or Applications folder (Mac) to see if Adobe Bridge CC is installed. If it is not, launch the Adobe Application Manager and select to install it from the Creative Cloud. Don't fret if you forget to do this. If you access Adobe Bridge from any application, and don't have it installed, you will automatically be taken to the Adobe Application Manager.

Opening an existing document in Mini Bridge

Mini Bridge works like the stand-alone Adobe Bridge application, but exists as a panel in Photoshop. You can access Mini Bridge by choosing File > Browse in Mini Bridge.

1   Launch Adobe Photoshop CC and choose File > Browse in Mini Bridge; Mini Bridge appears as a panel across the bottom of the workspace. If a message appears indicating that "Bridge must be running to browse files," click Launch Bridge.

If you are launching Bridge for the first time, you might be asked to enable application-specific extensions in Bridge; select "Yes". The first time Adobe Bridge launches, it could be slow because it is caching the files that it is preparing to display.

Even though you will be instructed to use Adobe Bridge throughout the lessons in this book, you can choose to use Mini Bridge.

2   From the drop-down menu in the navigation pod on the left side of Mini Bridge, select your User name. You now see personal folders that you can navigate to, such as Desktop, Documents, and Pictures.

3   Double-click Desktop to see the folders on your desktop appear in the Navigation pod, including the pslessons folder that you downloaded or dragged to the desktop from the DVD. If you do not see your folder on the Desktop, verify that you didn't save your folder to the Desktop of another User.

Select your user name to see the desktop folder,
if it is not immediately visible.

4   Double-click the pslessons folder to reveal the contents, and then click ps01lessons. The Mini Bridge now displays three images of an antique car in the folder.

Use Mini Bridge to locate your lesson files.

5   Locate and double-click to open the file named **ps0101_done.psd**. An image of an antique car appears. This is the finished project. You can keep it open as you work or close it once you have examined the file.

The completed lesson file.

As you practice with the files throughout this book, you will find that you are instructed to save a work file immediately after opening the original file.

6   Open the file named **ps0101.psd**, which is the starting file used for this lesson. Choose File > Save As to open the Save As dialog box.

7   Navigate to the ps01lessons folder. In the File name, or Save as text field, type **ps0101_work**, and choose Photoshop from the Format drop-down menu. Click Save.

Discovering the Tools panel

When you start Photoshop, the Tools panel appears docked on the left side of the screen—by default, it is docked on the left side of the workspace. There are four main groups of tools separated by functionality on the Tools panel: selection, cropping, and measuring; retouching and painting; drawing and type; and navigation. At the bottom of the Tools panel, you find Set foreground color and Set background color, as well as Quick Mask.

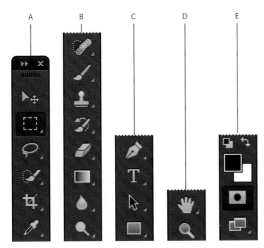

A. *Selection, cropping, and measuring tools.*
B. *Retouching and painting tools.*
C. *Drawing and type tools.*
D. *Navigation tools.*
E. *Foreground/Background and Quick Mask.*

Selection, Cropping, and Measuring Tools

ICON	TOOL NAME	USE
▸₊	Move (V)	Moves selections or layers.
⬚	Marquee (M)	Makes rectangular, elliptical, single row, and single column selections.
◯	Lasso (L)	Makes freehand, polygonal (straight-edged), and magnetic selections.
⬚	Quick Selection (W)	Makes selections by painting.
🔪	Crop (C)	Crops an image.
🖋	Eyedropper (I)	Samples pixels.

Retouching and Painting Tools

ICON	TOOL NAME	USE
	Spot Healing (J)	Removes imperfections.
	Brush (B)	Paints the foreground color.
	Clone Stamp (S)	Paints with a sample of the image.
	History Brush (Y)	Paints with the selected state or snapshot.
	Eraser (E)	Erases pixels—or reverts to a saved history state.
	Gradient (G)	Creates a gradient.
	Blur (no shortcut)	Blurs pixels.
	Dodge (O)	Lightens pixels in an image.

You can create a floating Tools panel by clicking the dark gray title bar at the top of the Tools panel and then dragging it to a new location. You can dock it again by dragging it back to the left side of the workspace; release when you see the blue vertical bar appear.

Drawing and Type Tools

ICON	TOOL NAME	USE
	Pen (P)	Draws a vector path.
T	Horizontal Type (T)	Creates a type layer.
	Path Selection (A)	Allows you to manipulate a path.
	Rectangle (U)	Draws vector shapes.

Navigation Tools

ICON	TOOL NAME	USE
	Hand (H)	Navigates the page.
	Zoom (Z)	Increases and decreases the relative size of the view.

Can't tell the tools apart? You can view tooltips that reveal a tool's name and keyboard shortcut by positioning your cursor over the tool.

The Tools panel is in a space-saving, one-column format. Click the double-arrows in the gray title bar area above the Tools panel to bring the Tools panel into the two-column view. Click the double-arrows again to bring the Tools panel back to the default, single-column view. Keep the Tools panel set to whichever format works best for you.

Accessing tools and their options

With the selection of most tools comes the opportunity to change options. In this exercise, you will have the opportunity to use the Brush tool and change its options to become even more powerful.

1   With the **ps0101_work.psd** image open, select the Brush tool (✏). Look in the Options bar to see a variety of options you can change.

*A. Brush Preset Picker. **B.** Painting Mode. **C.** Opacity. **D.** Flow. **E.** Airbrush. **F.** Pressure.*

Most tools have additional options available in the Options bar at the top of the workspace.

Note that by default, your brush is loaded with black paint. The paint color is indicated at the bottom of your Tools panel in the Foreground and Background color swatches. If you have not reset preferences, you might have a different color in your foreground.

2   Click once on the foreground color to open the picker so you can select a different color.

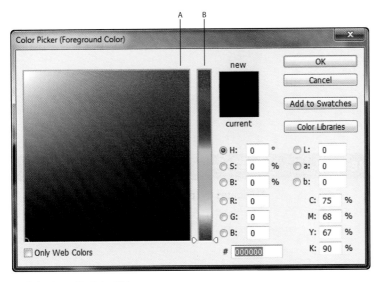

*A. Color Pane. **B.** Color Slider.*

Using the Color Picker, you can select a blue color that you will use to brighten up the sky.

3   In the Color Picker, click once on the section of the Color Slider that contains blue hues, and then choose a bright blue color from the large Color Pane. In our example, we pick a color that is created R: **37**, Green: **100**, B: **227**. Click OK.

Keep in mind that, depending upon the destination of your image, you might not be able to achieve the same color of blue that you see in the screen. Lesson 5, "Painting and Retouching," discusses color and how to use it in your images, in more detail.

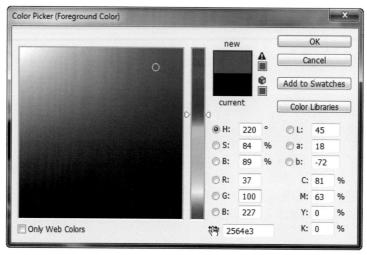

Click once in the blue section of the Color Slider, and then choose a bright blue color from the Color Pane.

Now you will change some of the Brush tool options in the Options bar at the top of the workspace.

4   Click the Brush Preset Picker to see your options for size and hardness. There are several options that you can change; for now you will focus on two.

5   Click and drag the size slider, which controls the size of the brush, to the right until you reach approximately 100 px. If the Hardness slider, which controls the hardness or softness of the brush, is not all the way to the left at 0%, slide it to the left now. This is now a large soft brush that will blend well at the edges of the strokes

In the next step, you will paint and then undo it. This is to help you understand the concept of blending and how it can make a difference when you paint.

Change the brush size and hardness.

6   Click and drag anywhere in the image one time to create a brush stroke across your image. Note that you have created a large opaque streak.

7   Choose Edit > Undo Brush Tool, or use the keyboard shortcut Ctrl+Z (Windows) or Command+Z (Mac OS) to undo the paint streak.

8   Now click and hold the Painting Mode drop-down menu; you see a list of options that allow you to change how your paint interacts with the image underneath. Select Color from the bottom of the list.

9   Click the arrow to the right of the Opacity option to see the slider. Click and drag the Opacity slider to the left until it reaches approximately 20%.

Select the paint blending mode named Color, and change the Opacity to 20%.

10 Now click and drag to paint in the upper-right corner of the image. You see that the result is quite different and you are brightening the sky.

Click and drag to paint blue in the upper-right corner of the image.

11 Notice that you can build up the color by releasing the paint brush and painting over the same area. If you make a mistake, choose Edit > Undo, or press Ctrl+Z (Windows) or Command+Z (Mac OS) to undo.

To go back multiple steps, choose Edit > Step Backward, or use the keyboard shortcut Ctrl+Alt+Z (Windows) or Command+Option+Z (Mac OS)

12 Choose File > Save. Keep this file open for the next part of this lesson.

Using panels

Much of the functionality in Photoshop resides in the panels, so you will learn to navigate them and quickly find the ones you need. In this section, you will learn how to resize, expand, and convert panels to icons and then back to panels again. You will also learn how to save your favorite workspaces so you don't have to set them up every time you work on a new project.

1   Choose Window > Workspace > Reset Essentials to put the panels back to their default locations.

The default panel locations.

Putting the panel system to use

Photoshop has a default setting for all the panels: it's what you see when you initially launch Photoshop. There are many panels, and not all of them are needed for all projects. This is the reason Photoshop has defined workspaces, which can help you streamline your workflow. There are many prebuilt workspaces available under the Window > Workspace menu; you can pick the one that helps you find the features you need for the task at hand.

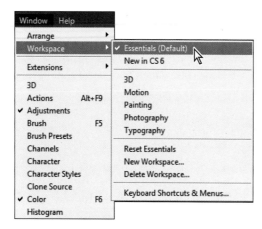

You can select different workspaces that help you find features depending upon the task at hand.

At this point, you have just reset the Essentials workspace. Test different workspaces by selecting Painting, and then Photography from the Window > Workspace menu. Once you have seen how panels can be collapsed and others made visible, return to Window > Workspace > Essentials.

Keep in mind that all these panels are accessible at all times from the Windows > Workspace menu.

To open panels that are not visible, choose the Window menu. If there is a check mark to the left of the panel listed, it means that the panel is already open. Photoshop CC can determine whether a panel is hidden behind another; panels that are hidden this way will not be marked as open, so you can select it in the Window menu to bring the hidden panel forward.

1   Select the Brush tool (✐).

2   Click the Swatches tab that is hidden behind the Color panel in the docking area to the right.

3   Click the color called Pure Red Orange in the Swatches panel. Notice that when you cross over a color, a Tooltip appears. If it is easier for you to read the color, you can select Small List from the Swatches panel menu (▾☰) in the upper-right corner.

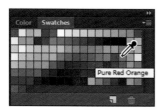

Click the Swatches tab to bring it forward.   *Choose to view the Swatches panel as a list.*

4   With the Brush tool selected, start painting in the upper-left corner of the image, adding orange to the sky. If necessary, press Ctrl+Z (Windows) or Command+Z (Mac OS). Keep in mind that by masking, or selecting parts of the image, you can have much more control over where you paint in an image. Read Lesson 4, "Making Selective Changes in Photoshop CC," for more information about selective changes.

Add orange to the sky in the upper-left part of the image.

Choosing other panels

You will now select another panel, the History panel. The History panel allows you to undo and redo steps, as well as save versions of your image while you work. In this exercise, you will use the History panel to undo and redo steps. In Lesson 5, "Painting and Retouching," you will spend more time in the History panel.

1 Click the History panel icon (⬚⁵) that is visible in the Essentials workspace. If you cannot locate it, choose Window > History.

Selecting the History panel.

Each row in the History panel represents a history state (or step). You can click back on earlier states to undo steps that you have taken, or redo by clicking the grayed-out history state. Keep in mind that if you step back in history and then complete a new step, all the gray history states disappear. This history default can be changed by selecting History Options from the History panel menu and checking Allow Non-Linear History.

2 Click back on the various history states to see how your steps are undone. Click forward again to see your steps redone.

Undoing a step in the History panel.

Expanding and collapsing your panels

To better manage your space, you can collapse and expand your panels. You can do this automatically with a preconfigured workspace, or you can choose to expand only the panels you want to see.

1   You might find that you need to reset your workspace to bring it back to its original configuration. If this is necessary, choose Window > Workspace > Reset Essentials.

2   Collapse groups of panels by double-clicking the dark gray bar (title bar) at the top of the panels. Double-click the dark gray bar again to expand them.

Collapse the panel by double-clicking the title bar.

You can also collapse a panel by clicking the double-arrows in the upper-right corner of the panel.

3   If the History panel is no longer open, click the icon for the History panel. Click the double-arrow in the upper-right area to collapse that panel back to an icon.

You can collapse a panel by clicking the double-arrows.

Customizing your panels

A panel group is made up of two or more panels that are stacked on top of each other. To view the other panels in a group, select the name on the tab of the panel. You will now learn to organize your panels according to your preferences.

1   If the Swatches panel is not forward, select the tab that reads Swatches; the Swatches tab is brought forward.

2   Now, select the Color tab to bring the Color panel to the front of the panel group.

3   Click the tab of the Color panel, drag it away from the panel group and into the image area, and then release the mouse—you have just removed a panel from a panel group and the docking area. Rearranging panels can help you keep frequently-used panels together in one area.

The Color panel as it is dragged away from a panel group.

4   Click the tab area at the top of the Swatches panel and drag it over the Color panel. As soon as you see an outline around the Color panel, release the mouse. You have now made a panel group.

The Swatches panel dragged into the Color panel, creating a new panel group.

You'll now save a custom workspace. Saving a workspace is a good idea if you have production processes that often use the same panels. Saving workspaces is also helpful if you are in a situation where multiple users are sharing Photoshop on one computer.

5   Select Window > Workspace > New Workspace; the New Workspace dialog box appears.

6   In the File name text field, type **First Workspace**, and then click Save.

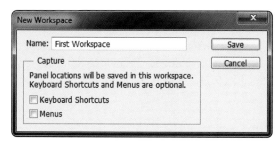

Name your new workspace.

7   Whenever you want to reload a workspace, whether it's one that you created or one that comes standard with Photoshop, select Window > Workspace and select the desired workspace from the list.

Hidden tools

Some of the tools in the Tools panel display a small triangle at the bottom-right corner. This indicates that there are additional tools hidden under the tool.

1   Click and hold the Brush tool to see the hidden Pencil, Color Replacement, and Mixer Brush tools. You can also access the hidden tools by right-clicking (Windows) or Ctrl+clicking (Mac OS).

Selecting a hidden tool.

2   Select the Mixer Brush tool (✔) and release. The Color Mixer tool is now the visible tool, and the options in the Options bar have been changed.

The Mixer Brush simulates realistic painting techniques, such as mixing colors on the canvas, combining colors on a brush, or varying paint wetness across a stroke.

You will now change the foreground color by selecting Set the foreground color in the Tools panel.

3   Click once on the foreground color at the bottom of the Tools panel; the Color Picker appears.

4   Position your cursor on the Color Slider (hue) to the right of the Color Pane and click and drag it up until shades of orange appear in the Color Pane.

5   Click once in the Color Pane to select an orange color. Any orange color will do for this exercise, but you can also type a value into the text fields for a more accurate selection. In this example, a color with the RGB value of R: **236**, G: **169**, B: **24** was selected.

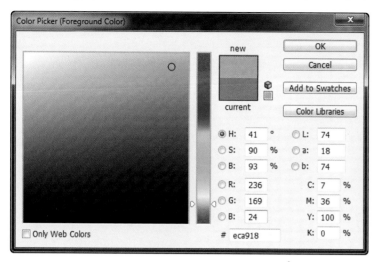

Select an orange color from the Color Picker.

6   Click the Brush Preset picker button in the Options bar and set the following attributes for the Mixer Brush tool:

- **Size**: **175 px** (This indicates the size of the brush; in this example, a very large brush is indicated.)

- **Hardness**: **20%** (A value of 100% would be a hard-edged brush.)

Leave all other settings at their defaults.

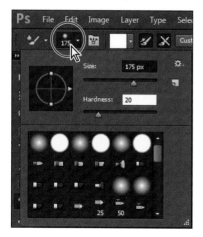

Changing the Mixer Brush tool.

There are many options for the Mixer Brush, but for this example, you will use a preset that will adjust all the settings to give you a smooth blended result in your image.

7   Click once on mixer brush combinations drop-down menu—this drop-down menu may have defaulted to Custom—and select the Moist, Light Mix preset.

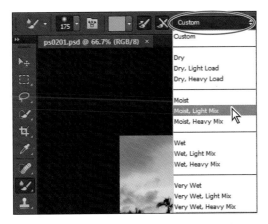

Change the Useful mixer brush combination to Moist, Light Mix.

8   Press Ctrl+0 (zero) (Windows) or Command+0 (zero) (Mac OS.) This is the keyboard shortcut for Fit on Screen, and it assures that you see the entire image area.

9   With the Mixer Brush tool still selected, start painting in the upper-left area of your image to create a shade of orange blending in from the corner. Repeat this for all four corners in the image. If you want to repaint, press Ctrl+Z (Windows) or Command+Z (Mac OS) to revert to the previous image and try again.

An orange tint is blended into the corners for an artistic effect.

10   Choose File > Save, or use the keyboard shortcut Ctrl+S (Windows), or Command+S (Mac OS) to save your file.

Navigating the image area

To work most efficiently in Photoshop, you'll want to know how to zoom (magnify) in and out of your image. Changing the zoom level allows you to select and paint accurately and helps you see details that you might otherwise have overlooked. The zoom function has a range from a single pixel up to a 3,200 percent enlargement, which gives you a lot of flexibility in terms of viewing your images.

You'll start by using the View menu to reduce and enlarge the document view, and end by fitting the entire document on your screen.

1   Choose View > Zoom In to enlarge the display of **ps0101_work.psd**.

2   Press Ctrl+plus sign (Windows) or Command+plus sign (Mac OS) to zoom in again. This is the keyboard shortcut for the Zoom In command that you accessed previously from the View menu.

3   Press Ctrl+minus sign (Windows) or Command+minus sign (Mac OS) to zoom out. This is the keyboard shortcut for View > Zoom Out.

Now you will fit the entire image on the screen.

4   Choose View > Fit on Screen, or use the keyboard shortcut Ctrl+0 (zero) (Windows) or Command+0 (zero) (Mac OS), to fit the document to the screen.

5   You can also display artwork at the size it will print by choosing View > Print Size.

Using the Zoom tool

When you use the Zoom tool (🔍), each click increases the view size to the next preset percentage, and centers the display of the image around the location in the image that you clicked. By holding the Alt (Windows) or Option (Mac OS) key down (with the Zoom tool selected), you can zoom out of an image, decreasing the percentage and making the image view smaller. The magnifying glass cursor is empty when the image has reached either its maximum magnification level of 3,200 percent or the minimum size of one pixel.

1   Choose View > Fit on Screen.

2   Select the Zoom tool, and click two times on the license plate to zoom in. You can also use key modifiers to change the behavior of the Zoom tool.

3   Press Alt (Windows) or Option (Mac OS) while clicking with the Zoom tool to zoom out.

You can accurately zoom into the exact region of an image by clicking and dragging a marquee around that area in your image. To do this, you must disable a new Zoom tool option.

4   Uncheck the Scrubby Zoom check box in the Zoom tool's Option bar to disable this feature. The Scrubby Zoom feature allows you to click and drag to zoom immediately. In this example, you need a more predictable zoom area.

If Scrubby Zoom is disabled; you may not have sufficient VRAM to enable this feature. Make sure you check the requirement needs to run Photoshop in the Getting started portion of this book.

Disable the Scrubby Zoom in the Zoom tool's Option bar.

5   With the Zoom tool still selected, press and hold the mouse and click and drag from the top left corner of the car's grill to the lower-right of the bumper. You are creating a rectangular marquee selection around the front of the car. Once you release the mouse, the area that was included in the marquee becomes enlarged to fill the document window.

Drag a marquee over the front of the car.

6   Double-click the Zoom tool in the Tools panel to return to a 100 percent view.

Because the Zoom tool is used so often, it would be tiresome to continually have to change from the Zoom tool back to the tool you were using. Read on to see how you can activate the Zoom tool at any time without deselecting your current tool.

7   Select the Move tool (✛) at the very top of the Tools panel.

8   Press and hold Ctrl+spacebar (Windows) or Command+spacebar (Mac OS). (Note that on the Mac OS, you must press and hold the spacebar before the Command key, otherwise you trigger Spotlight.) The Move tool is temporarily converted into the Zoom In tool. While still pressing and holding Ctrl/Command+spacebar, click and drag over the front of the car again, then release. Note that although you have changed the zoom level, the Move tool is still active.

You can zoom out by pressing and holding Alt+spacebar (Windows) or Option+spacebar (Mac OS).

9   Choose View > Fit on Screen.

Using the Hand tool

The Hand tool allows you to move or pan around the document. It is a lot like pushing a piece of paper around on your desk.

1   Select the Zoom tool (🔍), then click and drag on an area surrounding the front of the car.

2   Select the Hand tool (✋), then click and drag to the right to push the picture to the right. Notice that when the Hand tool is active, three view buttons appear in the Options bar (at the top of the work area) that allow you to change your current view to Actual Pixels, Fit Screen, or Fill Screen.

3   Select the Zoom tool and hold the spacebar. Notice that the cursor turns into the Hand tool. Click and drag left to view the front of the car again. By pressing and holding the spacebar, you can access the Hand tool without deselecting the current tool.

4   Double-click the Hand tool in the Tools panel to fit the entire image on your screen. This is the same as using Ctrl+0 (zero) (Windows) or Command+0 (zero) (Mac OS).

NAVIGATION SHORTCUTS	WINDOWS	MAC OS
Zoom In	Ctrl+plus sign or Ctrl+spacebar	Command+plus sign or Command+spacebar
Zoom Out	Ctrl+minus sign or Alt+spacebar	Command+minus sign or Option+spacebar
Turn Zoom In tool into Zoom Out tool	Alt	Option
Fit on Screen	Ctrl+0 (zero) or double-click the Hand tool	Command+0 (zero) or double-click the Hand tool
Hand tool (except when Type tool is selected)	Press spacebar	Press spacebar

Tabbed windows

In Photoshop, you have control over how your windows appear in the workspace. You can work with floating image windows, or choose to tab your windows across the top of the workspace. In this section, you find out how to use the new tabbed workspace.

1   If the Mini Bridge is not visible, choose File > Browse in Mini Bridge. In the Navigation pod, double-click the image named **ps0102.psd** to open it in Photoshop.

2   The image is displayed as a separate tab within Photoshop, allowing you to click the tab in order to switch between active images.

Multiple open images appear as tabs at the top of the screen.

3   Click the **ps0102.psd** tab, click and drag the tab away from its tabbed position, and then release the mouse button. The image second window is now floating.

4   Click the title bar of the floating window and drag upward until your cursor is next to the tab of the other image. When you see a blue bar appear, release the mouse button. The image is now back to being a tabbed window. You can stop a window from tabbing accidently by pressing and holding the Ctrl (Windows) or Command (Mac OS) key while dragging the floating window.

If you would prefer not to take advantage of the tabbed window feature, you can choose Edit > Preferences (Windows) or Photoshop > Preferences (Mac OS), then choose Interface. In the Options section, uncheck Open Documents as Tabs and click OK.

To quickly move all floating windows back to tabbed windows, choose Window > Arrange > Consolidate All to Tabs.

Maximizing productivity with screen modes

Now that you can zoom in and out of your document, as well as reposition it in your image window, it's time to learn how to take advantage of screen modes. You have a choice of three screen modes in which to work. Most users start and stay in the default—Standard Screen mode—unless they accidentally end up in another. Screen modes control how much space your current image occupies on your screen, and whether you can see other Photoshop documents as well. The Standard Screen mode is the default screen mode when you open Photoshop for the first time. It displays an image on a dark gray background for easy and accurate viewing of color without distractions, and also provides a flexible work area for dealing with panels.

1   Click the tab of the **ps0101_work.psd** image to make that image active.

2   Press the Tab key; the Tools panel and other panels disappear, creating much more workspace. Press the Tab key again to bring the Tools panel and other panels back.

3   Press Shift+Tab to hide the panel docking area while keeping the rest of the panels visible. Press Shift+Tab to bring the hidden panels back. Both the Tools panel and the panel docking area should now be visible.

As you position your cursor over various tools, you see a letter to the right of the tool name in the tooltip. This letter is the keyboard shortcut that you can use to access that tool. You could, in fact, work with the Tools panel closed and still have access to all the tools via your keyboard.

You will hide the panels once more so that you can take advantage of a hidden feature in Photoshop CC.

4   Press the Tab key to hide the panels. Then position your cursor over the thin gray strip where the Tools panel had been, and pause. The Tools panel reappears. Note that the Tools panel appears only while your cursor is in the Tools panel area, and it disappears if you move your cursor out of that area. Try this with the panel docking area to the right of the screen, and watch as that also appears and disappears as your cursor moves over the gray border off to the right. Keep in mind that this may not function as expected if you are using multiple monitors.

By changing the screen modes, you can locate over-extended anchor points and select more accurately up to the edge of your image. Changing modes can also help you present your image to clients in a clean workspace.

5   Press the Tab key again to display all the panels.

6   Press **F** to cycle to the next screen mode, which is Full Screen Mode With Menu Bar. This view surrounds the image out to the edge of the work area with a dark gray (even behind the docking area) and displays only one image at a time, without tabs, and centered within the work area. You can access additional open images by choosing the image name from the bottom of the Window menu.

You can also change your screen mode by selecting View > Screen Mode.

7   Notice that the gray background area (pasteboard) now extends to fill your entire screen and your image is centered within that area. One of the benefits of working in this mode is that it provides more area when working on images.

The Full Screen mode with Menu bar.

8   Press **F** on the keyboard again to see the last screen mode, Full Screen Mode.

Full Screen mode.

This is Full Screen mode. A favorite with multimedia users, it allows you to show others your document full-screen with no distracting screen elements. All menus and panels are hidden automatically in this mode; however, they are still accessible by hovering the cursor over the area where the panels normally reside. The panels temporarily reappear for easy access. If you'd like to see the panels while in this mode, press the Tab key to display and hide them.

9   Press the **F** key once to cycle back into Standard Screen mode, or click and hold the Change Screen Mode button at the bottom of the Tools panel and select Standard Screen Mode. If you do not see the Tools panels, you can press Tab.

Self study

Choose File > Browse to access a practice file in your ps01lessons folder. You can double-click **ps0102.psd** to explore workspaces further.

1   Using Window > Arrange, you can arrange several open document windows in different ways. Explore the different views that Photoshop provides by choosing various image arrangements.

2   Click the tabs of various panels and practice clicking and dragging panels from one group to another. You can put your panels back in order when you are finished experimenting by selecting Window > Workspace > Essentials, or Reset Essentials.

3   Use the Window menu to open the Info, Histogram, and Layers panels, and then save a new workspace called Color Correction. These panels are covered in Lesson 6, "Color Correcting an Image."

4   Take a look at some of the pre-built workspaces Photoshop has already provided for you. They will change the panel locations, and some will highlight things in the menu that are relevant to each workspace. For instance, by selecting What's New, you see the new panels and new features highlighted in the menus.

Review

Questions

1   What is the Full Screen mode?

2   Name two ways to fit your image to the screen.

3   What happens in the Essentials workspace when you exit one panel and select another?

4   How do you save a workspace?

Answers

1   The Full Screen mode displays a document window on a black background and hides all interface elements from view.

2   You can fit your image to the screen by using the View menu, or by double-clicking the Hand tool, right-clicking while you have the Zoom or Hand tool selected, or by pressing Ctrl+0 (zero) (Windows) or Command+0 (zero) (Mac OS).

3   When you leave one panel to select another, the initial panel returns to its original location in the docking area.

4   You can save your own workspace by selecting Window > Workspace > New Workspace.

What you'll learn in this lesson:

- Opening a file
- Checking the size of an image
- Cropping an image
- Quick color correction
- Saving a file

Introduction to Photoshop CC

In this lesson, you'll learn the basic skills that you need to start to work in Photoshop. Simple tasks are covered, such as opening a file, cropping it to the size you need, and adjusting the image's color. You will also find out what formats are best to save your image in, depending upon its use.

Starting up

Before starting, make sure that your tools and panels are consistent by resetting your preferences. See "Resetting Adobe Photoshop CC preferences" in the Starting up section of this book.

You will work with a file from the ps02lessons folder. Make sure that you have loaded the pslessons folder onto your hard drive from the supplied DVD. See "Loading lesson files" in the Starting up section of this book.

In this lesson, you will open a file that represents a typical candid image that you might have in your own library. You will learn to crop, color correct, and resize the image. You will also learn to save it in the right format for both print and web or screen presentation.

See Lesson 2 in action!

Use the accompanying video to gain a better understanding of how to use some of the features shown in this lesson. You can find the video tutorial for this lesson on the included DVD.

Opening a file

You can open a file using multiple methods in Adobe Photoshop. The easiest method is to open the file directly from Photoshop. Using this method avoids the image file from opening in a preview mode, which is typical when file type confusion occurs.

1   Launch Adobe Photoshop CC.

2   Choose File > Open. When the Open dialog box appears, navigate to the Desktop or to the location where you saved the pslessons folder, and then open it to find the ps02lessons folder.

3   Click the **ps0201.psd** file once to select it, and then click Open. The image file from a hockey practice appears. The image needs to be cropped to create a closer cropped image of the boys, and also needs to be color corrected a bit.

Saving the work file

You will now save a copy of your image to work with.

1   Choose File > Save As.

2   When the Save As dialog box appears, navigate to the ps02lessons folder and type **ps0201_work** in the File name text field. Choose Photoshop from the format drop-down menu and click Save. If the Photoshop Format Options dialog box appears, click OK.

Cropping an image

In this next part of the lesson, you will crop the image. Keep in mind that there are many methods for cropping your image area; in this lesson we focus on the easiest method, which is also the most commonly used method.

1   Select the Crop tool (⊟). When the Crop tool is selected, you see a selection indicator around the image and four corner markers. You can just click and drag on these corner markers to crop the image, but in this lesson, you will learn to create your own new custom cropped area.

2   The purpose of cropping this image is to allow it to proportionally fit into a 4″×6″ area, and also to create a closer crop around the boys' faces.

3   Note that when the Crop tool is selected, you have additional options available in the options bar across the top of the window. Click once on the Select an aspect ratio drop-down menu and select 2:3 (4:6). A crop area is created, but you will adjust it.

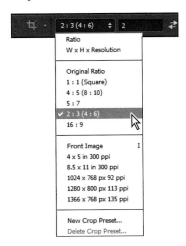

Select the Ratio for 2:3 (4:6).

Note that when you click and drag on the corner of the crop area, the aspect ratio of the crop remains intact. Also note that a default grid that represents the "rule of thirds" appears. You will use this grid to create a more dynamic crop.

4   Switch the proportions of the crop area to be horizontal by clicking the Swap height and width button (⇵) located in the Crop tool's options bar.

Swap the height and width of the crop.

About the rule of thirds grid

The rule of thirds is a guideline that photographers and designers use to create more dynamic layouts and imagery. According to the guideline, important elements of the photograph should be placed on or along the lines, or at the intersections of the lines.

Original image.   *Cropping grid.*   *The result.*

Example of an image before and after the rule of thirds crop was applied.

5   Click the upper-right corner marker of the active crop area and click and drag down closer to the taller boy's face. Ignore the guidelines that appear for now.

Click and drag to reposition the upper-left of the crop area.

6   Now click and drag from the lower-right corner. This time, as you position, pay
attention to the guidelines. Try to position the crop area so that the center of the taller
boy's face is directly in the middle of the intersection of the guideline in the upper-left
area.

Click and drag to reposition the lower-right corner of the crop area.

7   Uncheck the Delete Cropped Pixels check box that is in the middle of the Crop tool
options bar. By unchecking this box, you will not delete any image information, and
will be able to reposition your crop at a later point.

8   Once you have the crop area surrounding the two boys, with the intersection of the taller boy in the guideline, and the smaller boy's face aligned with the third vertical gridline, click the Commit check box (✔) or press the Enter or Return key to commit the crop area.

The finished crop area.

Keep in mind that even though using the rule of thirds is only a guideline, it can provide you with some direction when cropping your image. If you do not like seeing the gridlines, or would like to use another grid, you can turn it off, or choose another by selecting the Set the overlay options button (⊞) in the Crop tool options.

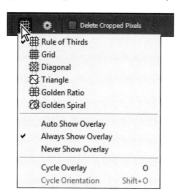

You can turn off the grid lines, or select another from the Crop tool options bar.

9   To see how the existing pixels are still stored, switch to your Move tool. You will move your image area, and then immediately undo that move so as to not change your cropped image.

10 Using the Move tool (✛), click the image area and drag to reposition your image area. Notice that, since you unchecked Deleted Cropped Pixels, the pixels still exist. Use this feature when you are not sure if you will need to reposition an image inside of the cropped area.

11 You can press Control+Z (Windows) or Command+Z (Mac OS) to undo your repositioning. If you made several moves, you can choose Windows > History, and go back several steps by clicking Crop in the History panel.

Go back in History to undo your moves.

Quick image correction

Anyone who has used Photoshop will tell you that there are multiple tools and features that perform the same tasks. This is especially true when adjusting image quality. In this lesson, you will be introduced to curves and adjustment layers, which can be as complex or as simple as you want. The approach is simple in this lesson, but look for more advanced features that you can use with Curves in Lesson 6, "Color Correcting an Image".

Why use Adjustment layers for image correction?

Throughout this book you find that adjustment layers are used rather than many of the menu items, which have duplicate features. For instance, in this lesson, you will select Curves from the Layers menu item, rather than selecting it from the Image > Adjustments > Curves. This is because changes performed using adjustment layers can be edited and updated, even after you save the file (in the .psd format). When using the standard Image > Adjustments menu items, you only have the option to undo your changes, and that opportunity is lost after you perform so many other steps, or close the file. More about adjustment layers is covered in Lesson 10, "Using Layer Styles and Adjustment Layers."

Increasing contrast using curves

In this next part of the lesson, you will use a simplified step in the curves panel. You will adjust the contrast of the image using a Preset. As you gain more skills in Photoshop, you will use presets less and make more custom changes.

1   With your cropped image still open, choose Layers > New Adjustment Layers > Curves. The New Layer dialog box appears; leave all the options set at the default and click OK. The Properties panel appears with a curve inside it. This may look confusing at first, but in this lesson, you will only be using this panel to balance the color in your image and lighten it slightly. It cannot be stressed enough that this tool is extremely powerful and covered in more detail throughout the lessons in this book.

2   In the Properties panel, select the Preset drop-down menu and note the available presets that you have to choose from. For this example, you will choose a preset that should improve any image, but typically you should be careful when using presets as they typically don't give the same professional result that can be achieved with custom changes.

3   Select Medium Contrast (RGB) from the Preset drop-down menu. You see that the contrast has been strengthened in this image.

Increase the contrast in the image using a preset.

Adjusting the neutral

4   Click the middle Sample in image to set the gray point eyedropper that appears on the left side of the Properties panel.

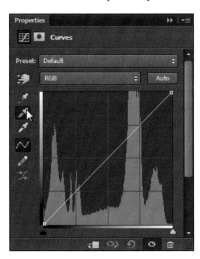

Select the Sample grey point eyedropper from the Properties panel.

With this eyedropper, you can locate an item in the image that is considered neutral, a gray or shade of gray, and use it to balance the color of your image. In this example, we will use the collar of the taller boy's shirt.

5   Click once on the grey collar. You see an immediate change in the balance of the image. This is because any color cast in the image has been neutralized. Read more about balancing color in your image in Lesson 6, "Color Correcting an Image."

Select the Sample grey point eyedropper from the Properties panel and click the gray in the collar.

6   If you don't already see the Layers panel, choose Windows > Layers now. When you created an adjustment layer, it was added on top of the layer that contains your image information. Click the bottom (Layer 0) layer to make it active.

Make sure to select the bottom layer, Layer 0, before moving on.

7   Choose File > Save to save the file.

Using the improved Smart Sharpen feature

In this next part of the lesson you will sharpen your image. By correctly applying sharpening to your image, you can make your image look more crisp and clean, whether its final destination is as a printed image or on-screen. Sharpening enhances the definition of edges in an image. The degree of sharpening that you need to apply to your own images varies depending on the quality of the original image. Keep in mind that sharpening cannot correct a severely blurred image.

1   Choose Filter > Sharpen > Smart Sharpen. The Smart Sharpen feature offers you the ability to sharpen edges of objects in your image without creating unnecessary graininess (noise). In this window, you see many controls but you will only change the value in the Amount slider.

    The amount of sharpening that you choose depends upon the subject matter and how defined you want the edges to be. Typically, you can start at about 150% and then move upwards from there, depending upon the content of your image.

2   Click and drag the value in the Amount slider to the right to about 250%. Leave all
other settings the same, but do not click OK yet.

Apply a sharpening amount of approximately 250%.

How much sharpening is enough?

Many users are confused about how much sharpening should be applied. The amount can
vary based upon the subject matter in the image, where it is going to be viewed, and even the
type of paper it will be printed on. Here are some generic suggestions to get you started.

Up to 150%

Images where you don't want a lot of edge detail, hence lower numbers, would be older
people, where you do not want to accentuate skin flaws and wrinkles.

Over 150–200%

Images that are OK to go higher in the amount value are images that include children,
product, or architectural images. By increasing the value of the sharpening, you can bring
out details such as wood grain and other important textures.

3   Click and hold the image preview to turn off the sharpening preview and see what the image looked like before the Smart Sharpen feature was applied. You should be able to see more detail when you release and let the preview show how the sharpening is applied.

Click and hold the Preview to turn off the preview of the sharpening.

4   Click OK to apply the sharpening.

A look back in History

Compare how your image looks now with the original by using the History panel.

1   If you do not see your History panel, choose Windows > History.

2   Click the topmost thumbnail in the History panel. This represents the original image that you opened.

3   Now, click the bottom History state, which should be named Smart Sharpen and note the difference. After comparing the images, remain on the Smart Sharpen state.

Compare your image with the original by using the History panel.

Saving files

Adobe Photoshop allows you to save your files in a variety of file formats, which makes it possible to use your images in many different ways. You can save images to allow for additional editing of things such as layers and effects that you have applied in Photoshop, or save images for sharing with users who need only the finished file for use on the Web or for printing. In all, Photoshop allows you to save your file in more than a dozen unique file formats.

As you work on images, it is best to save them using the default Photoshop format, which uses the .psd extension at the end of the filename. This is the native Photoshop file format, and retains the most usable data without a loss in image quality. Because the Photoshop format was developed by Adobe, many non-Adobe software applications do not recognize the .psd format.

Additionally, the .psd format may contain more information than you need, and may be a larger file size than is appropriate for sharing through e-mail or posting on a web site. While you can create copies of images for sharing, it is a good idea to keep an original version in the .psd format as a master file that you can access if necessary. This is especially important because some file formats are considered to be *lossy* formats, which means that they remove image data in order to reduce the size of the file.

Understanding file formats

While Photoshop can be used to create files for all sorts of media, the three most common uses for image files are web, print, and video production. Following is a list of the most common formats and how they are used.

WEB PRODUCTION FORMATS	
JPEG (Joint Photographic Experts Group)	This is a common format for digital camera photographs and the primary format for full-color images shared on the web. JPEG images use lossy compression, which degrades the quality of images and discards color and pixel data. Once the image data is lost, it cannot be recovered.
GIF (Graphic Interchange Format)	GIF files are used to display limited (indexed) color graphics on the Web. It is a compressed format that reduces the file size of images, but it only supports a limited number of colors and is thus more appropriate for logos and artwork than photographs. GIF files support transparency.
PNG (Portable Network Graphics)	PNG was developed as an alternative to GIF for displaying images on the Web. It uses lossless compression and supports transparency.

PRINT PRODUCTION FORMATS

PSD (Photoshop document)	The Photoshop format (.psd) is the default file format and the only format, besides the Large Document Format (PSB), that supports most Photoshop features. Files saved as .psd can be used in other Adobe applications, such as Adobe Illustrator, Adobe InDesign, Adobe Premiere, and others. The programs can directly import .psd files and access many Photoshop features, such as layers.
TIFF or TIF (Tagged Image File Format)	TIFF is a common bitmap image format. Most image-editing software and page-layout applications support TIFF images up to 2GB in file size. TIFF supports most color modes and can save images with alpha channels. While Photoshop can also include layers in a TIFF file, most other applications cannot use these extended features and see only the combined (flattened) image.
EPS (Encapsulated PostScript)	EPS files can contain both vector and bitmap data. Because it is a common file format used in print production, most graphics software programs support the EPS format for importing or placing images. EPS is a subset of the PostScript format. Some software applications cannot preview the high-resolution information contained within an EPS file, so Photoshop allows you to save a special preview file for use with these programs, using either the EPS TIFF or EPS PICT option. EPS supports most color modes, as well as clipping paths, which are commonly used to silhouette images and remove backgrounds.
Photoshop PDF	Photoshop PDF files are extremely versatile, as they can contain bitmap and vector data. Images saved in the Photoshop PDF format can maintain the editing capabilities of most Photoshop features, such as vector objects, text, and layers, and most color spaces are supported. Photoshop PDF files can also be shared with other graphics applications, as most of the current versions of graphics software are able to import or manipulate PDF files. Photoshop PDF files can even be opened by users with the free Adobe Reader software.

VIDEO PRODUCTION FORMATS

TIFF or TIF	*See Print Production Formats, above.*
TARGA (TrueVision Advanced Raster Graphics Adapter)	This legacy file format is used for video production. The TARGA format supports millions of colors, along with alpha channels.

Choosing a file format

In this section, you will save your file to share online and for printing. You will use two common formats, JPEG and Photoshop PDF.

Saving a JPEG file

To save a copy of your image for sharing online, whether on a web site or to send through e-mail, you will save it using the JPEG file format. In this lesson, you will use the Save menu, but in Lesson 13, "Creating Images for Web, Video, and Interactive Use," you will discover additional features when saving files for use online, including how to use the Save for Web feature in Photoshop.

1   Choose File > Save As.

2   In the Save As dialog box, type **hockey** in the File name text field. From the Format drop-down menu, choose JPEG. If necessary, navigate to the ps02lessons folder so the file is saved in this location, then click the Save button. The JPEG Options dialog box appears.

3   In the JPEG Options dialog box, confirm that the quality is set to maximum, and leave the format options set to their defaults. Click OK. This completes the Save process for your file.

4   Choose File > Close to close the file and click Save when prompted.

Because JPEG is supported by web browsers, you can check your file by opening it and using any web browser, such as Firefox, Internet Explorer, or Safari. Open the browser and choose File > Open, which can appear as Open File or Open Location, depending upon the application. Navigate to the ps02lessons folder and double-click to open the file you saved.

Saving for print

In this part of the lesson, you will change the color settings to choose a color profile more suitable for print to help you preview and prepare your file for printing. You will change the resolution of the image before saving it.

Changing the color settings

You will now change the color settings to get a more accurate view of how the file will print.

1   If **ps0201_work.psd** is not open, choose File > Open Recent > **ps0201_work.psd**. You can use the Open Recent command to easily locate your most recently opened files. The file opens.

2   Choose Edit > Color Settings. The Color Settings dialog box appears.

3   From the Color Settings drop-down menu, choose North America Prepress 2. This provides you with a color profile based upon typical printing environments in North America. Click OK to close the Color Settings dialog box.

Select the North America Prepress 2 color setting.

4   Choose the Zoom tool ( ) from the Tools panel, and then click and drag to create a zoom area around the bar of the goal in the image.

5 Choose View > Proof Colors, or press Ctrl+Y (Windows) or Command+Y (Mac OS). Notice a slight change in the color of the red, as the colors appear more subdued. The Proof Colors command allows you to work in the RGB format while approximating how your image will look when converted to CMYK, the color space used for printing. While you will work on images in the RGB mode, they generally must be converted to CMYK before they are sent to a professional printer. Leave them in RGB mode if going to a desktop printer or copier.

The image before Proof Colors is turned on.   *The image after Proof Colors is turned on.*

Adjusting image size

Next, you will adjust the image size for printing. When printing an image, you generally want a resolution of at least 150 pixels per inch. For higher-quality images, you will want a resolution of approximately 266 pixels per inch. While this image was saved at 72 pixels per inch, it is larger than needed. By reducing the physical dimensions of the image, the resolution (number of pixels per inch) can be increased.

1 Choose Image > Image Size; the Image Size dialog box appears. The image currently has a resolution of 72 pixels per inch.

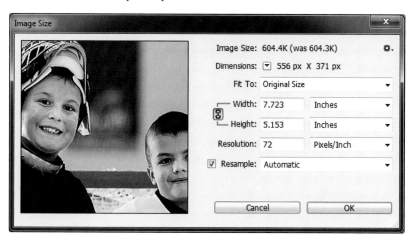

The image is at a low resolution of 72 pixels per inch.

This low resolution affects the image quality, and should be increased to print the best image possible. For this to occur, the dimensions of the image will need to be reduced so the image will be of a higher resolution, but will be smaller in size.

Resampling changes the amount of image data. When you resample up, you increase the number of pixels. New pixels are added, based upon the interpolation method you select. While resampling adds pixels, it can reduce image quality if it is not used carefully.

2   In the Image Size dialog box, uncheck Resample Image. By unchecking the Resample Image check box, you can increase the resolution without decreasing image quality.

You can use this method when resizing large image files, such as those from digital cameras that tend to have large dimensions but low resolution.

3   Type **266** in the Resolution field. The size is reduced in the Width and Height text boxes to accommodate the new increased resolution, but the Pixel Dimensions remain the same. For quality printing at the highest resolution, this image should be printed no larger than approximately 2.09 inches by 1.395 inches. Click OK.

In this image, you are not adding pixels; you are simply reducing the dimensions of the image to create a higher resolution.

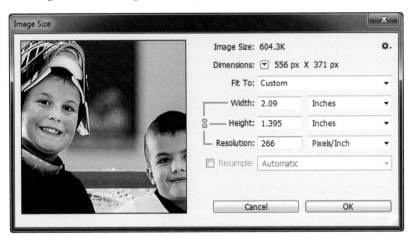

Increase resolution without decreasing quality.

4   Choose File > Save. Keep this file open for the next part of this lesson.

Saving a Photoshop PDF file

Images containing text or vector shapes may appear fine in low resolution when viewed on a computer display, even if the vector information is rasterized (converted into pixels.) When the same images are used for print projects, they should retain the resolution-independent vector elements. This keeps the text and other vector graphics looking sharp, so you do not need to worry about the jagged edges that occur when text and shapes are rasterized. To keep the vector information, you need to save the file using a format that retains both vector and bitmap data.

1   With the **ps0201_work.psd** image still open, choose File > Save As. The Save As dialog box appears.

2   In the Save As dialog box, navigate to the ps02lessons folder. In the Name text field, type **Hockey print version**. From the Format drop-down menu, choose Photoshop PDF, then click Save. Click OK to close any warning dialog box that might appear. The Save Adobe PDF dialog box appears.

3   In the Save Adobe PDF dialog box, choose Press Quality from the Adobe PDF Preset drop-down menu, and then click Save PDF. If a warning appears, indicating that older versions of Photoshop may not be able to edit the PDF file, click Yes to continue.

4   Your file has been saved in the Adobe PDF format, ready to be used in other applications such as Adobe InDesign, or shared for proofing with a reviewer who may have Adobe Acrobat or Adobe Reader.

Self study

1 Using the image named **ps0202.psd** found within your ps02lessons folder, create a more dynamic crop that centers more on the gorilla in the image. Remember to apply the rule of thirds.

2 Using Image > Image Size, change the image size of the **ps0202.psd** image to 500 px wide, and then choose to save your **ps0202.psd** image for the web as a .png file.

Review

Questions

1 What does unchecking the Delete Cropped Pixels allow you to do in your image?

2 What does Smart Sharpen do to an image?

3 Why is it important to use adjustment layers?

4 When would you save a file in the .jpeg or .png format?

Answers

1 By unchecking the Delete Cropped Pixels check box, you can reposition your crop area, since the pixels are hidden but not deleted.

2 Sharpening enhances the definition of edges in an image. The degree of sharpening that you need to apply to your own images varies depending on the quality of the original image.

3 It is important to use adjustment layers so you can make additional edits to your image adjustments after they have been applied.

4 Typically, you would save a file in the .png or .jpeg format if you are saving it for the web or for an on-screen presentation.

What you'll learn in this lesson:

- Navigating Adobe Bridge
- Using folders in Bridge
- Making a favorite
- Creating metadata
- Using automated tools

Organizing and Managing Your Files with Adobe Bridge

Using Adobe Bridge, you can manage and organize your files, use and modify XMP metadata for faster searches, and quickly preview files before opening them.

Starting up

Before starting, make sure that your tools and panels are consistent by resetting your preferences. See "Resetting Adobe Photoshop CC preferences" in the Starting Up section of this book.

Also confirm that you have Adobe Bridge CC installed in your system. You can launch the Adobe Application Manager to check the status of all your Creative Cloud applications. If the column to the right of Adobe Bridge states Up to date, you are all set. Otherwise, you can click Install to have Adobe Bridge CC installed on your system.

If you do not see Adobe Bridge, make sure to check the Updates in the Adobe Application Manager to see if it requires an update.

You will work with several files from the ps03lessons folder in this lesson. Make sure that you have loaded the pslessons folder onto your hard drive from the supplied DVD. See "Loading lesson files" in the Starting Up section of this book.

See Lesson 3 in action!

Use the accompanying video to gain a better understanding of how to use some of the features shown in this lesson. You can find the video tutorial for this lesson on the included DVD.

What is Adobe Bridge?

Adobe Bridge is an application that helps you locate, organize, and browse the documents you need to create print, web, video, and audio content.

This lesson covers the functionality of the complete Bridge application, not the Mini Bridge that is available as a panel in your Photoshop workspace.

You can use Bridge to access documents such as images, text files, and even non–Adobe documents, such as Microsoft Word or Excel files. Using Adobe Bridge, you can also organize and manage images, videos, and audio files, as well as preview, search, and sort your files without opening them in their native applications.

Once you discover the capabilities of Adobe Bridge, you'll want to make it the control center for your Photoshop projects. With Bridge, you can easily locate files using the Filters panel and import images from your digital camera right into a viewing area that allows you to quickly rename and preview your files. This is why the recommended workflow throughout this book includes opening and saving files in Adobe Bridge. Reading through this lesson will help you to feel more comfortable with Adobe Bridge, and will also make you aware of some of the more advanced features that are available to you for your own projects.

Navigating through Bridge

To use Adobe Bridge effectively, you'll want to know the available tools and how to access them.

1   From Photoshop CC, choose File > Browse in Bridge to launch the Adobe Bridge CC application. If you are taken directly to the Adobe Application Manager, select Adobe Bridge CC and install it.

2   Once Adobe Bridge is launched, click the Favorites panel to make sure it is forward. Click Desktop (listed in the Folders panel). You see the ps03lessons folder that you downloaded to your hard drive. Double-click the ps03lessons folder; notice that the contents of that folder are displayed in the Content panel, in the center of the Adobe Bridge window. You can also navigate by clicking folders listed in the Path bar that is located in the upper-left corner of the content window.

You can view folder contents by double-clicking a folder, or by selecting the folder in the Path bar.

In this folder, you see a variety of file types, including Adobe Illustrator, Adobe Photoshop, Adobe Acrobat, and video files. These files came from *istockphoto.com* and many still have their default names.

You can navigate through your navigation history by clicking the Go back and Go forward arrows in the upper-left corner of the window. Use the Reveal All Recent files icon (⟲) to find folders and files that you recently opened. Note that there are also helpful navigational tools that allow you to quickly return to Photoshop, load photos from a camera, and flip your images.

3   Click the Go back arrow (◀) to return to the desktop view.

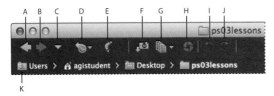

A. Go back. B. Go forward. C. Go to parent or Favorites.
D. Reveal recent file or go to recent folder. E. Return to Adobe Photoshop.
F. Get Photos From Camera. G. Refine. H. Open in Camera Raw.
I. Rotate 90° counterclockwise. J. Rotate 90° clockwise. K. Path bar.

This example might show a file path to the ps03lessons folder that is different from your example because this desktop is referencing a folder on a particular user's desktop.

4   Click the Go forward arrow (▶) to return to the last view, which is the ps03lessons folder.

Using folders in Adobe Bridge

Adobe Bridge is used for more than just navigating your file system. Bridge is also used to manage and organize folders and files.

1   Click the tab of the Favorites panel in the upper-left corner of the Bridge window to make sure it is still forward. Then click the arrow to the left of Desktop so that it turns downward and reveals its contents. If you are on the Mac OS, you can simply click Desktop to reveal the contents.

2   Click Computer to reveal its contents in the center pane of the Bridge window. Continue to double-click items, or click the arrows to the left of the folder names in the Folder panel, to reveal their contents.

You can use Adobe Bridge to navigate your entire system, much as you would by using your computer's directory system.

Managing folders

Adobe Bridge is a great tool for organizing folders and files. It is a simple matter of dragging and dropping to reorder items on your computer. You can create folders, move folders, move files from one folder to another, and copy files and folders to other locations; any organizing task that can be performed on the computer can also be performed in Adobe Bridge. This is a great way to help keep volumes of images organized for easy accessibility, as well as easy searching. One advantage of using Adobe Bridge for these tasks is that you have bigger and better previews of images, PDF files, and movies, with much more information about those files at your fingertips.

3   Click Desktop in the Folders panel to reveal its contents again.

4   Click ps03lessons to view its contents. You'll now add a new folder into that lessons folder.

5   Click the Create a New Folder icon (📁) in the upper-right corner of the Bridge window to create a new untitled folder inside the ps03lessons folder. Type the name **Graphics**.

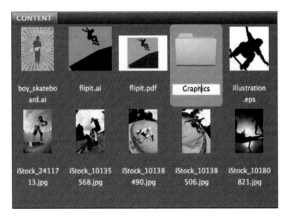

Creating a new folder in Bridge.

You can use Adobe Bridge to organize images. Since you are able to see a preview of each file, you can more easily rename them, as well as relocate them to more appropriate locations in your directory system. In the next step, you will move files from one folder to the new Graphics folder you have just created.

6   Click once on the image named **boy_skateboard.ai**, and then Shift+click the image named **flipit.ai**. Both images are selected.

You can easily reduce and enlarge the size of your thumbnails by pressing Ctrl+plus sign or Ctrl+minus sign in Windows or Command+plus sign or Command+minus sign in Mac OS.

7 Click and drag the selected images to the Graphics folder. When the folder becomes highlighted, release the mouse. The files have now been moved into that folder.

You can select multiple images and organize folders directly in Adobe Bridge.

8 Double-click the Graphics folder to view its contents. You see the **boy_skateboard** and the **flipit** Adobe Illustrator (.ai) files that you moved.

9 Click ps03lessons in the file path bar at the top to return to the ps03lessons folder content.

Making a Favorite

As you work in Photoshop, you will find that you frequently access the same folders. One of the many great features in Bridge is that you can designate a frequently used folder as a Favorite, allowing you to quickly and easily access it from the Favorites panel. This is extremely helpful, especially if the folders that you are frequently accessing are stored deep in your file hierarchy.

1 Select the Favorites panel in the upper-left corner of the Bridge window to bring it to the front. In the list of Favorites, click Desktop. Double-click the ps03lessons folder to see the skateboarding images. Since the Graphics folder is going to be used again in this lesson, you'll make it a Favorite.

2   Place your cursor over the Graphics folder in the center pane (Content), and click and drag the Graphics folder until you see a horizontal line appear in the Favorites panel. Be careful not to drag this folder into a folder (highlighted with a blue box) in the Favorites panel. When a cursor with a plus sign (⤵) appears, release the mouse. On the Mac OS you will see a circle with a plus sign. The folder is now listed as a Favorite.

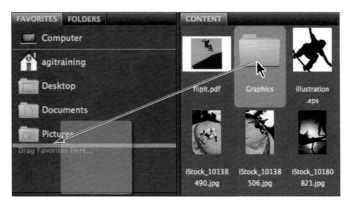

Drag a folder to the bottom of the Favorites panel to make it easier to locate.

3   Click the Graphics folder shown in the Favorites panel to view its contents. Note that creating a Favorite simply creates a shortcut for quick access to a folder; it does not copy the folder and its contents.

4   When you are finished looking inside the Graphics folder, click the Go back arrow to return to the ps03lessons folder.

If your Favorite is created from a folder on an external hard drive or server, you will need to have the hard drive or server mounted in order to access it.

Creating and locating metadata

Metadata is information that can be stored with images. This information travels with the file, and makes it easy to search for and identify the file. In this section, you are going to find out how to locate and create metadata.

1   Make sure that you are viewing the contents of the ps03lessons folder in the center pane of Adobe Bridge. If not, navigate to that folder now.

2   Choose Window > Workspace > Reset Standard Workspaces. This ensures that you are in the Essentials view and that all the default panels for Adobe Bridge are visible. Alternatively, you can click Essentials in the Application bar at the top-right of the Bridge workspace. You might need to maximize your Bridge window after you reset the workspace.

Note that if you click the arrow to the right of the workspace presets, you can choose other workspaces, and even save your own custom workspace.

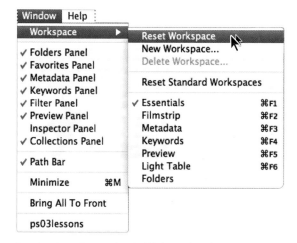

Resetting the workspace using the Workspace drop-down menu.

3   Click once on **iStock_1771975.jpg**, and look for the Metadata and Keywords panels in the lower-right area of the Adobe Bridge workspace.

4   If the Metadata panel is not visible, click the Metadata panel tab. In this panel, you see the image data that is stored with the file. Take a few moments to scroll through the data and view the information that was imported from the digital camera that was used to take the photo.

Click and drag the bar to the left of the Metadata panel farther to the left if you need to open up the window.

5   If necessary, click the arrow to the left of IPTC Core to reveal its contents. IPTC Core is the schema for XMP that provides a smooth and explicit transfer of metadata. Adobe's Extensible Metadata Platform (XMP) is a labeling technology that allows you to embed data about a file, known as metadata, into the file itself. With XMP, desktop applications and back-end publishing systems gain a common method for capturing and sharing valuable metadata.

6   On the right side of this list, notice a series of pencil icons. The pencil icons indicate that you can enter information in these fields. Some of the information about the creator has already been included, such as the creator's name and his location. You will add additional information.

If you are not able to edit or add metadata information to a file, it could be locked. Make sure that you are not working directly from the Lesson DVD, and then right-click the file (in Adobe Bridge) and choose Reveal in Explorer (Windows) or Reveal in Finder (Mac OS). In Windows, right-click the file, choose Properties, and uncheck Read-only; in Mac OS, right-click the file, choose Get Info, then change the Ownership (Sharing) and Permissions to Read and Write.

7   Scroll down until you can see Description Writer, and click the pencil next to it. All editable fields are highlighted, and a cursor appears in the Description Writer field.

8   Type your name, or type **Student**.

9   Scroll up to locate the Description text field. Click the Pencil icon to the right and type **Skateboarder catching air**, to add a description for the image.

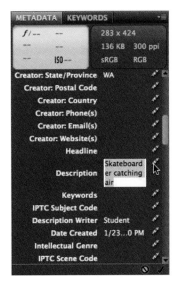

Reveal the IPTC contents and enter metadata information.

10 Click the Apply button (✔), located in the bottom-right corner of the Metadata panel, to apply your changes. You have now edited metadata that is attached to the image; this information will appear whenever someone opens your image in Bridge or views the image information in Adobe Photoshop using File > File Info.

Using keywords

Keywords can reduce the amount of time it takes to find an image on a computer by using logical words to help you locate images more quickly.

1 Click the Keywords tab, which appears behind the Metadata panel. A list of commonly used keywords appears.

2 Click the New Keyword button (✣) at the bottom of the Keywords panel. Type **Skateboarder** into the active text field, and then press Enter (Windows) or Return (Mac OS).

3 Select the empty check box to the left of the Skateboarder keyword. This adds the Skateboarder keyword to the selected image.

4 With the Skateboarder keyword still selected, click the New Sub Keyword button (✣). Type **Male** into the active text field, then press Enter (Windows) or Return (Mac OS).

5 Select the empty check box to the left of the Male keyword. You have now assigned a keyword and a sub keyword to the **iStock_1771975.jpg** image.

6 Select the Skateboarder keyword, and then click the New Keyword button (✣) at the bottom of the Keywords panel; a blank text field appears. Type **Sunset** and press Enter (Windows) or Return (Mac OS). Then select the check box next to Sunset to assign the keyword to this image.

7   Right-click (Windows) or Ctrl+click (Mac OS) on the Sunset keyword, and choose the option Rename. When the text field becomes highlighted, type **Orange**, press Enter (Windows) or Return (Mac OS). Make sure the Orange check box remains selected.

A. *New Sub Keyword.* B. *New Keyword.*
C. *Delete Keyword.*

You can also enter information directly into the image by opening the image in Adobe Photoshop, and then choosing File > File Info. The categories that appear on the top include Description, Camera Data, IPTC, and IPTC Extension, among others. Once it is entered in the File Info dialog box, the information is visible in Adobe Bridge.

Creating a Metadata Template

Once you have added metadata to an image, you can easily apply it to more images by creating a metadata template. In this exercise, you will apply the metadata template from the **iStock_1771975.jpg image** to other images in the same folder.

1   Make sure that **iStock_1771975.jpg** is selected in Adobe Bridge.

2   Choose Tools > Create Metadata Template. The Create Metadata Template window appears.

3   In the Template File name text field (at the top), type **Sunset Skateboarders**.

In the Create Metadata Template window, you can choose the information that you want to build into a template. In this exercise, we will choose information that already exists in the selected file, but if you wanted to, you could add or edit information at this point.

4   Select the check boxes to the left of the following categories: Creator, Creator: City, Creator: State/Province, Description, Keywords, and Description Writer, then click Save.

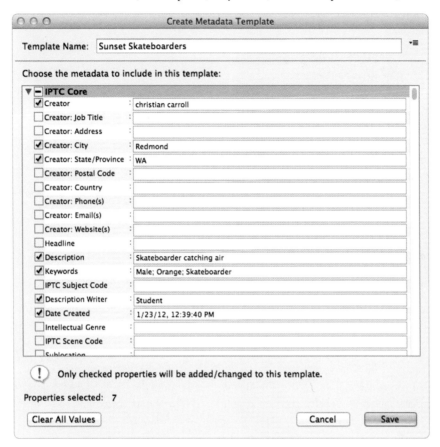

Select a file and check the information you want to save into a metadata template.

You have just saved a template. Next, you will apply it to the other two sunset images in this folder.

5   Select the **iStock_1771975.jpg** image, press and hold the Ctrl (Windows) or Command (Mac OS) key, and select the **iStock_10135568.jpg** image. Both images are selected.

6   Choose Tools > Append Metadata and select Sunset Skateboarders. Note that you can also choose Replace Metadata if you want to eliminate existing metadata. The same metadata has now been applied to all the images at once.

Choose the metadata template you want to use to add metadata to an image or images.

Opening a file from Adobe Bridge

Opening files from Adobe Bridge is a great way to begin the work process in Adobe Photoshop. Not only is it very visual, but important data stored with the files also makes it easier to locate the correct file.

1   In the ps03lessons folder, double-click **iStock_10138490.jpg** to open the file in Adobe Photoshop.

Sometimes you will find that double-clicking a file opens it in a different application than expected. This can happen if you are working in generic file formats such as JPEG and GIF. To avoid this problem, you can right-click (Windows) or Ctrl+click (Mac OS) the image, and choose Open With to select the appropriate application.

2   Choose File > Close and then select File > Browse in Bridge to return to Adobe Bridge.

3   You can also click once to select an image and then choose File > Open, or use the keyboard shortcut Ctrl+O (Windows) or Command+O (Mac OS).

Searching for files using Adobe Bridge

Find the files that you want quickly and easily by using the Search tools built directly into Adobe Bridge and taking advantage of the Filter panel.

In this example, you have a limited number of files to search within, but you will have the opportunity to see how helpful these search features can be.

Searching by name or keyword

The benefit of adding metadata to your images is that you can use it to find your files later. Using the Find dialog box in Adobe Bridge, you can narrow your criteria down to make it easy to find your files when needed.

1   Make sure that you are still viewing the content in the ps03lessons folder.

2   Choose Edit > Find, or use the keyboard shortcut Ctrl+F (Windows) or Command+F (Mac OS). The Find dialog box appears.

3   Select Keywords from the Criteria drop-down menu, and type **Skateboarder** into the third text field (replacing Enter Text.) Then press Enter (Windows) or Return (Mac OS). Because you are looking within the active folder only, you get a result immediately. The image files **iStock_1771975.jpg**, **iStock_10138490.jpg**, **iStock_10138506.jpg**, and **iStock_10135568.jpg** appear.

Search your folders using the tools built right into Adobe Bridge.

4   Clear the search by clicking the X icon (⊗) to the right of the New Search icon at the top of the results pane.

Using the Filter panel

You can use the Filter panel to locate files that you can't remember where you saved them. With the Filter panel, you can look at attributes such as file type, keywords, and date created or modified to narrow down the files that appear in the content window of Adobe Bridge.

1   Make sure that you are still viewing the content of the ps03lessons folder. Notice that the Filter panel collects the information from the active folder, indicating the keywords that are being used, as well as modification dates and more.

2   Click to turn down the arrow next to Keywords in the Filter panel, and select Skateboarder from the list; notice that only images with the Skateboarder keyword applied are visible. Click Skateboarder again to deselect it and view all the images.

Find files quickly by selecting different criteria in the Filters panel.

3   Click the Clear filter button (⊙) in the lower-right of the Filter panel to turn off any filters.

4   Experiment with investigating file types as well. Only file types that exist in the selected folder appear in the list. If you are looking for an Adobe Illustrator file, you might see that there are none located in this folder, but you will see a QuickTime video file that you can select and preview right in Adobe Bridge.

You can select File Types from the Filter panel to locate them easily.

5   Again, click the Clear filter button (⊘) in the lower-right area of the Filter panel to turn off any filters.

Saving a Collection

If you like using Favorites, you'll love using Collections. A Collection allows you to take images from multiple locations and access them in one central location. Understand that Adobe Bridge essentially creates a shortcut (or alias) to your files and does not physically relocate them or copy them to a different location.

1   If your Collections tab is not visible, Choose Window > Collections Panel or click the tab next to Filter. The Collections panel comes forward.

2   Click the gray area in the content pane to make sure that nothing is selected, and then click the New Collection button in the lower-right area of the Collections panel. Type **Redmond Skateboarding** into the new collection text field. Press Return or Enter to confirm your new collection.

Create a new Redmond Skateboarding collection.

3 Navigate back to the ps03lessons folder, and then take two random skateboarding images and drag them to the Redmond Skateboarding collection. In this example, the two images of the girl skateboarding were selected.

4 Click the Redmond Skateboarding collection folder; notice that even though you can easily access the files you added to the collection, the files remain intact in their original location.

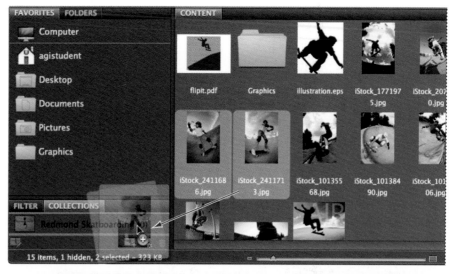

A collection helps you to organize files without moving them to new locations.

Automation tools in Adobe Bridge

Adobe Bridge provides many tools to help you automate tasks. In this section, you will learn how to access and take advantage of some of these features.

Batch renaming your files

You might have noticed that in the ps03lessons file, there are many files that contain iStock in the filename. These images were downloaded from *iStockphoto.com*, and instead of changing the names immediately, we have opted to change them simultaneously using the batch rename feature in Adobe Bridge.

1   Click the Go back arrow (◄) in the upper-left area of the Adobe Bridge window to go back to the ps03lessons folder.

2   Choose Edit > Select All, or press Ctrl+A (Windows) or Command+A (Mac OS.) All the images are selected. Don't worry if the Graphics folder is selected; the files inside will not be affected.

3   Choose Tools > Batch Rename. The Batch Rename dialog box appears.

    In this instance, we want a simple, uncomplicated name. If you look in the Preview section at the bottom of the Batch Rename dialog box, you can see that the Current filename and New filename are long strings of text and numbers. You will simplify this by eliminating some of text from the filenames.

4   In the New File names section, type **Skateboard** in the Text field.

5   In the Sequence Number row, verify that it is set to Two Digits.

6   Confirm that the sequence number is starting at 1. You can start it anywhere if you are adding additional images to a folder later.

7   If there is any other criteria, click the Minus sign button (⊟) (Remove this text from the file names) to remove them. The New file name in the Preview section becomes significantly shorter.

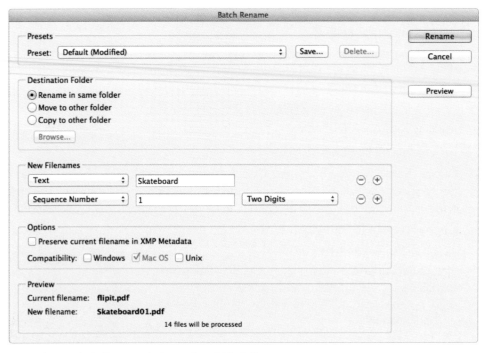

You can change multiple files names simultaneously in Adobe Bridge.

If you look in the Preview section at the bottom of the dialog box, you can see that the new filename is a very simple **Skateboard01.jpg** now. Click the Rename button. All the selected files automatically have their name changed.

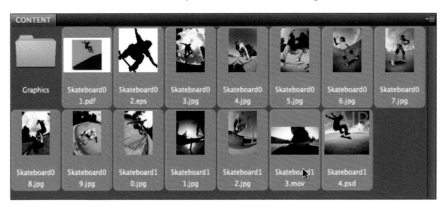

The content panel after the images were renamed.

Additional Photoshop Tools

Adobe Bridge comes with a variety of Photoshop tools that you can use in Bridge as well. In this example, you will select three images that you want to incorporate into one composited image. Instead of opening all three images and cutting and pasting or dragging them into one file, you will use the Load Files into Photoshop layers feature.

Make sure that you are still in the ps03lessons folder; select the **Skateboard03.jpg**, and then Shift+click the **Skateboard05.jpg** image. All three images are selected.

Select Tools > Photoshop. Note that there are many tools that you can use in this menu item; for this example, select the Load Files into Photoshop Layers option. A script immediately launches Photoshop (if it is not already open) and a new layered file is created from the selected images.

You should ensure that your selected images are approximately the same pixel dimensions before running this script; otherwise, you might have to make some transformation adjustments in Photoshop. In this example, the images are approximately the same size.

Select multiple files in Adobe Bridge and open them in one layered file.

The result is three layers in one Photoshop file.

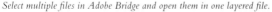

Changing the view

You can work in a way that's more effective for you by adjusting the look and feel of Adobe Bridge. Changing the view can help you focus on what is important to see in the Content section of the Bridge workspace. Whether you need to focus on content or thumbnails, there is a view that can help you.

1   Before experimenting with the views, make sure that you are in the Essentials workspace by selecting the Essentials button located in the upper-right area of the Bridge workspace.

2   Click the Click to Lock to Thumbnail Grid button (⊞) in the lower-right corner of the Bridge workspace. The images are organized into a grid.

3   Now click the View content as details button (▬▬) to see a thumbnail and details about creation date, last modified date, and file size.

Changing the view of Adobe Bridge.

4   Choose the View Content as List button (☰) to see the contents consolidated into a neat list, which you can easily scroll through.

5   Click the View Content as Thumbnails button (⠿) to return to the default thumbnail view.

6   Experiment with changing the size of the thumbnails in the Content panel by using the slider to the left of the preview buttons. Don't forget that you can also change the thumbnail size by pressing Ctrl++ (plus sign) or Ctrl+- (minus sign) (Windows) or Command++ (plus sign) or Command+- (minus sign) (Mac OS).

Self study

As you work with Bridge, create some new Favorites of folders that you frequently use. You might also want to practice removing Favorites: highlight one of the Favorites and choose File > Remove from Favorites. Also, explore creating and opening up multiple files as layers in Photoshop.

Review

Questions

1   How do you access Photoshop automation features from within Adobe Bridge?

2   Where do you find the metadata for an image, and how do you know if the metadata is editable?

3   Which panel in Adobe Bridge enables you to organize your files on your computer?

Answers

1   You can access automated tools for Adobe Photoshop by choosing Tools > Photoshop.

2   You find metadata information in the Metadata and Keywords panels in the lower-right corner of the Bridge workspace. Metadata is editable if it has the pencil icon next to it.

3   You can use the Folders panel to organize your files.

What you'll learn in this lesson:

- Using the selection tools
- Refining your selections
- Transforming selections
- Using the Pen tool
- Saving selections

Making Selective Changes in Photoshop CC

Creating a good selection in Photoshop is a critical skill. Selections allow you to isolate areas in an image for retouching, painting, copying, or pasting. If done correctly, selections are inconspicuous to the viewer; if not, images can look contrived, or over-manipulated. In this lesson, you will discover the fundamentals of making good selections.

Starting up

Before starting, make sure that your tools and panels are consistent by resetting your preferences. See "Resetting the Photoshop workspace" in the Starting up section of this book. Keep in mind that if you do not reset your Photoshop preferences, you could have additional dialog boxes appear that reference mismatched color profiles and more.

You will work with several files from the ps04lessons folder in this lesson. Make sure that you have loaded the pslessons folder onto your hard drive from the supplied DVD. See "Loading lesson files" in the Starting up section of this book.

See Lesson 4 in action!

Use the accompanying video to gain a better understanding of how to use some of the features shown in this lesson. You can find the video tutorial for this lesson on the included DVD.

The importance of a good selection

"You have to select it to affect it" is an old saying in the image-editing industry. To make changes to specific regions in your images, you must activate only those areas. To do this, you can use selection tools such as the Marquee, Lasso, and Quick Selection tools, or you can create a selection by painting a mask. For precise selections, you can use the Pen tool. In this lesson, you'll learn how to select pixels in an image with both pixel and pen (vector) selection techniques.

You'll start with some simple selection methods and then progress into more difficult selection techniques. Note that even if you are an experienced Photoshop user, you will want to follow the entire lesson; there are tips and tricks included that will help all levels of users achieve the best selections possible.

Using the Marquee tools

The first selection tools you'll use are the Marquee tools, which include Rectangular, Elliptical, Single Row, and Single Column tools. Some of the many uses for the Rectangular and Elliptical Marquee tools are to isolate an area for cropping, to create a border around an image, or to use that area in the image for corrective or creative image adjustment.

1   In Photoshop, choose File > Browse in Bridge. Navigate to the ps04lessons folder and double-click **ps0401_done.psd** to open the image of a car. The completed image appears. You can leave the file open for reference, or choose File > Close to close it.

The completed selection file.

2   Return to Adobe Bridge by choosing File > Browse in Bridge. Navigate to the ps04lessons folder and double-click **ps0401.psd** to open the image. The start file for this lesson appears.

3   Choose File > Save As. When the Save As dialog box appears, navigate to the ps04lessons folder. In the File name text field, type **ps0401_work**. Choose Photoshop from the Format drop-down menu and click Save. If the Photoshop Format Options dialog box appears, click OK.

4   Select the Rectangular Marquee tool (⬚), near the top of the Tools panel.

5   Make sure that Snap is selected by choosing View > Snap. If the check box shows a checkmark, it is already active.

6   Position your cursor in the upper-left side of the guide in the car image, and drag a rectangular selection down toward the lower-right corner of the guide. A rectangular selection appears as you drag, and it stays active when you release the mouse.

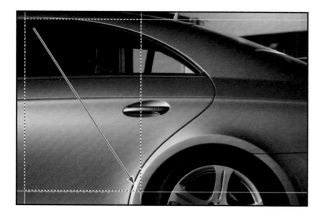

Creating a rectangular selection in the image.

You'll now apply an adjustment layer to lighten just the selected area of the image. You are lightening this region so that a text overlay can be placed over that part of the image.

7   If the Adjustments panel is not visible, choose Window > Adjustments and click the Curves icon; the Properties panel appears.

Click the Curves button to create a new Curves adjustment layer.

8   To ensure consistent results, first click the panel menu (▾≡) in the upper–right corner of the Properties panel and choose Curves Display Options. In the Show Amount of section, select Pigment/Ink %. Choosing Pigment for corrections makes the curves adjustment more representative of ink on paper. Click OK to close the Curves Display Options dialog box.

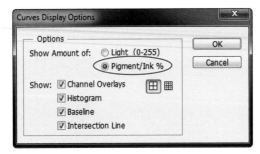

Select Pigment/Ink % in the Curve Display options.

9   Make sure that you can see additional options at the bottom of the Properties panel, such as Input and Output. If you do not see these options, click and drag the bottom of the Properties panel to expose them.

If necessary, expand the Properties panel to see additional options at the bottom.

10 Click and drag the upper-right anchor point (shadow) straight down, keeping it flush with the right side of the Properties window, until the Output text field reads approximately 20, or type **20** into the Output text field. The rectangular selection in the image is lightened to about 20% of its original value.

Because you used an adjustment layer, you can double-click the Curves thumbnail in the Layers panel to re-open the Curves panel as often as you need to readjust the lightness in the rectangular selection.

Make a curve adjustment to the selection.   *The result.*

11 Now go back to the Layers panel, click the box to the left of the text layer named poster text; the Visibility icon (👁) appears, and the layer is now visible. The text appears over the lightened area.

12 Choose File > Save to save this file. Keep the file open for the next part of this exercise.

Creating a square selection

In this section, you'll learn how to create a square selection using the Rectangular Marquee tool.

1   Click the Background thumbnail in the Layers panel to select it.

2   Select the Rectangular Marquee tool (□) and position your cursor over the taillight of the car. Click and drag while holding the Shift key. Note that your selection is constrained, creating a square selection. When you have created a square (size doesn't matter), first release the mouse and then the Shift key.

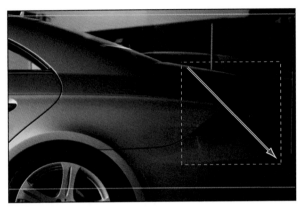

Click and drag while holding the Shift key.

3   With the square selection still active, position your cursor over the selected region of the image. Notice that an arrow with a dashed box appears (▷▫). This indicates that the selection shape can be moved without moving any of the pixel information in the image.

4   Click and drag the selection to another location. Only the selection moves. Reposition the selection over the taillight.

5   Select the Move tool (▸✛) and position the cursor over the selected region. Notice that an icon with an arrow and scissors appears (▷✂). This indicates that if you move the selection, you will cut, or move, the pixels with the selection.

6   Click and drag the selection; the selected region of the image moves with the selection.

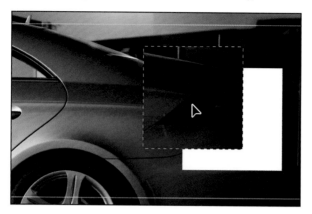

When the Move tool is selected, the pixels are moved with the selection.

7   Select Edit > Undo Move, or use the keyboard shortcut Ctrl+Z (Windows) or Command+Z (Mac OS) to undo your last step.

8   You'll now alter that section of the image. Note that in this example you edit a region of an image without creating a layer; you are affecting the pixels of the image and cannot easily undo your edits after the image has been saved, closed, and reopened. You will discover more ways to take advantage of the Adjustments panel later in this lesson.

9   Choose Image > Adjustments > Hue/Saturation.

You will now adjust the hue, or color, of this region. Click and drag the Hue slider to change the color of the selected region. Select any color. In this example, the Hue slider is moved to **–150**. Click OK. The new hue is applied to the taillight region.

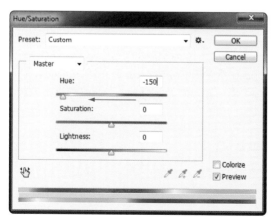

Changing the hue of the selected region.

The result.

10   Choose File > Save; keep the image open for the next part of this lesson.

Creating a selection from a center point

1   Select the Background layer in the Layers panel, then click and hold the Rectangular Marquee tool (⬚) and select the hidden Elliptical Marquee tool (⬭).

The selection technique you're about to use requires you to press and hold two modifier keys as you drag.

2   You'll now draw a circle selection from the center of the image. Place your cursor in the approximate center of the tire, and then press and hold the Alt (Windows) or Option (Mac OS) key and the Shift key. Click and drag to pull a circular selection from the center origin point. Release the mouse (before the modifier keys) when you have created a selection that is surrounding the tire. If necessary, you can click and drag the selection while you still have the Elliptical Marquee tool selected, or use your arrow keys to nudge the selection.

Press and hold Alt/Option when dragging to create a selection from the center.

While pressing and holding the Alt (Windows) or Option (Mac OS) key and the Shift key, you can add the spacebar to reposition the selection as you are dragging with the Marquee tool. Release the spacebar to continue sizing the selection.

3 Choose Select > Transform Selection. A bounding box with anchor points appears around your selection. Use the bounding box's anchor points to adjust the size and proportions of the selection. Note that you can scale proportionally by pressing and holding the Shift key when you transform the selection.

Transform your selection.

4 When you are finished with the transformation, click the check mark (✔) in the upper-right corner of the Options bar, press the Enter (Windows) or Return (Mac OS) key to confirm your transformation change, or press the Esc key in the upper-left corner of your keyboard to cancel the selection transformation.

5 Choose File > Save. Keep this file open for the next part of this lesson.

Changing a selection into a layer

You will now move your selection up to a new layer. By moving a selection to its own independent layer, you can have more control over the selected region while leaving the original image data intact. You'll learn more about layers in Lesson 8, "Introduction to Photoshop Layers."

1   With the tire still selected, click the Background layer to make it active. Press Ctrl+J (Windows) or Command+J (Mac OS). Think of this as the *Jump my selection to a new layer* keyboard shortcut. Alternatively, to create a new layer for your selection, you can select Layer > New > Layer Via Copy. The selection marquee disappears and the selected region is moved and copied to a new layer called Layer 1.

A new layer created from the selection.

2   Now you will apply a filter to this new layer. Choose Filter > Blur > Motion Blur. The Motion Blur dialog box appears.

3   In the Motion Blur dialog box, type **0** (zero) in the Angle text field and **45** in the Distance text field; then click OK. A motion blur is applied to the tire.

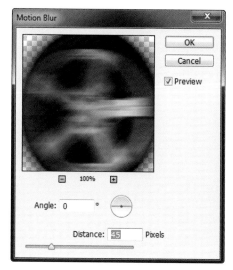

Applying the motion blur.   *The result.*

4   Select the Move tool (✛), move the tire slightly to the right, and type **5**. By typing 5, you have changed the Opacity of this layer to 50 percent.

5   Choose File > Save, and then File > Close.

Working with the Magic Wand tool

The Magic Wand makes selections based on tonal similarities; it lets you select a consistently colored area, for example a blue sky, without having to trace its outline. You control the range it automatically selects by adjusting the tolerance.

1   Choose File > Browse in Bridge to bring Adobe Bridge forward. Then navigate to the ps04lessons folder and open the image **ps0402.psd**. An image of a kite appears.

2   Choose File > Save As; the Save As dialog box appears. Navigate to the ps04lessons folder and type **ps0402_work** into the File name text field. Make sure that Photoshop is selected from the Format drop-down menu, and click Save.

3   Click and hold the Quick Selection tool (✐) to locate and select the hidden Magic Wand tool (✾).

4   In the Options bar, make sure the tolerance is set to **32**.

5   Position your cursor over the red portion of the kite and click once. Notice that similar tonal areas that are contiguous (touching) are selected. Place your cursor over different parts of the kite and click to see the different selections that are created. The selections pick up only similar tonal areas that are contiguous; in this case, this is not the most effective way to make a selection.

6   Choose Select > Deselct, or use the keyboard shortcut Ctrl+D (Windows) or Command+D (Mac OS).

7   Click once in the sky at the top center of the image. The sky becomes selected. Don't worry if the sky is not entirely selected; it is because those areas are outside of the tolerance range of the area that you selected with the Magic Wand tool.

Image with the background selected.

To see what is included in a selection, position any selection tool over the image. If the icon appears as a hollow arrow with a dotted box next to it, it is over an active selection. If the icon of the tool or crosshair appears, that area is not part of the active selection.

8   Press Ctrl+0 (zero) (Windows) or Command+0 (zero) (Mac OS) to fit the picture to the screen. Then press and hold the Shift key and click the area of sky that was left unselected. Those areas are added to the selection of the sky.

9   Choose Select > Inverse. Now the selection has been turned inside out, selecting the kite. Inversing a selection is a helpful technique when solid colors are part of an image, since you can make quick selections instead of focusing on the more diversely colored areas of an image.

If you have control over the environment when you capture your images, it can be helpful to take a picture of an object against a solid background. That way, you can create quick selections using tools like Quick Selection and the Magic Wand.

10 Don't worry if you accidentally deselect a region, since Photoshop remembers your last selection. With the selection of the kite still active, choose Select > Deselect, and the selection is deselected; then choose Select > Reselect to reselect the kite.

11 Now you will sharpen the kite without affecting the sky. Choose Filter > Sharpen > Smart Sharpen. The Smart Sharpen dialog box appears.

12 Drag the Amount slider to the right to about 200, or type **200** into the Amount text field. Leave the Radius text field at 1. Change the Reduce Noise slider to about 10%, or type **10** into the Reduce Noise text field. There are reasons that you have entered these settings; they are just not addressed in this lesson that is focused on selections. Read more about Sharpening in Lesson 6, "Color Correcting an Image."

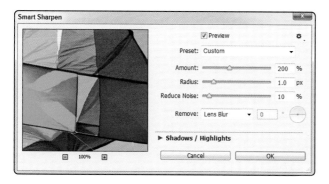

Sharpening the selection only.

13 Click and drag in the preview pane to bring the kite into view. Notice that in the preview pane of the Smart Sharpen dialog box, only the kite is sharpened. Position your cursor over the kite in the preview pane, and then click and hold. This temporarily turns the preview off. Release the mouse to see the Smart Sharpen filter effect applied. Click OK.

14 Choose File > Save. Then choose File > Close to close this file.

The Lasso tool

The Lasso tool is a freeform selection tool. It is great for creating an initial rough selection, and even better for cleaning up an existing selection. The selection that you create is as accurate as your hand on the mouse or trackpad allows it to be, which is why it lends itself to general cleaning up of selections. The best advice when using this tool is not to worry about being too precise; you can modify the selection, as you will see later in this section.

1 Choose File > Browse in Bridge to bring Adobe Bridge forward. Navigate to the ps04lessons folder inside the pslessons folder you copied to your computer. Double-click **ps0403.psd** to open the image. An image of a snowboarder appears.

2 Choose File > Save As. When the Save As dialog box appears, navigate to the ps04lessons folder. In the File name text field, type **ps0403_work**. Choose Photoshop from the Format drop-down menu and click Save.

You will now create a selection using the Lasso tool.

3 Select the Lasso tool (⌀) in the Tools panel.

4   Click slightly outside the snowboarder and drag the Lasso tool around him. The lasso selection that you are making does not have to be perfect, as you will have an opportunity to edit it shortly.

Click and drag around the snowboarder using the Lasso tool.

Adding to and subtracting from selections

You created a selection that surrounds the snowboarder. You'll now use the Lasso tool to refine that selection.

Deleting from the selection

In this part of the exercise, you learn to subtract from your active selection.

1   Select the Lasso tool (⌽) in the Tools panel.

2   Look at your image and determine the areas of your selection that you want to delete. This might include the area between the snowboarder and the selection of the sky surrounding him.

3   Press and hold the Alt (Windows) or Option (Mac OS) key and notice that the cursor turns into a Lasso with a minus sign. While holding the Alt/Option key, click and drag outside the selected area and into the active selection. Release the mouse when you have circled back to your original starting point. The new Lasso selection you made is deleted from the existing selection.

4   To practice this skill, press and hold the Alt/Option key, and click to start your lasso path on the edge of the snowboarder. Then, click and drag along the edge of the snowboarder for a short bit. When you want to end the lasso path, make sure to circle back around to the start point.

Carefully drag along the edge of the snowboarder, and then circle back to your starting point, enclosing the section that you want to delete from the active selection.

You do not have to delete the sky from all the edges of the snowboarder for this exercise. However, to prepare for the next section, you will delete the section between the snowboarder's legs and the board.

5   With the Alt/Option key pressed, click anywhere on the inside edge of one of the snowboarder's legs and drag all the way around the inner edge, over the mitten, and back to the starting point. Release the mouse when you are back at the initial clicking point.

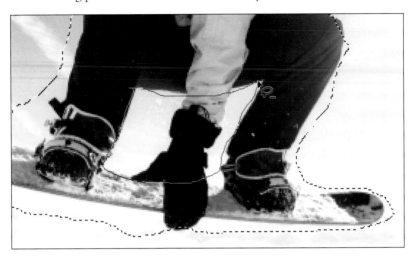

Delete the section between the snowboarder's legs from the selection.

Adding to the selection

If you want to add to an active selection, press and hold the Shift key and create a closed area. Follow these steps to bring the mitten back into the active selection.

1   Press and hold the Shift key and click and drag along the edge of the mitten. Make sure you drag beyond the mitten and down into the active area at the top and bottom to create a fully encompassed area to add to the selection.

2   You can continue to Shift+drag to add areas that you missed, or Alt/Option+Drag to subtract areas that you might have selected in error.

Using the Shift key to add to a selection and the Alt (Windows) or Option (Mac OS) key to delete from a selection, you can edit selections created with any of the selection tools.

Saving a selection

You should always save your selection because you might accidentally delete it or you might need to reactivate it at another time.

1 Choose Select > Save Selection; the Save Selection dialog box appears.

2 Type **snowboarder** into the File name text field, and then click OK. Anytime that you might need to reactivate the selection, choose Select > Load Selection, and then choose the Channel named snowboarder. Keep the other settings at the default and click OK.

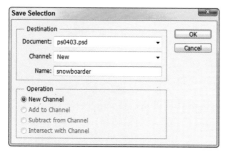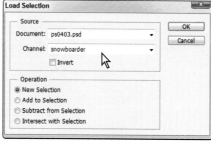

You can save a selection and then reload it when needed.

3 Choose File > Save to save this file. Keep the file open for the next part of the lesson.

Feathering the selection

In this part of the lesson, you will feather your selection (don't worry if your selection is less than perfect). Feathering is the term that Photoshop uses to describe a vignette, or fading of an image around the edges of a selection. There are many ways to feather a selection; in this section, you will learn the most visual method, which is the Refine Edge feature.

1 With the Lasso tool still selected, click Refine Edge in the Options bar. The Refine Edge dialog box appears.

2 Use the Feather slider to change the feather amount to about **5** pixels. By using the Refine Edge feature, you see a preview of the vignette immediately.

3   From the Output To drop-down menu, select Layer Mask and click OK. The image is faded, and a mask is added to the layer in the Layers panel.

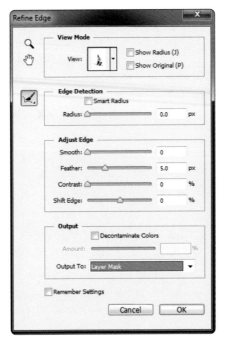

Change the Feather to 5 pixels.   *The result.*

Layer masks essentially cover any area that was not selected at the time the mask was created. Your selection is now in a state that can be reactivated, turned off, and turned on at any time. Layer Masks are discussed in more detail in Lesson 8, "Introduction to Photoshop Layers."

4   Press and hold the Shift key and click the Layer Mask in the Layers panel to turn off the mask; press and hold the Shift key and click the Layer Mask again to turn it on.

*Press and hold the Shift Key and click
the layer mask to turn it off and on.*

5   Choose File > Save, and then File > Close.

Using the Quick Selection tool

The Quick Selection tool allows you to paint your selection on an image. As you drag, the selection expands outward and finds defined edges of contrast to use as boundaries for the selection. In this part of the lesson, you'll re-open the original **ps0403.psd** image to make a selection using the Quick Selection tool.

1   Choose File > Browse in Bridge to open Adobe Bridge. Navigate to the ps04lessons folder inside the pslessons folder. Double-click **ps0403.psd** to open the image.

2   Choose File > Save As. When the Save As dialog box appears, navigate to the ps04lessons folder. In the File name text field, type **ps0403_workv2**. Choose Photoshop from the Format drop-down menu and click Save.

3   Choose View > Fit on Screen to see the entire image in your document window.

4   Choose the Quick Selection tool (⟋) in the Tools panel. Keep in mind that this could be hidden underneath the Magic Wand (✦) tool.

5   Position your cursor over the snowboarder. You see a circle with a small crosshair in the center (⊹).

Only the crosshair will appear if you have the Caps Lock key depressed.

6   From the Options bar, click the Brush drop-down menu, and either slide the size slider to the right to a value of 10, or enter **10** into the Size text field.

7   Now, click and drag to paint over the snowboarder. You can release the mouse and continue painting the snowboarder; notice that you are adding to the selection.

Adding to the Selection (⟋) is the default action that you can expect, as you can see by the selected option in the Options bar.

Initial selection with the Quick Selection tool.

If you accidently grab a part of the image that you do not want to select, press and hold the Alt key (Windows) or Option key (Mac OS), and paint over the region to deselect it.

Adjust the Quick Selection brush size by pressing the [(left bracket) repeatedly to reduce the selection size, or the] (right bracket) to increase the selection size.

8   Save your selection by choosing Select > Save Selection; the Save Selection dialog box appears.

9   In the File name text field, type **Boarder**, and then click OK, leaving the other settings at their defaults. Now you have a saved selection. Keep in mind that if you deselect your selection, or close your saved file, you can reload your selection by choosing Select > Load Selection.

10 Choose File > Save, and then File > Close to close the file.

Making difficult selections with the Refine Edge feature

Using the Refine Edge feature can help you improve your selection of difficult items, such as fur and hair. There is still no *magic tool* for making a perfect selection, but the Refine Edge improvements certainly help.

1   Choose File > Browse in Bridge and open the image named **ps0404.psd**. Choose File > Save As. When the Save As dialog box appears, navigate to the ps04lessons folder. In the File name text field, type **ps0404_work**. Choose Photoshop from the Format drop-down menu and click Save. If the Photoshop Format Options dialog box appears, click OK.

2   Click and hold the Quick Selection tool, and then select the hidden Magic Wand tool (✦).

3   Click the white area off to the right of the woman; the white area becomes selected.

4   Choose Select > Inverse to invert the selection. The woman is now selected.

5   Click the Refine Edge button in the Options bar; the Refine Edge dialog box appears.

6 To get a better view of the hair selection, choose the Black & White option from the View drop-down menu. Black & White is a viewing option that you can use to see your selection better.

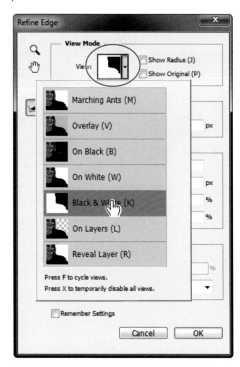

Change the View to Black & White to better see the selection edges.

7 Using the Radius slider, in the Edge Detection section, change the Radius value to **100**. This might seem like a drastic radius selection, but you can see that this masked the hair fairly well.

The issue you now have is that by increasing the radius to get a better selection of hair, you also degraded the edge selection of the shoulder beneath the hair. You will use the Erase Refinements tool to clean up your selection.

8 Click and hold the Refine Radius tool and select the Erase Refinements tool.

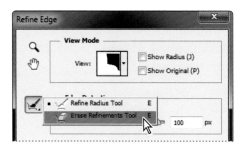

Clean up your selection using the Erase Refinements tool.

9   Position your cursor over an area in your image where you would like to clean up the selection. Note that you can increase or decrease your brush size by pressing the [(left bracket) or] (right bracket) keys.

10 Start painting over the areas that you do not want the refinements to take place. In this example, this is in the shoulder area, at the edge of the suit.

Refine edge went into the shoulder. *Use the Erase Refinements tool.* *The result, a more accurate selection of the shoulder.*

11 Select Layer Mask from the Output drop-down menu and click OK. Since you have applied a layer mask, your results are shown as a transparent selection. Save and close the file.

The completed selection.

Using Quick Mask

Earlier in this lesson, you learned how to add to and subtract from selections. Another method for modifying selections is to use Quick Mask. Rather than using selection tools to modify the selection, you'll use the Paint Brush tool in the Quick Mask mode and paint to modify your selection. Note that when creating a mask, by default it is the inverse of a selection; it covers the unselected part of the image and protects it from any editing or manipulations you apply.

In this lesson, you will create a mask using the Quick Mask feature, save the selection, and then copy and paste the selection into another image.

1   To see the file in its completed stage, choose File > Browse in Bridge and navigate to the ps04lessons folder. Locate the file named **ps0405_done.psd** and double-click to open it in Photoshop. A picture with a duck and penguins appears. You can keep the file open for reference or choose File > Close now.

The completed exercise.

2   Choose File > Browse in Bridge to bring Adobe Bridge forward. Then navigate to the ps04lessons folder and open the image named **ps0405.psd**; an image of a duck appears.

Choose File > Save As. When the Save As dialog box appears, navigate to the ps04lessons folder. In the File name text field, type **ps0405_work**. Choose Photoshop from the Format drop-down menu and click Save. If the Photoshop Format Options dialog box appears, click OK.

3   Select the Lasso tool (⌐) and make a quick (and rough) selection around the duck. Make sure that as you click and drag, creating a selection that encompasses the duck, the Lasso tool finishes where it started, creating a closed selection around the duck. Don't worry about the accuracy of this selection, since you are going to paint the rest of the selection using Photoshop's painting tools in the Quick Mask mode.

4   Select the Quick Mask Mode button (▢) at the bottom of the Tools panel, or use the keyboard shortcut **Q**. Your image is now displayed with a red area (representing the mask) over areas of the image that are not part of the selection.

5   Now you will use the painting tools to refine this selection. Select the Brush tool (✓) in the Tools panel.

Create a rough selection using the Lasso tool.   *The selection in the Quick Mask mode.*

6   Click the Default Foreground and Background Colors button at the bottom of the Tools panel (⬚), or press **D** on your keyboard, to return to the default foreground and background colors of black and white. Painting with black adds to the mask, essentially blocking that area of the image from any changes. Painting with white subtracts from the mask, essentially making that area of the image active and ready for changes.

As a default, the Quick Mask appears as red when you paint with black, and clear when you paint with white. The red indicates a masked area.

These tips will help you to make more accurate corrections on the mask.

BRUSH FUNCTION	BRUSH KEYBOARD SHORTCUTS
Make brush size larger	] (right bracket)
Make brush size smaller	[(left bracket)
Make brush harder	Shift+] (right bracket)
Make brush softer	Shift+[(left bracket)
Return to default black and white colors	D
Switch foreground and background colors	X

7   Choose View > 100% to view the image at 100 percent. Zoom in further if necessary.

8   With black as your foreground color, start painting close to the duck, where there might be some green grass that you inadvertently included in the selection. Keep in mind that the areas where the red mask appears will not be part of the selection.

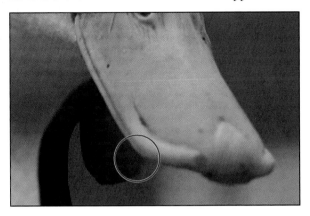

Paint the mask to make a more accurate selection.

9   If you accidentally paint into or select some of the duck, press **X** on your keyboard to swap the foreground and background colors, putting white in the foreground. Start painting with white, and you will see that this eliminates the mask, thereby making the regions that you paint with white part of the selection.

10 Continue painting until the selection is more accurate. When you are satisfied with your work, view the selection by clicking the Quick Mask Mode button (⬚) at the bottom of the Tools panel, or by pressing **Q** on your keyboard. This exits the Quick Mask mode and displays the selection that you have created as a marquee. You can press **Q** to re-enter the Quick Mask mode to fine-tune the selection even further, if necessary. Keep the selection active for the next section.

Saving selections

You spent quite some time editing the selection in the last part of this lesson. It would be a shame to lose that selection by closing your file or clicking somewhere else on your image. As mentioned earlier in this lesson, you should save your selections. In this part of the lesson, you'll save a selection so you can close the file, reopen it, and retrieve the duck selection whenever you need it.

1   With your duck selection active, choose Select > Save Selection.

2   Type **duck** in the File name text field and click OK.

3 If you cannot see the Channels panel, choose Window > Channels to see that you have a saved channel (or selection) named duck. Selections that are saved with an image are known as alpha channels. Channels are not supported by all file formats. Only Photoshop, PDF, PICT, Pixar, TIFF, PSD, and Raw formats save alpha channels with the file.

Name your saved selection.   *The Channels panel.*

4 Choose Select > Deselect, or press Ctrl+D (Windows) or Command+D (Mac OS), to deselect the active selection.

5 Once a selection is saved, you can easily reselect it by choosing Select > Load Selection, or by Ctrl+clicking (Windows) or Command+clicking (Mac OS) on the channel in the Channels panel. The duck selection is reactivated.

You can save multiple selections in an image, but take note: your file size will increase each time you save a new selection. When multiple selections are saved, you will need to click the Channel drop-down menu and choose which saved selection to display.

Copying and pasting a selection

There are many different methods for moving a selection from one image to another. In this lesson, you will simply copy a selection and paste it into another image.

1   Choose Edit > Copy, or use the keyboard shortcut Ctrl+C (Windows) or Command+C (Mac OS).

2   Choose File > Browse in Bridge, and navigate to the ps04lessons folder. Double-click the file named **ps0406.psd** to open it in Photoshop. A photograph of penguins appears.

3   Choose File > Save As. In the Save As dialog box, navigate to the ps04lessons folder and type **ps0406_work** in the File name text field. Leave the format set to Photoshop and click Save.

4   With the image of the penguins in front, select Edit > Paste, or use the keyboard shortcut Ctrl+V (Windows) or Command+V (Mac OS). The duck selection is placed in the penguin image on its own independent layer, making it easy to reposition.

A new layer is created when the selection is pasted.   The result.

5   Select the Move Tool (▸+) and reposition the duck so that it is flush with the bottom of the image.

6   Choose File > Save, then choose File > Close to close the file. Close any other open files without saving.

Using the Pen tool for selections

The Pen tool is the most accurate of all the selection tools in Photoshop. The selection that it creates is referred to as a path. A path utilizes points and segments to define a border. Paths are not only more accurate than other selection methods, but they are also more economical, as they do not increase file size, unlike saved channel selections. This is because paths don't contain image data; they are simply outlines. In this section, you will learn how to make a basic path, and then use it to make a selection that you can use for adjusting an image's tonal values.

Pen tool terminology

Bézier curve: Originally developed by Pierre Bézier in the 1970s for CAD/CAM operations, the Bézier curve became the underpinning of the entire Adobe PostScript drawing model. The depth and size of a Bézier curve is controlled by fixed points and direction lines.

Anchor points: Anchor points are used to control the shape of a path or object. They are automatically created by the shape tools. You can manually create anchor points by clicking from point to point with the Pen tool.

Direction lines: These are essentially the handles that you use on anchor points to adjust the depth and angle of curved paths.

Closed shape: When a path is created, it becomes a closed shape when the starting point joins the endpoint.

Simple path: A path consists of one or more straight or curved segments. Anchor points mark the endpoints of the path segments. In the next section, you will learn how to control the anchor points.

---

1   Choose File > Browse in Bridge to bring Adobe Bridge forward. Then navigate to the ps04lessons folder and open image **ps0407.psd**.

2   Choose File > Save As. When the Save As dialog box appears, navigate to the ps04lessons folder. In the File name text field, type **ps0407_work**. Choose Photoshop from the Format drop-down menu and click Save. If the Photoshop Format Options dialog box appears, click OK.

    This part of the exercise will guide you through the basics of using the Pen tool.

3   Select the Pen tool (✐) from the Tools panel.

4   Position the cursor over the image, and notice that an asterisk appears in the lower-right corner of the tool. This signifies that you are beginning a new path.

5   When the Pen tool is selected, the Options bar displays three path buttons in a drop-down menu: Shape layers, Paths, and Fill pixels. If the default is not already set to Paths, select it now.

Select Paths in the Pen tool options.

6   Increase the zoom level by pressing the Ctrl+plus sign (Windows) or Command+plus sign (Mac OS) so that you can view the exercise file in the image window as large as possible. If you zoom too far in, zoom out by pressing Ctrl+minus sign (Windows) or Command+minus sign (Mac OS).

7   Place the pen tip at the first box in Example A, and click once to create the first anchor point of the path. Don't worry if it's not exactly on the corner; you can adjust the path later.

8   Place the pen tip at the second box on Example A and click once. Another anchor point is created, with a line connecting the first anchor point to the second.

9   Continue clicking each box in the exercise until you reach the last box on the path. If you're having difficulties seeing the line segments between the points on your path, you can temporarily hide the Exercise layer by clicking the Visibility icon next to that layer.

10 Press and hold the Ctrl (Windows) or Command (Mac OS) key, and click the white background to deactivate the path that was just drawn to prepare for the next path.

In Example A, only straight line segments were used to draw a path; now you'll use curved line segments.

11 Reposition the document in the window so that Example B is visible.

12   With the Pen tool selected, click and hold the small square (the first anchor point in the path) and drag upward to create directional handles. Directional handles control where the following path will go. Note that when you create directional handles, you should drag until the length is the same or slightly beyond the arch that you are creating.

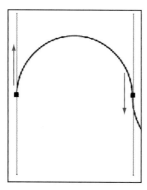

Click and drag with the Pen tool to create directional handles.

13   Click and hold the second box in Example B, and drag the directional handle downward. Keep dragging until the path closely matches the curve of Example B. Don't worry if it's not exact for this part of the lesson.

14   Click the third box in Example B, and drag upward to create the next line segment. Continue this process to the end of the Example B diagram.

15   To edit the position of the points on the path, you'll use the Direct Selection tool (⬚). Click and hold the Path Selection tool (▶) and select the hidden Direct Selection tool.

16   Position the Direct Selection tool over a path segment (the area between two anchor points) and click once; the directional handles that control that line segment are displayed. Click and drag any of the directional handles to fine-tune your line segments. You can also click directly on each anchor point to reposition them if necessary.

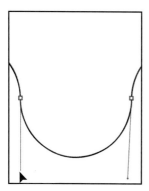

Adjusting the directional handles using the Direct Selection tool.

17   Choose File > Save, then choose File > Close to close the file.

Using the Pen tool to select an area of an image

1   Choose File > Browse in Bridge to bring Adobe Bridge forward. Then navigate to the ps04lessons folder and open image **ps0408.psd**.

2   Choose File > Save As. When the Save As dialog box appears, navigate to the ps04lessons folder. In the File name text field, type **ps0408_work**. Choose Photoshop PSD from the Format drop-down menu and click Save. If the Photoshop Format Options dialog box appears, click OK.

3   On the keyboard, press and hold the Ctrl (Windows) or Command (Mac OS) key; then press the plus sign (+) once to zoom in at 200 percent. You'll see the zoom % in the lower-left corner of your workspace. Position the apple on the left side of the image that is in focus so that you can see the entire apple in the document window.

4   Select the Pen tool (✐) and begin drawing a path around the apple using the skills you learned in the previous exercise by clicking and dragging at the top edge of the apple and dragging a handle to the right.

5   Move the Pen tool further along the apple, and click and drag again, dragging out directional handles each time, creating curved line segments that match the shape of the apple.

6   When you get back to the area where you began the path, the Pen cursor will show a circle next to it, indicating that when you click back on that first anchor point, it will close the path.

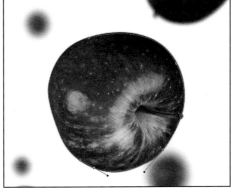

Creating a path around the edge of the apple.

7   If the Paths panel is not visible, select Window > Paths. Path information is stored in the Paths panel. You see one path in the panel, named Work Path.

8 Double-click the name Work Path in the Paths panel. The Save Path dialog box appears. Type **Apple** in the File name text field and click OK.

The Paths panel with the renamed path.

9 In the Paths panel, click below the name of the path to deselect the path. To reselect the path, click the path name.

10 Now you'll apply an adjustment to this path selection. If the Layers panel is not visible, choose Window > Layers.

11 Click and hold the Create new fill or adjustment layer button (⬤) at the bottom of the Layers panel and select Hue/Saturation. The Properties panel becomes active and the Hue/Saturation adjustment is displayed.

12 Drag the Hue slider to **+116** or type **+116** into the Hue text field. You should see only the apple turn green.

13 A new adjustment layer is created, named Hue/Saturation 1. The pen path you created is visible to the right of the Hue/Saturation adjustment layer thumbnail and acts as a mask, blocking the adjustment from occurring outside of the path.

The Hue/Saturation adjustment layer.   Adjustment layer with a   The result.
                                        vector mask.

If you want to have multiple paths in the Paths panel, deselect any active path before you begin drawing a new path. If you don't deselect, the new path you create will be added to, and become part of, the currently active path.

14 Choose File > Save, then choose File > Close to close the file.

More Pen tool selection techniques

In the last exercise, you created a curved path. Now you'll create a path with a combination of straight lines and curves.

1 Choose File > Browse in Bridge to bring Adobe Bridge forward. Then navigate to the ps04lessons folder and open image **ps0409.psd**.

Choose File > Save As. When the Save As dialog box appears, navigate to the ps04lessons folder. In the File name text field, type **ps0409_work**. Choose Photoshop PSD from the Format drop-down menu and click Save. If the Photoshop Format Options dialog box appears, click OK.

2 Choose View > Fit on Screen, or use the keyboard shortcut Ctrl+0 (zero) (Windows) or Command+0 (zero) (Mac OS).

3 With the Pen tool (✐), create the first anchor point at the bottom-left side of the door by clicking once.

4   Staying on the left side of the door, click again at the location that is aligned with the top of the door frame's crossbar.

The second path point.

5   Now, to set up the path for a curve segment around the arc of the door window, place the pen over the last anchor point. When you see a right slash next to the pen cursor, click and drag to pull a Bézier directional handle. Drag until the directional handle is even with the top horizontal bar inside the door window. The purpose of this handle is to set the direction of the curve segment that follows.

The Bézier handle.

6   To form the first curve segment, place the Pen tool cursor at the top of the arc of the door window, and then click, hold, and drag to the right until the curve forms around the left side of the window's arc; then release the mouse button.

The curve and its anchor point.

7   To finish off the curve, place your cursor at the right side of the door, aligned with the top of the door frame's crossbar. Click and drag straight down to form the remainder of the curve.

The completed curve.

8   Because the next segment is going to be a straight line and not a curve, you'll need to remove the last handle. Position the cursor over the last anchor point; a left slash appears next to the Pen cursor. This indicates that you are positioned over an active anchor point. Click with the Alt (Windows) or Option (Mac OS) key depressed; the handle disappears.

9   Click the bottom-right side of the door to create a straight line segment.

10 To finish the path, continue to click straight line segments along the bottom of the door. If you need some help, look at the example.

The completed, closed path, selected with the Direct Selection tool.

11 Editing paths requires a different strategy when working with curved segments. With the Direct Selection tool (⬐), select the path in the image to activate it, and then select the anchor point at the top of the door. Two direction handles appear next to the selected anchor point. You also see handles at the bottom of each respective curve segment to the left and the right. These are used for adjusting the curve.

12 Select the end of one of the handles and drag it up and down to see how it affects the curve. Also drag the handle in toward and away from the anchor point. If you need to adjust any part of your path to make it more accurate, take the time to do so now.

13 Double-click the name Work Path in the Paths panel, and in the File name text field, type **door**. Keep the image open for the next section.

Converting a path to a selection

Paths don't contain image data, so if you want to copy the contents of a path, you need to convert it to a selection.

1   Make sure that the file from the last exercise is still open.

2   Click the path named door in the Paths panel to make the path active.

3   At the bottom of the Paths panel, there are seven path icons next to the panel trash can:

- **Fill path with foreground color** (⊙) fills the selected path with the current foreground color.

- **Stroke path with brush** (○) is better used if you first Alt/Option+click the icon and choose the tool from the drop-down menu that includes the brush you want to stroke with.

- **Load path as a selection** (○) makes a selection from the active path.

- **Make work path from selection** (⌒) creates a path from an active selection.

- **Add a Mask** (▣) makes an active selection into a layer mask. If you have an active path, you can click this button twice to make a layer mask from the path.

- **Create new path** (▣) is used to start a new blank path when you want to create multiple paths in an image.

- **Delete current path** (🗑) deletes the selected path.

4   Choose Load path as a selection to create a selection from the door path, or press Ctrl+click (Windows) or Command+click (Mac OS) on the path in the Paths panel.

5   Choose Select > Deselect, or use the keyboard shortcut Ctrl+D (Windows) or Command+D (Mac OS), to deselect the selection.

6   Choose File > Close, without saving the document.

Self study

Take some time to work with the images in this lesson to strengthen your selection skills. For instance, you used **ps0403.psd** with the Lasso and Quick Selection tools. Try making different selections in the image as well as using the key commands to add and subtract from the selection border. Also experiment with Quick Mask.

Open the image named **ps0410.psd** Using what you have learned in this lesson, make a circular selection of the face of the clock. Use Select > Transform, if needed, to adjust the shape, and then change the Hue, or color, of the clock face to any other color.

Review

Questions

1   Which selection tool is best used when an image has areas of similar color?

2   Which key should you press and hold when adding to a selection?

3   What can you do to select the image data inside a path?

4   Which dialog box allows you to edit your selection using different masking options?

5   When does Refine Edge appear in the Options bar?

Answers

1   The Magic Wand is a good tool to use when you have areas of an image with similar colors. The Magic Wand tool selects similar colors based on the Tolerance setting in the Options bar.

2   Press and hold the Shift key to add to a selection. This works with any of the selection tools.

3   To select the pixels inside of a path, you can activate the path by Ctrl+clicking (Windows) or Command+clicking (Mac OS) on the path in the Paths panel or by clicking the Load Path as Selection button at the bottom of the Paths panel.

4   The Refine Selection dialog box allows you to select the best masking technique and to preview edge selection changes that you are making.

5   Refine Edge will only appear in the Options bar when a Selection tool is active.

What you'll learn in this lesson:

- Selecting color
- Using the Brush tool
- Applying transparency
- Using blending modes
- Retouching images

Painting and Retouching

In this lesson, you'll get a quick primer in color and color models. You will then have an opportunity to practice using Photoshop's painting and retouching tools, such as the Brush, Clone Stamp, and a variety of healing tools.

Starting up

Before starting, make sure that your tools and panels are consistent by resetting your preferences. See "Resetting the Photoshop workspace" in the Starting up section of this book.

You will work with several files from the ps05lessons folder in this lesson. Make sure that you have loaded the pslessons folder onto your hard drive from the supplied DVD. See "Loading lesson files" in the Starting up section of this book.

See Lesson 5 in action!

Use the accompanying video to gain a better understanding of how to use some of the features shown in this lesson. You can find the video tutorial for this lesson on the included DVD.

Setting up your color settings

Before you begin selecting colors for painting, you should have an understanding of color modes and Photoshop's color settings. Let's start with a basic introductory overview of the two main color modes that you will use in this lesson, RGB and CMYK.

Color primer

This lesson is about painting, adding colors, and changing and retouching images. It is important to understand that what you see on the screen is not necessarily what your final viewers will see on the variety of paper stocks and devices available to them. Bright colors tend to become duller when output to a printer, and some colors can't even be reproduced on the screen or on paper. This is because each device—whether it's a monitor, printer, or TV screen—has a different color gamut.

Understanding color gamut

The gamut represents the number of colors that can be represented, detected, or reproduced on a specific device. You might not realize it, but you have experience with different gamuts already; your eyes can see many more colors than your monitor or a printing press can reproduce.

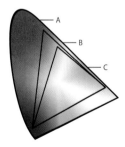

A. Colors that your eye recognizes.
B. Colors that your monitor recognizes.
C. Colors that your printer reproduces.

In this lesson, you will learn how you can address some of the color limitations that are inherent when working with color that is displayed or output by different devices. A quick introduction to the RGB and CMYK color models will help you get a better grasp on what you can achieve. There are entire books on this subject; in this section, you will gain enough information to apply effectively to your images in Photoshop.

If you receive a Missing or Mismatched Profile warning dialog box on any images used in this lesson, click OK to accept the default setting.

The RGB color model

The RGB (Red, Green, Blue) color model is an additive model in which red, green, and blue are combined in various ways to create other colors.

1   Choose File > Open, and navigate to the ps05lessons folder. Open the file named **ps05rgb.psd**. An image with red, green, and blue circles appears. Try to imagine the three color circles as light beams from three flashlights with red, green, and blue colored gels.

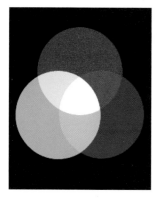

Red, green, blue.

2   Select the Move tool (⊹), and then select the Auto-Select check box in the Options bar. By selecting Auto-Select Layer, you can automatically activate a layer by choosing pixel information on that layer. One at a time, click and drag the red, green, and blue circles around on the image.

Notice that white light is generated where the three colors intersect.

3   Now, turn off the visibility of the layers by selecting the Visibility icon (👁) to the left of each layer name, with the exception of the black layer. It is just like turning off a flashlight; when there is no light, there is no color.

4   Choose File > Close. Choose to not save changes.

The CMYK color model

CMYK (Cyan, Magenta, Yellow, and Black [or Key]—black was once referred to as the *Key* color) is a subtractive color model, meaning that as ink is applied to a piece of paper, these colors absorb light. This color model is based on mixing CMYK pigments to create other colors.

Ideally, by combining CMY inks together, the color black should result. In reality, the combination of those three pigments creates a dark, muddy color, and so black is added to create a panel with true blacks. CMYK works through light absorption. The colors that are seen are the portion of visible light that is reflected, not absorbed, by the objects on which the light falls.

In CMYK, magenta plus yellow creates red, magenta plus cyan creates blue, and cyan plus yellow creates green.

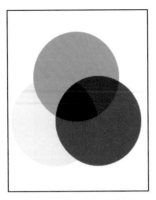

Cyan, magenta, yellow, and black.

1   Choose File > Open, and navigate to the ps05lessons folder. Open the file named **ps05cmyk.psd**. An image with cyan, magenta, and yellow circles appears. Think of the colors in this file as being created with ink printed on paper.

2   With the Move tool (⊕) selected, and the Auto-Select Layer check box selected, individually click and drag the cyan, magenta, and yellow circles around on the image to see the color combinations that are created with ink pigments of these three colors. Notice that black appears at the intersection of all three, but, as mentioned earlier, it would never reproduce that purely on a printing press.

3   Choose File > Close to close the **ps05cmyk.psd** image. Do not save your changes.

4   Uncheck the Auto-Select Layer check box in the Options bar.

Working in the RGB mode

Unless you use an advanced color management system, you should do much of your creative work in the RGB mode. The CMYK mode is limited in its capabilities (fewer menu selections), and if you work in this mode, you have already made some decisions about your final image output that might not be accurate. Follow this short color primer to help you achieve the results that you expect.

In this lesson, you'll use generic profiles for your monitor and output devices. If you want to create a custom monitor profile, follow the instructions in the Photoshop Help menu, under the heading, "Calibrate and profile your monitor." You can also type **Calibrate Monitor** into the Search field on *adobe.com* to find additional helpful tips for calibrating your display.

1   Choose File > Browse in Bridge to bring Adobe Bridge to the front.

2 Navigate to the ps05lessons folder and open the image **ps0501.psd**. A very colorful image of a woman appears.

A colorful RGB image.

3 Press Ctrl+Y (Windows) or Command+Y (Mac OS); some of the colors become duller. By pressing Ctrl+Y/Command+Y, you have turned on the Proof Colors. This is a toggle keyboard shortcut, which means you can press Ctrl+Y/Command+Y again to turn the preview off. Note that the text in your title bar indicates whether this preview is active or not. Keep the file open for the next part of this lesson.

The Proof Colors preview attempts to visually simulate what the colors in this image would look like if it were to be printed. This simulation is controlled by the choices you make in the color settings. This is why understanding the color settings is important, since the settings you choose not only affect your preview, but also how the image appears in its final destination, print or on-screen.

Editing color settings

For this lesson, you will adjust the color settings for Photoshop as if the final destination for this image were print. Note that if you have other applications from the Creative Cloud installed, you can adjust your color settings throughout all of them using Adobe Bridge CC. Applying color settings through Adobe Bridge saves you the time of making sure that all the colors are consistent throughout your production process. If you want to adjust color settings throughout all your Creative Cloud applications, follow the instructions for using Adobe Bridge. If you only want to change the color settings in Adobe Photoshop, follow the steps starting at step 4.

1 Choose File > Browse in Bridge to bring Adobe Bridge to the front. If you do not have Bridge installed, you can install it when the Adobe Application manager launches.

2   Choose Edit > Color Settings and select North America Prepress 2, if it is not already selected. Click the Apply button.

The new color settings are applied to all of your Creative Cloud applications. Note that the setting you selected is a generic setting created for a printing process that is typical in North America. If your selections are not exactly the same, choose the setting that states it is a prepress setting.

3   Click the Return to Adobe Photoshop boomerang icon ( ) at the top of Bridge.

4   In Photoshop, choose Edit > Color Settings, even if you have already set them in Adobe Bridge.

5   If North America Prepress 2 is not selected in the Settings drop-down menu, choose it now. Leave the Colors Settings dialog box open.

6   While still in the Color Settings dialog box, press Ctrl+Y (Windows) or Command+Y (Mac OS) to use the toggle shortcut for the CMYK preview. You can tell if you are in the CMYK preview by looking at the title bar of the image window. Notice that CMYK appears in parentheses at the end of the title.

The title bar indicates that this image is in the CMYK preview mode.

It is good to get this sneak peek into what your CMYK image will look like, but there is still the issue of having many different kinds of CMYK output devices. You might have one printer that produces excellent results and another that can hardly hold a color. In the next section, you will learn about the different CMYK settings and how they can affect your image.

7   Make sure that the CMYK preview is still on. If not, press Ctrl+Y (Windows) or Command+Y (Mac OS). From the CMYK drop-down menu in the Working Spaces section of the Color Settings dialog box, choose **U.S. Sheetfed Uncoated v2**.

Notice the color change in the image. You might need to reposition the Color Settings dialog box to see your image. Photoshop is now displaying the characteristics of the color space for images printed on a sheetfed press. This would be the generic setting you might choose if you were sending this image to a printing press that printed on individual sheets of paper.

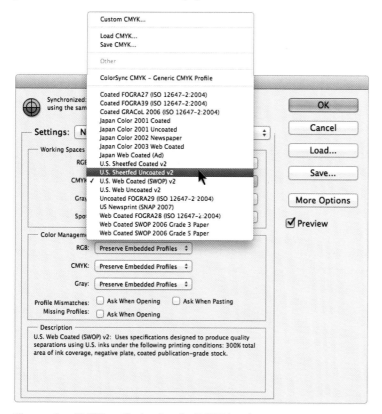

Choose various CMYK specifications from the CMYK drop-down menu.

8   From the CMYK drop-down menu, choose **Japan Web Coated (Ad)**. Notice that the color preview changes again. You might use this selection if you were sending this image overseas to be printed on a large catalog or book press. A web press is a high-volume, high-speed printing press that prints on large rolls of paper rather than individual sheets.

You do not want to pick a CMYK setting simply because it looks good on your screen; you want to choose one based upon a recommendation from a printer, or you should use the generic settings that Adobe provides. The purpose of selecting an accurate setting is not only to keep your expectations realistic; it also helps you accurately adjust an image to produce the best and most accurate results.

9 From the Settings drop-down menu, choose the **North America Prepress** 2 setting again, and click OK. Keep the file open for the next part of this lesson.

Keep in mind that if you are using your images for web only, you can use the preview feature to view your image on different platforms. To make this change, choose View > Proof Setup and choose either Internet Standard RGB or Legacy Macintosh RGB from the menu.

Selecting colors

There are many methods that you can use to select colors to paint with in Photoshop. Most methods end up using the Color Picker dialog box. In this section, you will review how to use the Color Picker to choose accurate colors.

1 Click once on the Set foreground color box at the bottom of the Tools panel. The Color Picker appears. It is tough to represent a 3D color space in 2D, but Photoshop does a pretty good job of interpreting colors in the Color Picker. Using the Color Picker, you can enter values on the right, or use the Color slider and color field on the left to create a custom color.

2 Now, with the Color Picker open, click and drag the color slider to change the hue of your selected color. The active color is represented as a circle in the color field.

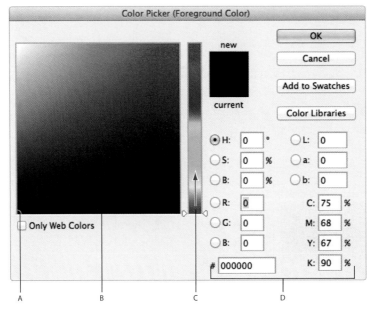

A. Selected color. B. Color field. C. Color slider. D. Color values.

3   Now, click in the color field, and then click and drag your selected color toward the upper-right corner of the color field, making it a brighter, more saturated color. To choose a lighter color, click and drag the selected color to the upper-left corner of the color field. Even though you can select virtually any color using this method, you might not achieve the best results.

4   Press Ctrl+Shift+Y (Windows) or Command+Shift+Y (Mac OS) to see how Proof Colors affects the colors in the Color Picker. Notice that colors that will not print well in CMYK show up with in gray (gamut warning). Press Ctrl+Shift+Y/ Command+Shift+Y again to turn off Proof Colors.

Perhaps you are creating images for the Web and you want to work with web-safe colors only. This is very restrictive, but you can limit your color choices by selecting the Only Web Colors check box in the Color Picker.

5   Select and deselect the Only Web Colors check box to see the difference in selectable colors in the color field.

There are warning icons in the Color Picker to help you choose the best colors for print and the Web.

6   Click in the lower-left corner of the color field and drag up toward the upper-right corner. Note that at some point, when you enter into the brighter colors, an Out of gamut for printing warning icon (⚠) appears. This indicates that, although you might have selected a very nice color, it is never going to print based on your present color settings. Click the Out of gamut warning icon, and Photoshop redirects you to the closest color you can achieve.

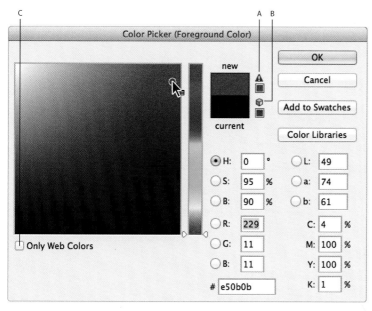

A. Out of gamut for printing warning. B. Not a web safe color warning. C. Only Web Colors.

7   Click and drag your selected color in the color field until you see the Not a web safe color alert icon (⊛) appear. Click the Not a web safe color icon to be redirected to the closest web-safe color.

8   Position the Color Picker so that you can see part of the **ps0501.psd** image, then position the cursor over any part of the image. Notice that the cursor turns into the Eyedropper tool (✐). Click to select any color from the image.

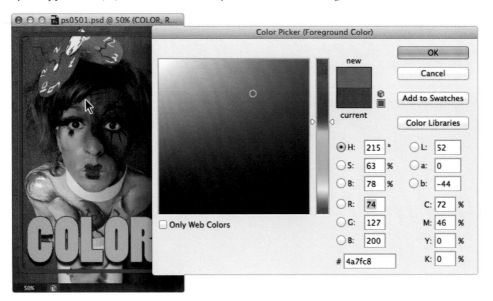

Click outside the Color Picker to sample a color from your image.

9   Click OK in the Color Picker dialog box.

10   Choose File > Close. If asked to save changes, select No.

Starting to paint

Now that you know a little more about color and how to find it in Photoshop, you will start to do some painting. You will work on a new blank document to begin with, but once you have the basics of the painting tools down, you'll put your knowledge to work on actual image files.

1   Under the File menu, choose New. The New dialog box appears.

2   Type **painting** in the File name text field. From the preset drop-down menu, choose Default Photoshop Size. Leave all other settings at their defaults and click OK. A new blank document is created; keep it open for the next part of this lesson.

Using the Color panel

Another way to select color is to use the Color panel.

1   If the Color panel is not visible, choose Window > Color.

Place your cursor over the color ramp at the bottom of the panel, then click and drag across the displayed color spectrum. Notice that the RGB sliders adjust to indicate the color combinations creating the active color. If you have a specific color in mind, you can individually drag the sliders or key in numeric values.

Note that the last color you activated appears in the Set foreground color swatch, located in the Color panel, as well as near the bottom of the Tools panel.

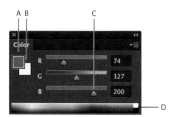

A. *Set foreground color.*
B. *Set background color.*
C. *Slider.*
D. *Color ramp.*

2   Click once on the Set Foreground Color box to open the Color Picker. Type the following values in the RGB text fields on the right side of the Color Picker dialog box: R: **74** G: **150** B: **190**. Click OK.

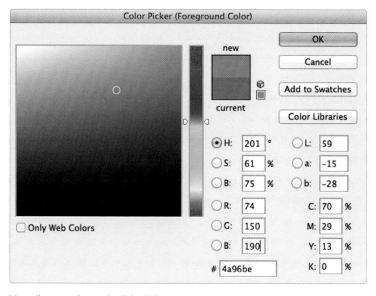

Manually enter values in the Color Picker.

Using the Brush tool

The Brush tool paints using the foreground color. You can control the brush type, size, softness, mode, and opacity with the Brush tool Options.

1   Select the Brush tool (✏) in the Tools panel.

2   Click the arrow next to the brush size in the Options bar to open the Brush Preset picker.

Click the arrow in the Brush Options bar to open the presets.

3   If you are not in the default panel view, click and hold the panel menu, which looks like a gear icon (⚙), in the upper-right corner of the Brush Preset picker, and choose Small Thumbnail View.

You can use the panel menu to choose different views.

4   Position your cursor over any of the brushes to see a tooltip appear. The tooltip provides a description of the brush, such as soft, airbrush, hard, or chalk. Some will also display the brush size in pixels.

5   Locate the brush with the description Soft Round Pressure Size pixels, toward the top of the panel, and click it.

6   Use the Size slider or enter **45 px** into the Size text field to change the diameter of the brush to 45 pixels, and press the Enter (Windows) or Return (Mac OS) key. The brush is selected and the Brushes Preset picker is closed.

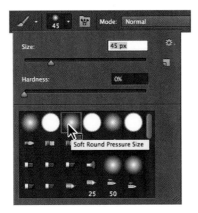

*The Brush Preset picker and the
Soft Round 45 pixel brush.*

7   Position your cursor on the left side of the image window, then click and drag to paint a curved line similar to the example below. If you do not see your brush stroke, make sure that the Mode in the Options bar is set to Normal.

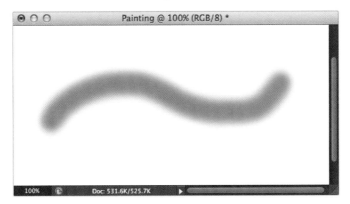

Painted brush stroke.

8 Using the Color panel, click a different color from the color ramp (no specific color is necessary for this exercise). Then paint another brush stroke that crosses over, or intersects, with the first brush stroke.

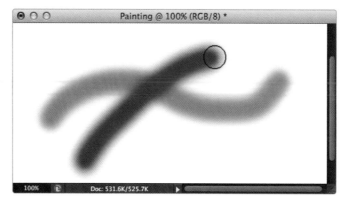

Painting a second brush stroke.

Note that when you paint, the Brush tool cursor displays the diameter of the brush that is selected. To resize the brush, you can return to the Brush Preset picker in the Options bar, but it is more intuitive to resize your brush dynamically, using a keyboard shortcut.

If you have the Caps Lock key pressed, your Brush tool cursor appears as a crosshair.

9 Press the] (right bracket) key to increase the brush size. Now press the [(left bracket) key to decrease the size of the brush. As this blank document is for experimentation only, you can paint after resizing to see the size difference.

10 Choose File > Save to save the file. Keep the file open for the next part of this lesson.

Changing opacity

Changing the level of opacity affects how transparent your brush strokes look over other image information. In this section, you will experiment with different opacity percentages.

1 If the Swatches panel is not visible, choose Window > Swatches. The Swatches panel appears with predetermined colors ready for you to use.

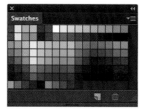

The Swatches panel.

2 Position your cursor over any swatch color and you'll see an eyedropper, along with a tooltip indicating the name of the color. Click any one of the swatches; it becomes your current foreground color.

3 Now, to change its opacity, go to the Options bar at the top and click the arrow next to 100%. A slider appears. Drag the slider to the left to lower the opacity to about 50 percent, and then click the arrow to collapse the slider. Alternatively, you can type **50** into the Opacity text field. Understand that changing the opacity of a color does not affect any of the painting that you have already completed, but it will affect future painting.

Change the opacity of the brush to 50 percent.

 You can change the opacity by hovering over the word Opacity in the Options bar. A double-arrow appears (⇔), allowing you to slide the opacity down or up without revealing the slider.

4 Click and drag with the Brush tool to paint over the canvas. Make sure to overlap existing colors to see how one color interacts with another. Take some time here to experiment with different colors, opacity settings, and brush sizes.

5 Choose File > Save and then File > Close to close the file.

Save time—learn the shortcuts

There are many keyboard shortcuts to help you when painting in Photoshop, most of which are integrated into the exercises in this lesson. Here is a list that will help you save time and work more efficiently.

BRUSH FUNCTION	BRUSH KEYBOARD SHORTCUTS
Open the Brush Preset picker	Right-click (Windows) Ctrl+click (Mac OS)
Increase Brush size	] (right bracket)
Decrease Brush Size	[(left bracket)
Make Brush Harder	Shift+] (right bracket)
Make Brush Softer	Shift+[(left bracket)
Change Opacity	Type a value, such as **55** for 55 percent or **4** for 40 percent
100% Opacity	Type **0** (zero)

Using the Brush Presets

In this section, you find out how to take advantage of the preset brushes that come with Photoshop.

1   Choose File > Browse in Bridge, and then navigate to the ps05lessons folder and open image **ps0502.psd**. An image of a woman playing a guitar appears.

The file before you apply new brush strokes.

2   Choose File > Save As. In the Save As dialog box, name the file **ps0502_work**. Navigate to your ps05lessons folder and click Save.

3   Select the Brush tool (✐) and then select the Toggle the Brush panel button (▣) in the Options bar. The Brush panel appears.

4   Select the Brush Presets tab to bring it forward, and then select Small List from the panel menu. This will make it easier for you to identify the brushes by name.

5   Click the Round Curve Low Bristle Percent preset.

6   Using the Size slider, click and drag the size of the brush to approximately 205 px. You can preview the tip by activating the Toggle the Live Tip Brush Preview button ( ). Note that this brush preview does not work with all the brush tips.

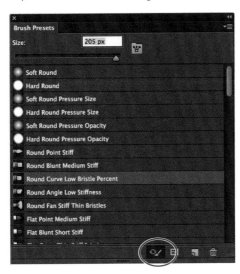

Select the Round Curve Low Bristle brush and change the size to 205 px.

7   With the Brush tool still selected, press and hold the Alt (Windows) or Option (Mac OS) key and sample a color of the woman's skin color. Choose a darker shade if possible.

8   In the Options bar, click the Mode drop-down menu and select Multiply.

9   Using large wide brush strokes paint over the woman playing the guitar. Since you are using a blending mode with a light color, the image is still visible. If you want to erase and try again, press Ctrl+Z (Windows) or Command+Z (Mac OS)

Note that as you paint, a preview of your brush appears and shows the movement of the bristles as you paint.

The image after you apply the brush stroke.

You can store your brushes for future use by taking advantage of the Brush preset feature.

10 Click the Create new brush (≡) button in the lower right of the Brush Presets panel. The Brush Name dialog box appears. Type the name **My Large Rounded Brush**, and click OK. This brush now appears in the Brush Preset panel for future use.

Store your brush for future use.

Using the Airbrush feature

In this section, you discover how to change the brush characteristics to act more like an airbrush. Using the airbrush option allows your paint to spread, much like the effect you would have using a true (non-digital) airbrush.

1   Select Round Fan Stiff Thin Bristles from the Brush Preset panel. Make sure the size is still close to 205 px. If not, use the slider to change it to that value now.

2   Press **D** to return to the Photoshop default colors of Black and White.

3   If the Mode drop-down menu (in the Options bar) is not set to Normal, set that to Normal now.

4   Click and release with your cursor anywhere on the image to stamp a brush stroke onto the image. Do this a couple more times. You can press the **[** (left bracket) or **]** (right bracket) keys to change the size of the stamped brush.

Stamp the brush stroke to produce the effect of dabbing the brush onto the image.

5   Now, Select the Enable airbrush-style build-up effects (✍) in the Options bar. Notice that you can change the flow, or pressure, of the paint coming out of the airbrush using the Flow control to the left. In this example, this is set to 50%.

6   Using the same brush preset, click and hold your image to notice that the paint spreads as you hold.

With the Enable airbrush option, the paint spreads as you click and hold the brush.

Experiment with different flows and sizes to see the effects that you have created.

7   When you are finished experimenting, return the Flow control back to 100%.

Creating a Border using the Bristle brushes

In this next section, you use a bristle brush to create an artistic border around the edge of the image.

1   Select the Round Blunt Medium Stiff bristle brush from the Brush Presets panel.

2   Choose any color that you want to use for the border you are about to create. In this example, we use the default black.

3   Click in the upper-left corner of the image. This is the top-left corner for your border.

Press and hold the Shift key and click in the lower-left corner. By Shift+clicking, you have instructed Photoshop that you want a stroke to connect from the initial click to the next.

4   Shift+click in the lower-right corner, and then continue this process until you return to your original stroke origin in the upper-left corner.

The completed border.

5   Press Ctrl+S (Windows) or Command+S (Mac OS) to save this image, then choose File > Close.

Applying color to an image

You can color anything realistically in Photoshop by using different opacity levels and blending modes. In this part of the lesson, you'll take a grayscale image and tint it with color. Understand that you can also paint color images to change the color of an object, like clothing for a catalog, or just to add interesting tints for mood and effect.

1   Choose File > Browse in Bridge, and then navigate to the ps05lessons folder and open image **ps0503.psd**. A grayscale image of a small boy appears.

The original grayscale image.

2   Double-click the Zoom tool (🔍) in the Tools panel to change the view to 100 percent. You might need to resize the image window to view more of the image.

3   Choose Image > Mode > RGB Color. This will not change the visual look of the image, but in order to colorize a grayscale image, it needs to be in a mode that supports color channels.

4   Choose File > Save As; the Save As dialog box appears. Navigate to the ps05lessons folder and type **ps0503_work** into the File name text field. Choose Photoshop from the Format drop-down menu and click Save.

5 Select the Brush tool and right-click (Windows) or Ctrl+click (Mac OS) on the canvas to open the contextual Brush Preset picker. Select the Soft Round brush (this is the first brush.) Slide the Size slider to 25 and the Hardness slider to 5. Press Enter (Windows) or Return (Mac OS) to exit.

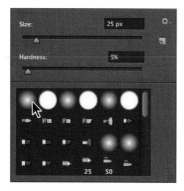

Change the brush size to 25 pixels, and the hardness to 5%.

6 Using the Opacity slider in the Options bar, change the opacity of the brush to 85 percent, or type **85** into the Opacity text field.

7 If you do not see the Swatches panel, choose Window > Swatches.

8 Position your cursor over a brown color in the Swatches panel. In this example, Dark Warm Brown is selected, but you can choose any color you want.

9 Using the Brush tool, paint the boy's hair. Notice that at 85 percent, the color is slightly transparent but still contains some of the image information underneath. You'll now paint the boy's hair more realistically.

Painting the hair at 85 percent opacity.

10 Choose File > Revert to return the image to the last saved version. Leave the file open.

Changing blending modes

Opacity is one way to alter the appearance or strength of a brush stroke. Another method is to change the blending mode of the painting tool you are using. The blending mode controls how pixels in the image are affected by painting. There are many modes to select from, and each creates a different result. This is because each blending mode is unique, but also because the blending result is based upon the color you are painting with and the color of the underlying image. In this section, you will colorize the photo by adjusting the opacity and changing the blending mode.

1   Make sure that **ps0503_work.psd** is still open and double-click the Zoom tool (🔍) in the Tools panel to verify that your view is still set to 100 percent.

Also, make sure the Swatches panel is forward and the Brush tool (✐) is selected for this part of the lesson.

2   Make sure that you still have the brown color selected in the Swatches panel.

3   In the Options bar, change the opacity to 50 percent.

4   Select Color from the Mode drop-down list. This is where you select various blending modes for your painting tools. Color is close to the bottom of this drop-down menu, so you might have to scroll to see it.

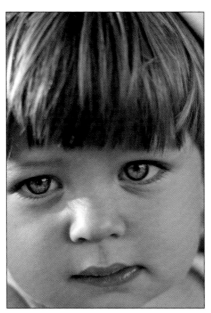

Change the blending mode to Color.

5   Using the Brush tool, paint over the boy's hair. Notice that the strength or opacity of the color varies according to the tonality of the painted area. This is because using the color blending mode you selected (Color) retains the grayscale information in the image. Where the image is lighter, the application of the brown color is lighter, and where the image is darker, the application of the brown color is darker.

6   Finish painting the hair brown, and then choose File > Save at this point so you can experiment with painting and blending modes.

In this example, you are changing actual pixels in the image; you will find out how to make non-destructive changes in Lessons 9 and 10 of this book.

Experiment with different colors to colorize the photo. Try using different modes with the same color to see how differently each mode affects the colorization. Some modes might have no effect at all. Experiment all you want with painting at this point. You can choose Ctrl+Z (Windows) or Command+Z (Mac OS) to undo a brush stroke that you do not like, or use Ctrl+Alt+Z (Windows) or Command+Option+Z (Mac OS) to undo again and again.

Don't like what you have done in just one area of the image? Select the Eraser tool and press and hold Alt (Windows) or Option (Mac OS); then click and drag to erase to the last version saved. You can also change the brush size, opacity, and hardness of the Eraser tool using the Options bar.

7   Choose File > Revert to go back to the last saved version; leave the file open for the next section.

The Eyedropper tool

The Eyedropper tool is used for sampling color from an image. This color can then be used for painting, or for use with text color. In this section, you will sample a color from another image to colorize the boy's face.

1   Make sure that **ps0503_work.psd** is still open, choose File > Browse in Bridge, and then navigate to the ps05lessons folder and open the file named **ps0504.psd**.

2   Select Window > Arrange > 2-up Vertical to see both images.

3   Click the title bar for the **ps0504.psd** image to bring that image forward.

Images tiled vertically.

4   Choose the Eyedropper tool (✐) and position it over the boy's face in the color image. Click once on his left cheek. The color is selected as the foreground color in the Tools panel.

You can access the Eyedropper tool while you have the Brush tool selected by pressing the Alt (Windows) or option (Mac OS) Keys. When you release the Alt/Option key, you are returned to the Brush tool.

5   Select the Brush tool, then using the Options bar at the top, make sure that Color is selected from the Mode drop-down menu and that the Opacity slider is set at 15 percent.

6   Position your cursor over the image to see the brush radius size. Press the] (right bracket) key several times until the brush is approximately 150 pixels wide. You can see the size reflected in the Options bar.

7   Click the title bar for the **ps0503_work.psd** image and with the Brush tool (✐) selected, paint the boy's face with the color you just sampled. Paint without releasing the mouse to give the face a good coverage of color.

8   Keep in mind that you have an opacity setting of 15%, which means that you can build up the skin tone color by painting over areas again. You can sculpt the image by adding more tone in the areas where you want more color.

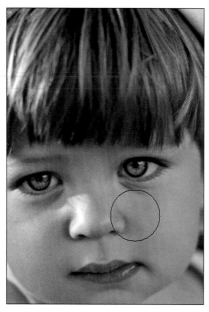

Add a light tint of skin color to the image.

9   With your Brush tool still selected, press and hold the Alt (Windows) or Option (Mac OS) key and sample the blue color from the striped shirt in the color image.

10 Press the [(left bracket) key until the brush size is about 60 pixels.

11 Press the number 5. By pressing 5 you can indicate that you want 50% opacity. This works with all values; for instance, you can press 43 for 43%, or 2 for 20%. To change the opacity to 100% you would press 0 (zero).

12 Position the paint brush over one of the boy's eyes in the grayscale image and click to paint it blue. Repeat this with the other eye.

13 Choose File > Save, then File > Close All to close both the **ps0503_work.psd** and the **ps0504.psd** files.

Retouching images

There are many techniques you can use to clean up an original image, from using any of the healing tools to the Clone Stamp tool. In this lesson, you will retouch an image using a variety of tools available in Photoshop CC.

1   To view the final image, choose File > Browse in Bridge and then navigate to the ps05lessons folder and open image **ps0505_done.psd**.

The image after using the retouching tools.

2   You can choose File > Close after viewing this file, or leave it open for reference.

Using the Clone Stamp tool

One of the problems with old photographs is that they most likely contain a large number of defects. These defects can include watermarks, tears, and fold marks. There are many different ways to fix these defects; one of the most useful is the Clone Stamp tool. The Clone Stamp tool lets you replace pixels in one area of the image by sampling from another area. In this part of the lesson, you'll use the Clone Stamp tool, and you will also have an opportunity to explore the Clone Source panel.

1   Choose File > Browse in Bridge, and then navigate to the ps05lessons folder and open image **ps0505.psd**.

2   Choose File > Save As; the Save As dialog box appears. Navigate to the ps05lessons folder and type **ps0505_work** into the File name text field. Choose Photoshop from the Format drop-down menu and click Save.

    You'll first experiment with the Clone Stamp tool (🏷). Don't worry about what you do to the image at this stage, since you will revert to saved when done.

3   Select the Zoom tool and click and drag a marquee around the top half of the image to zoom in closer to the face.

4   Select the Clone Stamp tool.

5   Position your cursor over the nose of the girl in the image and press and hold the Alt (Windows) or Option (Mac OS) key. Your cursor turns into a precision crosshair. When you see this crosshair, click with your mouse. You have just defined the source image area for the Clone Stamp tool.

6   Now position the cursor to the right of the girl's face, then click and drag to start painting with the Clone Stamp tool. The source area that you defined is recreated where you are painting. Watch carefully, since you will see a coinciding crosshair indicating the area of the source that you are copying.

The clone source and results.

7   Press the] (right bracket) key to enlarge the Clone Stamp brush. All the keyboard commands you reviewed for the Brush tool work with other painting tools as well.

8   Type **5**. By typing a numeric value when a painting tool is active, you can dynamically change the opacity. Start painting with the Clone Stamp tool again and notice that it is now cloning at 50 percent opacity.

9   Type **0** (zero) to return to 100 percent opacity.

10   You have completed the experimental exercise using the Clone Stamp tool.

     Choose File > Revert to go back to the original image.

Repairing fold lines

You will now repair the fold lines in the upper-right corner of the image.

1   Select the Zoom tool from the Tools panel, and if it is not already selected, choose the Resize Windows To Fit check box in the Options bar. By selecting this check box, the window will automatically resize when you zoom.

2   Click approximately three times in the upper-right corner of the image. There you see fold marks that you will repair using the Clone Stamp tool.

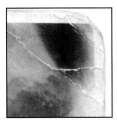

Fold marks that you will repair.

3   Select the Clone Stamp tool (✦) from the Tools panel.

4   Right-click (Windows) or Ctrl+click (Mac OS) on the image area to open the Brush Preset picker. Click the Soft Round brush and change the Size to **13** pixels. Press Enter or the Return key.

Select a soft round brush.

5   Position your cursor to the left of the fold mark, approximately in the center of the fold. Press and hold Alt (Windows) or Option (Mac OS), and click to define that area as the source.

6   Position the Clone Stamp tool over the middle of the fold line itself, and click and release. Depending upon what you are cloning, it is usually wise to apply a clone source in small applications, rather than painting with long brush strokes.

7   Press Shift+[(left bracket) several times to make your brush softer. This way, you can better disguise the edges of your cloning.

8 Continue painting over the fold lines in the upper-left corner. As you paint, you will see crosshairs representing the sampled area. Keep an eye on the crosshairs; you don't want to introduce unwanted areas into the image.

It is not unusual to have to redefine the clone source over and over again. You might have to Alt/Option+click in the areas outside of the fold line repeatedly to find better-matched sources for cloning. You might even find that you Alt/Option+click and then paint, and then Alt/Option+click and paint again, until you conceal the fold mark.

Don't forget some of the selection techniques that you learned in Lesson 4, "Making Selective Changes in Photoshop CC." You can activate the edge of the area to be retouched so you can keep your clone stamping inside the image area and not cross into the white border.

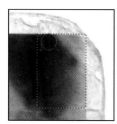

Create selections to help you control the cloning.

With the Clone Stamp tool, it is important to sample tonal areas that are similar to the tonal area you are covering. Otherwise, the retouching will look very obvious.

9 Choose File > Save. Keep this image open for the next part of this lesson.

The History panel

You can use the History panel to jump to previous states in an image. This is an important aid when retouching photos. In this section, you will explore the History panel as it relates to the previous section, and then continue to use it as you work forward in Photoshop.

1   Make sure that **ps0505_work.psd** is still open from the last section.

2   Choose Window > History. The History panel appears. Grab the lower-right corner of the panel and pull it down to expand the panel and reveal all the previous states in History.

Resizing the History panel.

3   You see many Clone Stamp states, or a listing of any function that you performed while the image was open. As you click each state, you reveal the image at that point in your work history. You can click back one state at a time, or you can jump to any state in the panel, including the top state, which is the state of the original image when it was first opened. You can use this as a strategy for redoing work that does not meet with your satisfaction.

4   If you need to redo some of the cloning that you did in the previous section, click a state in the History panel for your starting point, and redo some of your work.

All states in the History panel are deleted when the file is closed. If you want to save a state, click the Create new document button (⬚) to create a new file at the present history state.

5   Choose File > Save. Keep this file open for the next part of the lesson.

The Spot Healing Brush

The Spot Healing Brush tool paints with sampled pixels from an image and matches the texture, lighting, transparency, and shading of the pixels that are sampled to the pixels being retouched, or healed. Note that unlike the Clone Stamp tool, the Spot Healing Brush automatically samples from around the retouched area.

1   With the **ps0505_work.psd** file still open, select View > Fit on Screen, or use the keyboard shortcut Ctrl+0 (zero) (Windows) or Command+0 (zero) (Mac OS).

2   Select the Zoom tool (🔍), then click and drag the lower-right section of the image to zoom into the lower-right corner.

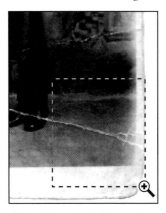

Click and drag with the Zoom tool.

Because you do not have to define a source with the Spot Healing tool, it can be easier to retouch. It is not the absolute answer to every retouching need, but it works well when retouching sections of an image that are not defined and detailed, like blemishes on skin or backgrounds.

3   Select the Spot Healing Brush tool (🖌), and then click and release repeatedly over the fold marks in the lower-right corner of the image. The tool initially creates a dark region, indicating the area that is to be retouched, but don't panic–it will blend well when you release the mouse. Now, using the Spot Healing Brush, repair the fold lines. Use the History panel to undo steps, if necessary. You can experiment with the brush size; sometimes a smaller brush size works better with this tool.

4   Choose File > Save. Keep this file open for the next part of this lesson.

The Healing Brush

The Healing Brush tool also lets you correct imperfections. Like the Clone Stamp tool, you can use the Healing Brush tool to paint with pixels you sample from the image, but the Healing Brush tool also matches the texture, lighting, transparency, and shading of the sampled pixels. In this section, you will remove some defects in the girl's dress.

1   Make sure that **ps0505_work.psd** is still open from the last section, and choose View > Fit on Screen.

2   Select the Zoom tool, then click and drag over the bottom area of the girl's dress.

Click and drag to zoom into the dress.

3   Click and hold the Spot Healing Brush (🖊) in the Tools panel to select the hidden tool, the Healing Brush (🖊).

4   Position your cursor over an area near to, but outside the fold line in the skirt, since you are going to define this area as your source. Press and hold Alt (Windows) or Option (Mac OS), and click to define the source for your Healing Brush tool.

5   Now, paint over the fold line that is closest to the source area you defined.

6   Repeat this process; Alt/Option+click in appropriate source areas near the folds across the dress, then paint over the fold lines, using the Healing Brush tool. Don't forget to change the size using the left and right brackets, if necessary.

Define a source and then paint with the
Healing Brush tool.

7   Choose File > Save, and leave this file open for the next part of this lesson.

Using the Patch tool

You might find that there are large areas of scratches or dust marks that need to be retouched. You can use the Patch tool to replace large amounts of an image with image data that you sample as your source. In this section, you will fix the large dusty area in the upper-left part of the image.

1   With the **ps0505_work.psd** file still open, choose View Fit on Screen, or use the keyboard shortcut Ctrl+0 (zero) (Windows) or Command+0 (zero) (Mac OS).

2   Select the Zoom tool ( ), and then click and drag to zoom into the upper-left area of the image.

Click and drag to zoom into the upper-left corner.

3   Click and hold the Healing Brush tool ( ) and select the hidden Patch tool ( ).

4   Click and drag a selection to choose a small area with defects. Then click and drag that selection over an area of the image with fewer defects, to use that area as a source.

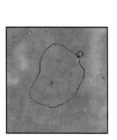 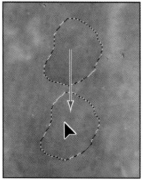 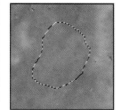

The original.   *Drag with the Patch tool.*   *The result.*

5   Continue to make selections and patch with the Patch tool to clean up most of the dust marks in the upper-left corner of the image.

6   Choose File > Save. Keep the file open for the next part of this lesson.

Using the Clone Source panel

When using the Clone Source panel, you can set up to five clone sources for the Clone Stamp or Healing Brush tools to use. The sources can be from the same image you are working on or from other open images. Using the Clone Source panel, you can even preview the clone source before painting, and rotate and scale the source. In this section, you will clone the upper-left corner of the **ps0505_work.psd** image and rotate it to repair the upper-right corner of the image. You will also define a second clone source to add an art deco border around the edge of the image.

1   Make sure that **ps0505_work.psd** is still open, and choose View > Fit on Screen.

2   Choose Window > Clone Source to open the Clone Source panel.

3   If it helps to zoom in to the image, press Ctrl+plus sign (Windows) or Command+plus sign (Mac OS), and then scroll to the upper-left corner.

The Clone Source panel.

The Clone Source panel displays five icons, each representing a sampled source. You will start out using the first clone source.

4   Choose the Clone Stamp tool (▲). Verify in the Options bar that the Mode is Normal and Opacity is 100 percent.

5   Press the] (Right bracket) until the Clone Stamp size is approximately 80 pixels. The size is indicated in the Options bar.

6   Click the first Clone Source icon in the Clone Source panel and position your cursor over the top-left corner of the image. Press and hold the Alt (Windows) or Option (Mac OS) key and click to define this corner as the first clone source.

You will now use this corner to replace the damaged corner in the upper right.

 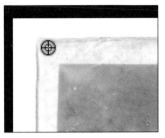

Select the first Clone Source icon.   *Alt/Option+click the upper-left corner.*

7   If you zoomed into the upper-left corner, press and hold the spacebar to turn your cursor into the Hand tool (✋), then click and drag to the left. Think of the image as being a piece of paper that you are pushing to the left to see the upper-right corner of the image.

8   When you are positioned over the right corner, select the Show Overlay check box (if it is not selected already) in the Clone Source panel. A ghost image of your clone source is displayed. If necessary, hover over Opacity in the Clone Source panel and drag it to a lower level.

Note that you can deselect the Clipped check box to see the entire clone source, but for this example, keep it selected.

Select Show Overlay to see your clone source before cloning.

9　Now, type **90** in the Rotate text field in the Clone Source panel. The corner is rotated so you can fit it in as a new corner in the upper-right area of the image.

Use the Clone Source panel to rotate your source.

10　Verify that your brush size is approximately the width of the white border. You can preview the brush size by positioning your cursor over the white border. If you do not see the brush size preview, you might have your Caps Lock key pressed. If necessary, make your brush smaller using the [(left bracket), or larger using the] (right bracket) keys repeatedly.

11　Make sure the corner is aligned with the outside of the underlying image (original upper-right corner). Don't worry about aligning with the original inside border.

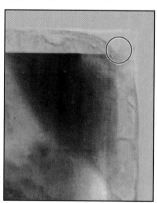
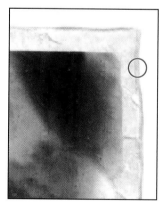

Align the corner before starting to clone.

12　Start painting only the corner with the Clone Stamp tool. Now the corner has been added to the image. Deselect the Show Overlay check box to better see your results.

13　Choose File > Save and keep this file open for the next part of this lesson.

Cloning from another source

In this section, you will open an image to clone a decoration, and then apply it to the
ps0505_work image.

1   Choose File > Browse in Bridge, and then navigate to the ps05lessons folder and
    double-click the image named **ps0506.psd**. An image with a decorative border
    appears.

2   If the Clone Source panel is not visible, choose Window > Clone Source. Make sure
    that the Show Overlay check box is deselected.

3   Select the Clone Stamp tool (♨), and then click the second Clone Source icon.

4   Position your cursor over the upper-left corner of the decorative border, and then
    press and hold the Alt (Windows) or Option (Mac OS) key and click to define this
    area of the image as your second clone source.

Define the upper-left corner as the second clone source.

5   Select the third Clone Source icon in the Clone Source panel.

6   Position your cursor over the upper-right corner of the decorative border, then press
    and hold the Alt (Windows) or Option (Mac OS) key and click to define this area of
    the image as your third clone source.

7   Choose Window > **ps0505_work.psd** to bring that image to the front.

8   If you cannot see your entire **ps0505_work.psd** image, choose View > Fit on
    Screen, or use the keyboard shortcut Ctrl+0 (zero) (Windows) or Command+0 (zero)
    (Mac OS).

9   To make the clone of the decorative border appear *antique*, you will make some
    modifications to the Clone Stamp tool options. With the Clone Stamp tool selected,
    go to the Options bar and select Luminosity from the Mode drop-down menu. Type
    50 into the Opacity text field.

10 Select the second Clone Source icon, and then select the Show Overlay check box in
    the Clone Source panel.

11 Position your cursor in the upper-left corner of the **ps0505_work.psd** image; you see the preview of the decorative border. When you have the decorative corner positioned roughly in the upper-left corner, start painting. Try to follow the swirls of the design as best you can, but don't worry about being exact. The blending mode and opacity that you set in the Options bar helps to blend this into the original image. Keep in mind that when you paint with a lighter opacity, additional painting adds to the initial opacity. If it helps to see the results, turn off the Show Overlay check box. Select it to turn it back on for the remainder of this lesson.

Paint with the Clone tool.   *The result.*

Now you will clone the third source to the upper-right corner of the image. This time, you can experiment with the position of the decoration on the image.

12 Navigate to the upper-right side of the **ps0505_work** image and select the third Clone Source icon from the Clone Source panel. You will now use the Clone Source panel to reposition the upper-right corner clone source.

13 Press and hold Alt+Shift (Windows) or Option+Shift (Mac OS) and press the left, right, up, or down arrow key on your keyboard to nudge the overlay into a better position. No specific position is required for this lesson; simply find a location that you feel works well.

14 Once you have the clone source in position, start painting. Lightly paint the decoration into the upper-right corner. If you feel your brush is too hard-edged, press Shift+[(left bracket) to make it softer.

15 Choose File > Save. Keep the **ps0505_work.psd** file open for the next part of this lesson. Choose Window > **ps0506.psd** to bring that image forward. Then choose File > Close. If asked to save changes, select Don't Save.

Self study

Return to the **ps0505_work.psd** image and use a variety of retouching tools, such as the Clone Stamp, Spot Healing, and Healing Brush tools to fix the rest of the damaged areas in the image. Also use the retouching tools to remove dust from the image.

Use the Clone Source panel to repair the lower-left and lower-right corners of the **ps0505_work.psd** image.

Review

Questions

1   If you have an image in the grayscale mode and you want to colorize it, what must you do first?

2   What blending mode preserves the underlying grayscale of an image and applies a hue of the selected color? Hint: it is typically used for tinting images.

3   What is the main difference between the way the Clone Stamp and Healing Brush replace information in an image?

4   How many clone sources can be set in the Clone Source panel?

Answers

1   To use color, you must choose a color mode that supports color, such as RGB or CMYK. You can change the color mode by selecting the Image > Mode menu.

2   The Color blending mode is used for tinting images.

3   The Clone Stamp makes an exact copy of the sampled area, whereas the Healing Brush makes a copy of the sampled area and matches the texture, lighting, transparency, and shading of the sampled pixels.

4   You can set up to five clone sources in the Clone Source panel.

What you'll learn in this lesson:

- Choosing your color settings
- Using the Histogram panel
- Discovering how to use a neutral
- Using Curves
- Understanding Unsharp mask
- Using Camera Raw

Color Correcting an Image

You can create interesting imagery in Photoshop, including complex compositions, filter effects, and even 3D imagery, but it is essential that you have a great looking image to start with.

Starting up

There are simple steps that you can take to create a brighter, cleaner, more accurate image. In this lesson, you'll learn how to use the Curves controls and how to sharpen your images. You'll learn what a neutral is and how to use it to color correct your images. You'll also have the opportunity to work with a Camera Raw image, using the improved Camera Raw plug-in.

Although the steps might at first seem time-consuming, they go quickly when not accompanied by the "whys and hows" included in this lesson. In fact, the process works almost like magic; a few steps and your image looks great!

Before starting, make sure that your tools and panels are consistent by resetting your preferences. See "Resetting Adobe Photoshop CC preferences" in the Starting up section of this book. You will work with several files from the ps06lessons folder in this lesson.

Make sure that you have loaded the pslessons folder onto your hard drive from the supplied DVD. See "Loading lesson files" in the Starting up section of this book.

See Lesson 6 in action!

Use the accompanying video to gain a better understanding of how to use some of the features shown in this lesson. You can find the video tutorial for this lesson on the included DVD.

Choosing your color settings

What many Photoshop users do not understand is the importance of knowing where an image is going to be published; whether for print, the Web, or even a digital device such as a cell phone. In Lesson 5, "Painting and Retouching," you read a little about color settings and discovered some of Photoshop's pre-defined settings. These help adapt the colors and values of an image for different uses. If not set properly, your images might appear very dark, especially in the shadow areas. For this lesson, you will use generic color settings that work well for a typical print image. You are also introduced to settings for other types of output, including the Web.

1   Choose Edit > Color Settings in Photoshop CC. The Color Settings dialog box appears.

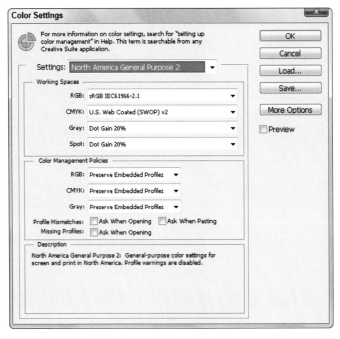

The Color Settings dialog box at its default settings.

2   As a default, North America General Purpose 2 is selected. This is a generic setting that basically indicates that Photoshop has no idea where you are using your image. Depending upon your image's final destination—print, web, or mobile, the results could vary widely. If you have another setting, it is most likely due to setting your Color Settings in Adobe Bridge.

3   For this example, make sure that the default settings of North America General Purpose 2 are selected. Click OK to exit the Color Settings dialog box.

Opening the file

You will now open a file that you will color correct.

1   Choose File > Browse in Bridge. When Adobe Bridge is forward, navigate to the ps06lessons folder that you copied onto your hard drive. Keep in mind that if you do not have Adobe Bridge installed, Adobe Application Manager launches, where you have the option to install Bridge.

2   Locate the image named **ps0601.psd** and double-click it to open it in Photoshop. You can also choose to right-click (Windows) or Ctrl+click (Mac OS) and select Open with Adobe Photoshop CC. An image of a boy appears; because this is not a professional photograph, it offers many issues that need to be addressed.

Note the comparison of images: the one on the left is uncorrected, and the one on the right is corrected. You'll correct the image on the left in the next few steps.

The image before correction.   *The image after correction.*

3   Choose File > Save As. The Save As dialog box appears. Navigate to the ps06lessons folder on your hard drive. Name this file **ps0601_work**, choose Photoshop from the Format drop-down menu, and click Save. Leave the image open.

Why you should work in RGB

In this lesson, you start and stay in the RGB (Red, Green, Blue) color mode. There are two reasons for this: you find more tools that are available in RGB mode, and changes to color values in RGB degrade your image less than if you are working in CMYK. If you were sending this image to a commercial printer, you would make sure your color settings were accurate, do all your retouching, and then convert your image to CMYK by choosing Image > Mode > CMYK Color.

If you want to see the CMYK preview while working in RGB, press Ctrl+Y (Windows) or Command+Y (Mac OS). This way, you can work in the RGB mode while you see the CMYK preview on your screen. This is a toggle keyboard shortcut, meaning that if you press Ctrl+Y or Command+Y again, the preview is turned off. You may not see a difference in the image, depending upon the range of colors, but the title tab indicates that you are in CMYK preview mode by displaying /CMYK after the title of the image.

Reading a histogram

Understanding image histograms is probably the single most important concept to becoming familiar with Photoshop. A histogram can tell you whether your image has been properly exposed, whether the lighting is correct, and what adjustments will work best to improve your image. It will also indicate if the image has enough tonal information to produce a quality image. You will reference the Histogram panel throughout this lesson.

1   If your Histogram panel is not visible, choose Window > Histogram. The Histogram panel appears.

A histogram shows the tonal values that range from the lightest to the darkest in an image. Histograms can vary in appearance, but typically you want to see a full, rich, mountainous area representing tonal values. See the figures for examples of a histogram with many values, one with very few values, and the images relating to each.

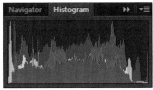

A good histogram and its related image.

A poor histogram and its related image.

Keep an eye on your Histogram panel. Simply doing normal corrections to an image can break up a histogram, giving you an image that starts to look posterized (when a region of an image with a continuous gradation of tone is replaced with several regions of fewer tones). Avoid breaking up the histogram by learning to use multi-function tools, such as the Curves panel, and making changes using adjustment layers that don't change your original image data.

2   To make sure that the values you read in Photoshop are accurate, select the Eyedropper tool (🖉). Notice that the Options bar (across the top of the document window) changes to offer options specific to the Eyedropper tool. Click and hold the Sample Size drop-down menu and choose 3 by 3 Average. This ensures a representative sample of an area, rather than the value of a single screen pixel.

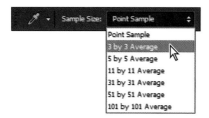

Set up the Eyedropper tool to sample more pixel information.

Making the Curve adjustment

You will now address the tonal values of this image. To do this, you will take advantage of the Curves Adjustments panel. Adjustment layers can be created by using the Adjustments panel, or in the Layers panel. To help you see the relationship between Adjustment layers and other layers, you will create one using the Layers panel.

1   If the Layers panel is not visible, choose Window > Layers. In this example, you will use an Adjustment layer to make color corrections to this image. By using an adjustments layer, you can make changes to an image's tonal values without destroying the original image data. See Lesson 10, "Using Layer Styles and Adjustment Layers," for more information about how to use the adjustment layers.

2   Click and hold the Create New Fill or Adjustment Layer button (●) at the bottom of
the Layers panel, select Curves, and release the mouse. The Properties panel appears
with the Curves options visible in it.

Select the Curves   *The Properties panel appears.*
Adjustment.

A. *Adjustment affects all layers below (click to clip to layer).*
B. *Press to view previous state.* **C.** *Reset to adjustment defaults.*
D. *Toggle layer visibility.* **E.** *Delete this adjustment layer.*

Once you choose to create an adjustment layer, it appears in the Properties panel; an
example is the Curves adjustment panel that you just revealed. If you accidently leave
the Curves adjustment, you can just click the Curves adjustment located in the Layers
panel, and then locate the Window > Properties panel.

3   Click the Properties tab and click and drag it out of the docking area toward the left.
Undocking the panel this way allows you to reposition the Properties panel. This
is important in later steps when you need to see the image at the same time as the
Properties panel.

*You can see all adjustment layer options in the Adjustments panel; you see a panel with links to
the other adjustments that you can make.*

If you make an error, you can undo one step by pressing Ctrl+Z (Windows) or Command+Z (Mac OS). If you want to return to the defaults for this adjustment, choose the Reset to Adjustment Defaults button (◙) in the lower-right portion of the Properties panel.

If you want to eliminate the adjustment layer, choose the Delete this adjustment layer button (🗑).

Defining the highlight and shadow

In this section, you'll set the highlight and shadow to predetermined values using the Set White Point and Set Black Point tools available in the Curves Adjustments panel. Before you do this, you'll determine what those values should be. This is a critical part of the process, since the default for the white point is 0, meaning that the lightest part of the image will have no value when printed, and any detail in this area will be lost.

Some images can get away with not having tonal values in very bright areas. Typically, reflections from metal, fire, and extremely sunlit areas, as well as reflections off other shiny objects such as jewelry, do not have value in those reflective areas.

These are referred to as specular highlights. By leaving them without any value, it helps the rest of the image look balanced, and allows the shine to pop out of the image.

This image has specular highlights, which should be left with a value of zero.

Locating the White and Black Point

Back before digital imagery became so accessible, highly skilled scanner operators used large drum scanners to scan and color-correct images. Back then, color experts followed many of the same steps that you will learn in this lesson. The most important step would be defining the tone curve based on what the operator thought should be defined as the lightest part of a tone curve, and the darkest.

There are many factors that can determine what appears to be a simple task. To produce the best image, you need to know where the image will be used; shiny coated paper, newsprint, or on screen only.

Before you get started, you will change a simple preference to make it easier for you to interpret the Curves in the Properties panel.

1   With the Properties panel open, click the panel menu in the upper-right area, and select Curves Display Options. The Curves Display Options dialog box appears.

2   Choose Show Amount of Pigment/Ink %, then click OK.

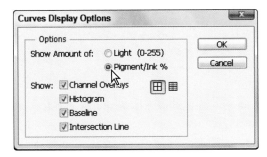

Change the Curves panel to display curve as if it was based upon ink.

Whether you work on print or web images, it can be helpful to visually interpret the curves panel based upon ink, since this puts the lightest colors of the image in the lower left and the darkest part of the image in the upper -right.

Inputting the white and black point values

The process of defining values for the lightest and darkest points in your image is not difficult, but it helps if you know where the image is going to be used. If you have a good relationship with a printer, they can tell you what white point (lightest) or black point (darkest) values work best for their presses and material that you are printing on. Alternatively, you can use the generic values suggested in this book. The values shown in this example are good for typical printing setups and for screen display.

1   Double-click the Sample in image to set White Point button (🖊) found in the Properties panel; the Color Picker (Target Highlight Color) dialog box appears. Even though you are in RGB, you can set values in any of the color environments displayed in this window. In this example, you'll use CMYK values.

2   Type **5** in the C (Cyan) text field, **3** in the M (Magenta) text field and **3** in the Y (Yellow) text field. Leave K (Black) at 0, and click OK. A warning dialog box appears asking if you would like to save the target values; click Yes.

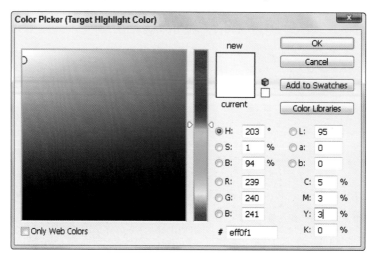

Setting the target highlight color.

3   Now, double-click the Sample in image to set Black Point button (✐). The Color Picker (Target Shadow Color) dialog box appears.

If you have properly defined ink and paper in your Color Settings dialog box, you do not need to change the Black Point values. If you are not sure where you are going to print, or if you are going to use your image on screen, you can use the values in the next step of this exercise.

4   Type **65** in the C (Cyan) text field, **53** in the M (Magenta) text field, **51** in the Y (Yellow) text box and **95** in the K (Black) text field. Click OK. A warning dialog box appears asking if you would like to save the target values; click Yes.

It is important to note that your printer might be able to achieve a richer black than the one offered here. If you have a relationship with a printer, ask for their maximum black value and enter it here. Otherwise, use these standard values.

5   Now, select the highlight slider (△), and then press and hold Alt (Windows) or Option (Mac OS) and slide it to the right. Notice that the image appears posterized: this is the automatic clipping that is visible when you press and hold the Alt/Option key. The clipping makes it easier to locate the darkest and lightest areas of an image—an essential task if you are trying to improve an image's tonal values.

6   In this example, the flames in the baseball hat are visible in the preview, indicating that the area is recognized as one of the lightest parts of this image. If you are working on your own image and don't immediately see the lightest part of the image, you can Alt/Option drag until a light part of your image is highlighted. Notice that there are other light areas in this image, but you are focusing on the primary subject, which is the boy.

 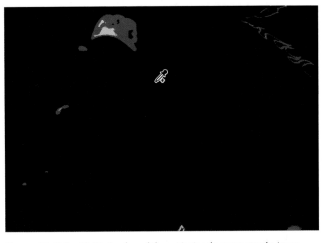

Select the highlight slider.   *Press and hold the Alt/Option key while positioning the cursor over the image.*

If you are working on a different image, you might notice that there are some other light areas that appear that could be considered specular highlights. It helps to remember that if a light point appears that belongs to something shiny, you should ignore it and drag the slider to the right until you find the first legitimate (non-spectacular) highlight.

In the next step, you will mark this light area with a color sampler on the image. This way, you can refer back to it at a later time.

7   With the Set white point eyedropper (🖊) selected, hover over the image and press and hold the Alt/Option key. The image now displays in the posterized view again.

Here is where it might get tricky: add the Shift key to this configuration; your cursor changes into the Color Sampler tool (🖋). Click the light area you found in the flame. A color sample appears on the image, but no change has yet been made to the image.

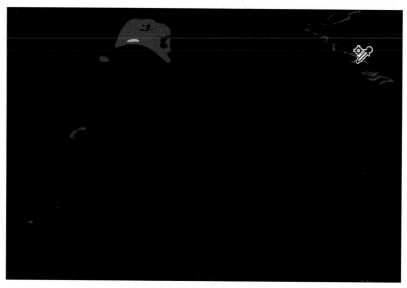

Add a color sample to mark the lightest point in the image.

If necessary, you can reposition the Color Sample by pressing and holding the Shift key and dragging it to a new location.

8   Make sure that the Set white point eyedropper is still selected, and click the color sampler you just placed. By clicking the color sampler, you defined this area of the image as the lightest point on the tone curve; it is adjusted to your newly defined highlight color values.

If this gives you unexpected results, you might have missed the color sampler. You can undo by pressing Ctrl+Z (Windows) or Command+Z (Mac OS), and then try clicking the white area of the flame again. Keep in mind that the color sample that you dropped is only a marker; you do not have to move the sampler to change the highlight.

Now you will set the black, or darkest, part of your image.

9   If you are not seeing the entire image, press Ctrl+0 (zero) (Windows) or Command+0 (zero) (Mac OS) to make the image fit in the window.

10   Select the shadow slider (◆) on the Properties panel, press and hold the Alt/Option key, and drag the slider toward the left.

When dragging the slider slowly, notice that clipping appears, indicating (with darker colors) the shadow areas of this image. Notice that there are many shadow areas in this image, but you see that the underside of the brim of the hat appears almost instantly, indicating that it is the darkest area in the image.

To see the darkest area of this image, press and hold the Alt/Option key and slide the shadow slider to the left.

Depending upon the input device you have, many areas display as the darkest areas of an image. This is an indication that the input device, whether a scanner or camera, does not have a large dynamic range of tonal values that it can record. You might have to take a logical guess as to what is the darkest part of the image.

11   Make sure that the Set black point eyedropper is selected, and then press and hold the Alt+Shift (Windows) or Option+Shift (Mac OS) keys and click the darkest shadow area to leave a color sampler.

Press and hold the Alt/Option key along with the Shift key and click the darkest area.

12   With the Sample in image to set black point eyedropper still selected, click the color sampler that you dropped on the image. This has now been set as the darkest area of the image, using the values you input earlier in this example.

You should already see a difference in the image—a slight color cast has been removed and the colors look a little cleaner—but you are not done yet. The next step involves balancing the midtones (middle values) of the image.

13   Leave the Curves Properties panel visible for the next exercise.

Adjusting the midtones

In many cases, you need to lighten the midtones (middle values of an image) in order to make details more apparent in an image.

1   Select the center (midtone area) of the white curve line and drag downward slightly to lighten the image in the midtones. This is the only visual correction that you will make to this image. You want to be careful that you do not adjust too much, as you can lose valuable information.

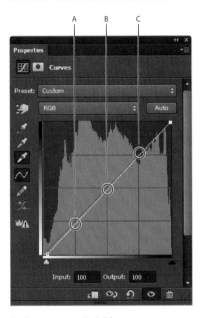

A. Quarter tones. *B.* Midtones.
C. Three-quarter tones.

2   Add a little contrast to your image by clicking the three-quarter tone area of the white curve line (the area between the middle of the curve and the top, as shown in the figure), then clicking and dragging up slightly. Again, this is a visual correction, so don't make too drastic a change.

Click and drag the three-quarter tone up slightly to lighten the image.

3   Keep the Curves Properties panel open for the next section of this lesson.

You can usually see a color cast by looking at the white and gray areas of an image, but, in some cases, you may not have any gray or white objects in your image. If these are art images, you might not want to neutralize them (for example, orange sunsets on the beach, or nice yellow candlelight images). Use the technique shown in this lesson at your discretion. It helps with a typical image, but it takes practice and experience to correct for every type of image.

Understanding neutral colors

A neutral is essentially anything in the image that is gray: a shade of gray, or even light to dark grays. A gray value is a perfect tool to help you measure color values, as it is composed of equal amounts of red, green, and blue. Knowing this allows you to pick up color inaccuracies by reading values in the Photoshop Info panel, rather than just guessing which colors need to be adjusted.

The first image you see below is definitely not correct. You can tell this by looking at the Info panel and seeing that the RGB values are not equal. In the second image, they are almost exactly equal. By looking at only the RGB values, you can tell that the image on the bottom is much more balanced than the image on the top.

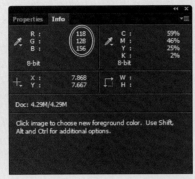

The neutrals in this image are not balanced; you can tell because the RGB values are not equal in value.

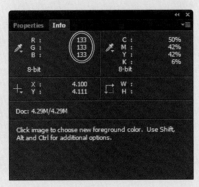

The neutrals in this image are balanced; you can tell because the RGB values are equal.

Setting the neutral

In this section, you'll balance the neutrals in the image.

1   With the Curves Properties panel still open, set another Color Sampler marker by Shift+clicking the gray area on the baseball that is located in lower-right corner of the image. In your images, you might find a neutral in a shadow on a white shirt, a gray piece of equipment, or a counter top.

Find a neutral gray in the image.

Some photographers like to include a gray card (available at photo supply stores) in their images to help them color-balance their images.

2   If the Info panel is not open, choose Window > Info. The Info panel appears.

In the Info panel, you see general information about RGB and CMYK values, as well as pinpoint information about the three Color Sampler markers you have created. You'll focus only on the #3 marker, since the first two were used to indicate highlight and shadow.

Notice that to the right of the #3 marker in the Info panel, there are two values separated by a forward slash. You'll focus only on the set of values to the right of the slash. Depending upon where you clicked in the gray area, you could have different values. The numbers to the left of the forward slash are the values before you started making adjustments in the Curves panel. The numbers to the right of the forward slash are the new values that you are creating with your curve adjustments.

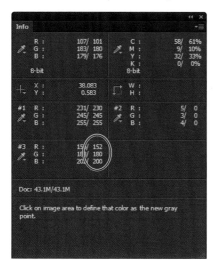

Focus on the values to the right of the forward slash.

3   Select the Sample in image to set Gray Point button (🖉).

4 Click once on the #3 marker you created. The new color values may not be exactly the same, but they come closer to matching each other's values.

The Info panel after the #3 marker is selected as a gray point.

If you want more advanced correction, you can enter each of the individual color curves and adjust them separately by dragging the curve up or down, while watching the values change in the Info panel.

5 Press Ctrl+S (Windows) or Command+S (Mac OS) to save your work file.

6 If your Layers panel is not visible, choose Window > Layers. On the Layers panel, click the Visibility icon (👁) to the left of the Curves 1 adjustment layer to toggle off and on the curves adjustment you just made. Make sure that the Curves layer's visibility is turned back on before you move on to the next section.

Click the Visibility icon to turn off and on the adjustment layer.

7 Choose File > Save. Keep this file open for the next part of this lesson.

Sharpening your image

Now that you have adjusted the tonal values of your image, you'll want to apply some sharpening to the image. In this section, you'll discover how to use unsharp masking. It is a confusing term, but is derived from the traditional (pre-computer) technique used to sharpen images.

To simplify this example, you'll flatten the adjustment layer into the Background layer.

If you are an advanced user, you can avoid flattening by selecting the Background layer, Shift+clicking the Curves 1 layer, then right-clicking (Windows) or Ctrl+clicking (Mac OS) and choosing Convert to Smart Object. This embeds the selected layers into your Photoshop file, but allows you to view and work with them as one layer. If further editing is needed, you can simply double-click the Smart Object layer, and the layers open in their own separate document.

1 Choose Flatten Image from the Layers panel menu.

Choose Flatten Image from the panel menu.

2 Choose View > 100%. The image may appear very large; you can pan the image by pressing and holding the spacebar and pushing the image around on the screen. Position the image so that you can see an area with detail, such as one of the eyes. Note that you should be in Actual Pixel view when using most filters, or you might not see accurate results on your screen.

Press and hold the spacebar, and click and drag on the image area to adjust the position of the image in the window.

3 Choose Filter > Convert for Smart Filters (this step is unnecessary if you already converted your layers into a Smart Object). If an Adobe Photoshop dialog box appears informing you that the layer is being converted into a Smart Object, click OK. Smart Objects allow you to edit filters more freely. Read more about Smart Objects in Lesson 12, "Using Smart Objects in Photoshop." An icon (⬛) appears in the lower-right corner of the layer thumbnail, indicating that this is now a Smart Object.

4 Choose Filter > Sharpen > Unsharp Mask. The Unsharp Mask dialog box appears.

You can click and drag inside the preview pane to change the part of the image that appears there.

Unsharp masking defined

Unsharp masking is a traditional film compositing technique used to sharpen edges in an image. The Unsharp Mask filter corrects blurring in the image, and it compensates for blurring that occurs during the resampling and printing process. Applying the Unsharp Mask filter is recommended whether your final destination is in print or online.

The Unsharp Mask filter assesses the brightness levels of adjacent pixels and increases their relative contrast: it lightens the light pixels that are located next to darker pixels as it darkens those darker pixels. You set the extent and range of lightening and darkening that occurs using the sliders in the Unsharp Mask dialog box. When sharpening an image, it's important to understand that the effects of the Unsharp Mask filter are far more pronounced on-screen than they appear in high-resolution output, such as a printed piece.

In the Unsharp Mask dialog box, you have the following options:

Amount determines how much the contrast of pixels is increased. Typically, an amount of 150 percent or more is applied, but this amount is reliant on the subject matter. Overdoing Unsharp Mask on a person's face can be rather harsh, so that value can be set lower (150 percent) as compared to an image of a piece of equipment, where fine detail is important (300 percent+).

Radius determines the number of pixels surrounding the edge pixels that are affected by the sharpening. For high-resolution images, a radius between 1 and 2 is recommended. If you are creating oversized posters and billboards, you might try experimenting with larger values.

Threshold determines how different the brightness values between two pixels must be before they are considered edge pixels and thus are sharpened by the filter. To avoid introducing unwanted noise into your image, a minimum Threshold setting of 10 is recommended.

5   Type **150** into the Amount text box. Because this is an image of a child, you can apply
a higher amount of sharpening without bringing out unflattering detail.

Click and hold the Preview pane to turn the preview off and on as you make changes.

6   Type **1** in the Radius text field and **10** in the Threshold text field, and click OK.

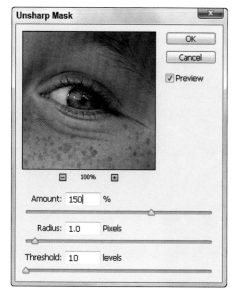

Using the Unsharp Mask dialog box.

7   Choose File > Save. Keep the file open for the next part of this lesson.

*Because you used the Smart Filter feature, you can turn the visibility of the filter off and on
at any time by clicking the visibility icon to the left of Smart Filters in the Layers panel. You
will find out how to apply masks and use other incredible Smart Object features in Lesson 12,
"Using Smart Objects in Photoshop".*

Comparing your image with the original

You can use the History panel in Adobe Photoshop for many functions. In this section,
you'll use the History panel to compare the original image with your finished file.

1   If the History panel is not visible, choose Window > History.

2   Make sure that you have the final step you performed selected. In this case, it
should be the Unsharp Mask filter. If you have some extra steps because you were
experimenting with the Smart Filter thumbnail, just click the Unsharp Mask state in
the History panel.

3 Click the Create New Document from Current State button (⊞) at the bottom of the History panel. A new file is created.

4 Click back on your original image, **ps0601_work.psd**, and press Ctrl+0 (zero) (Windows) or Command+0 (zero) (Mac OS) to fit the image on your screen.

5 Click the original snapshot located at the top of the History panel. This returns you to the original state.

6 Select Window > Arrange > 2-up Vertical to place the images side by side. Zoom into the area surrounding the small child to see that it appears almost as if a cast of color has been lifted from the image, producing a cleaner, brighter image.

Comparing your corrected image with the original image.

7 Choose File > Save, and then File > Close to close your **ps0601_work** file.

8 Choose File > Close for the unsharp mask file created from your History panel. When asked to save the changes, click No, or Don't Save.

Taking care of red eye

Red eye typically occurs when you use a camera with a built-in flash. The light of the flash occurs too fast for the iris of the eye to close the pupil, revealing the blood-rich area alongside the iris. There are many cameras that come with features to help you avoid this phenomenon, and most professional photographers don't experience this, since they typically use a flash that is not directly positioned in front of the subject. Also, there is a solution that is built right into Photoshop.

1 Open the image named **ps0602.psd**, click and click and hold the Spot Healing Brush tool (✐) and drag down to select the Red Eye tool (⊹).

Choose File > Save As. The Save As dialog box appears. Navigate to the ps06lessons folder on your hard drive. Name the file **ps0602_work**, choose Photoshop from the Format drop-down menu, and click Save.

2 Click and drag creating a marquee around the eye on the left side of the image; when you release the mouse, the red eye is removed. If you missed a section, you can repeat this without damaging the areas that are not part of the red eye.

3   Now, click and drag to surround the other eye, again repeating to add any areas that are not corrected.

4   Choose File > Save, or use the keyboard shortcut Ctrl+S (Windows) or Command+S (Mac OS).

5   Choose File > Close to close this file.

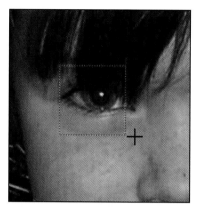

Click and drag, surrounding the iris of an eye, using the Red Eye tool to get rid of the red.

Using the Camera Raw plug-in

In this section, you'll discover how to open and make changes to a Camera Raw file. Camera Raw really deserves more than can be covered in this lesson, but this will give you an introduction, and hopefully get you interested enough to investigate further on your own.

What is a Camera Raw file?

A Camera Raw image file contains the unprocessed data from the image sensor of a digital camera; essentially, it is a digital negative of your image. By working with a Raw file, you have greater control and flexibility, while maintaining the original image file.

The Raw format is proprietary and differs from one camera manufacturer to another, and sometimes even between cameras made by the same manufacturer. This differentiation can lead to many issues, mostly that you also need the camera's proprietary software to open the Raw file, unless, of course, you are using Photoshop CC's Camera Raw plug-in. The Camera Raw plug-in supports more than 150 camera manufacturers, and allows you to open other types of files into the Camera Raw plug-in, including TIFFs and JPEGs. If you are not sure whether your camera is supported by the Camera Raw plug-in, go to *adobe.com* and type **Support Camera Raw cameras** in the Search text field.

1   Choose File > Browse in Bridge to launch Adobe Bridge. Navigate to the ps06lessons folder. Select the image named **ps0603.CR2**. This is a Camera Raw file from a Canon Rebel digital camera. Note that each manufacturer has its own extensions; the CR2 extension is unique to Canon cameras.

2   Double-click the **ps0603.CR2** file to automatically launch and open the file in Photoshop's Camera Raw plug-in.

The Camera Raw plug-in automatically launches when a Raw file is opened.

If you attempt to open a Raw file that is not recognized by the Camera Raw plug-in, you might need to update your plug-in. Go to adobe.com to download the latest version.

When the Camera Raw plug-in opens, you see a Control panel across the top, as well as additional tabbed panels on the right. See the table for definitions of each button in the Control panel.

ICON	TOOL NAME	USE
	Zoom (Z)	Increases or decreases the magnification level of a Camera Raw preview.
	Hand (H)	Allows you to reposition a Raw image, when magnified, in the preview pane.
	White Balance (I)	Balances colors in a Raw image when you click a neutral gray area in the image.
	Color Sampler (S)	Reads image data and leaves markers on the Raw image.
	Targeted Adjustment	Allows you to make changes in Curves, Hue, Saturation, Luminance and control grayscale conversion by clicking and dragging on the image.
	Crop (C)	Crops a Raw image right in the preview pane.
	Straighten (A)	Realigns an image.
	Spot Removal (B)	Heals or clones a Raw image in the preview pane.
	Red-Eye Removal (E)	Removes red eye from a Raw image.
	Adjustment Brush (K)	Paints adjustments of color, brightness, contrast, and more.
	Graduated Filter (G)	Replicates the effect of a conventional graduated filter, one that is composed of a single sheet of glass, plastic, or gel that is half color graduating to a half clear section.
	Open preferences dialog box (Ctrl+K, Command+K)	Changes preferences, such as where XMP files are saved.
	Rotate image 90 degrees counterclockwise (L)	Rotates an image 90 degrees counter-clockwise.
	Rotate image 90 degrees clockwise (R)	Rotates an image 90 degrees clockwise.

You'll have an opportunity to use several of these tools in the next lesson. Before starting, have a look at the panels on the right, and learn a bit about how they are used.

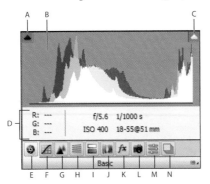

*A. Shadow Clipping Warning button. **B.** Histogram. **C.** Highlight Clipping Warning button. **D.** Info.
E. Basic panel. **F.** Tone Curve panel. **G.** Detail. **H.** HSL/Grayscale. **I.** Split Toning. **J.** Lens Corrections.
K. Effects. **L.** Camera Calibration. **M.** Presets. **N.** Snapshots.*

A. Shadow Clipping Warning button: Indicates if an image is underexposed, with large areas of shadow being clipped. Clipped shadows appear as a solid dark area if not corrected using the exposure controls.

B. Histogram: Shows you where image data resides on the tone curve.

C. Highlight Clipping Warning button: Indicates if an image is overexposed, with large areas of highlight being clipped. A clipped highlight appears as a solid white area if not corrected using the exposure controls.

D. Info: Displays the RGB readings that enable you to check your colors and balance.

E. Basic panel: Contains the main controls, such as White Balance, Exposure, and Fill Light, among others.

F. Tone Curve panel: Adjusts the tone curve. The Point tab must be brought to the front (by clicking it) to activate point-by-point controls.

G. Detail: Adjusts Sharpening and Noise Reduction.

H. HSL/Grayscale: Allows you to create grayscale images with total control over individual colors and brightness.

I. Split Toning: Introduces additional color tones into image highlights and shadows.

J. Lens Correction: Corrects for lens problems, including fringing and vignetting.

K. Effects: Applies filters and offers the ability to create post-cropping vignetting.

L. Camera Calibration: With the Camera Calibration tab, you can shoot a Macbeth color reference chart (available from camera suppliers). Then you can set Color Samplers on the reference chart, and use the sliders to balance the RGB values shown in the Info section. Settings can be saved by selecting the Presets tab and clicking the New Preset button in the lower-right corner, or by choosing Save Settings from the panel menu.

M. Presets: Stores settings for future use in the Presets tab.

N. Snapshots: Offers ability to save multiple versions of an image.

Using Camera Raw controls

In this section, you'll use a few of the controls you just reviewed.

1 Make sure that the Camera image is back to its original settings by pressing and holding the Alt (Windows) or Option (Mac OS) key and clicking Reset, located at the bottom-right corner. The Cancel button becomes Reset when you press and hold the Alt or Option key.

2 The first thing you are going to do with this image is balance the color. You can do this with the White Balance controls. In this instance, you'll keep it simple by selecting the White Balance tool (✐) from the Control panel.

A good neutral to balance from is the light gray section of the name tag. With the White Balance tool selected, click the white part of the name tag. The image is balanced, using that section of the image as a reference.

With the White Balance tool selected, click the name tag.

You'll now adjust some of the other settings available in the Basic tab, to make the image more colorful while still maintaining good color balance.

The image looks a bit underexposed; the girl's face is somewhat dark. You'll bring out more detail in the girl's face by increasing the exposure and then bringing down the highlights to recover some of the image detail.

3 Click the Exposure slider and drag to the right until you reach the +.80 mark, or type **.80** in the Exposure text field.

4 Click the Contrast slider in the Basic tab and drag to the right to about the +60 mark, or type **60** into the Contrast text field.

5 Recover some of the lost highlights by clicking and dragging the Highlight slider left, to the -85 mark, or by typing **-85** in the Highlights text field.

Increase the richness of color by using the Vibrance slider. Do not increase it too much if you plan on printing the image, since oversaturated, rich colors do not generally convert well to CMYK.

6   Drag the Vibrance slider right, over to the 25 mark, or type **25** into the Vibrance text field.

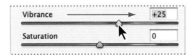

Drag the Vibrance slider to the right.

7   Select the Crop tool (⌶) from the Control panel, and click and drag to select an image area that is a little closer to the girl's face. Double-click in the image area to accept the crop.

Cropping an image in the Camera Raw Plug-in.

Now you'll save your settings.

8   Click the Presets tab. Press the Save Preset button (⊟) in the lower-right corner of the Presets panel. Type the name **Canon_outdoor** and click OK.

9   Keep the Camera Raw Plug-in window open for the next step.

Saving a DNG file

Next, you will save your image as a DNG file. A DNG file is essentially a digital negative file that maintains all the corrections you have made, in addition to the original unprocessed Raw image.

Adobe created the DNG format to provide a standard for Raw files. As mentioned previously, camera vendors have their own proprietary Raw formats and their own extensions and proprietary software to open and edit them. The DNG format was developed to provide a standard maximum-resolution format that all camera vendors would eventually support directly in their cameras. Right now, DNG provides you with the opportunity to save your original Camera Raw files in a format that you should be able to open for many years to come. Note that you can reopen the DNG over and over again, making additional changes without degrading the original image.

1   Click the Save Image button in the lower-left corner of the Camera Raw dialog box. The Save Options dialog box appears.

2   Leave the Destination set to Save in Same Location, then click the arrow to the right of the second drop-down menu in the File Naming section and choose 2 Digit Serial Number. This will automatically number your files, starting with the original document name followed by 01.

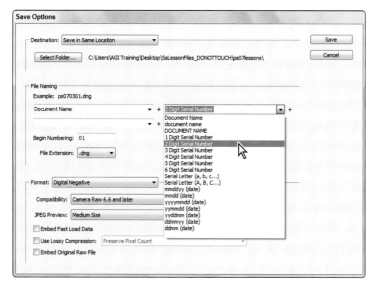

The Camera Raw Save Options dialog box.

3   Click Save. You are returned to the Camera Raw dialog box.

4   Click the Open Image button. The adjusted and cropped image is opened in Photoshop. You can continue working on this file. If you save the file now, you will see the standard Photoshop Save As dialog box. Note that whatever you save is a copy of the original Camera Raw file—your DNG file remains intact.

Reopening a DNG file

You'll now use Bridge to access your saved DNG file.

1   Access Bridge by choosing File > Browse in Bridge.

2   If you are not still in the ps06lessons folder, navigate to it now. Double-click the file you have created, **ps060301.dng**.

Note that the file reopens in the Camera Raw plug-in dialog box and that you can undo and redo settings, since the original has remained intact.

Self study

Try this exercise on your own.

In this section, you'll learn how to take advantage of the Smart Objects and Smart Filters features using a technique that includes painting on the Filter effects mask thumbnail.

1   Choose File > Browse in Bridge and locate the file named **ps0604.psd**, located in the ps06lessons folder.

2   Alt (Windows) or Option (Mac OS) double-click the Background layer to turn it into a layer (Layer 0).

3   Select Filter > Convert for Smart Filters, and click OK if a Photoshop dialog box appears. Then choose Filter > Blur > Gaussian Blur. Again, click OK if an Adobe Photoshop warning dialog box appears.

4   The Gaussian Blur dialog box appears. Use the slider at the bottom of the dialog box to apply a blur to the image. Move the slider until you can easily see the results; there's no exact number that you should set for this exercise, but make sure it is set at an amount high enough that you can see the results easily. Click OK when done. After you apply the Blur filter, a Smart Filter layer appears with a Filter effects mask thumbnail.

5   Select the Filter effects mask to activate it. This is the large white square to the left of Smart Filters in the Layers panel.

6   Choose the Brush tool (✔) from the Tools panel, and press D on your keyboard. This changes your foreground and background colors to the default colors of black and white.

7   If black is not set as your foreground color, press X to swap the foreground and background colors. Using the Paintbrush tool, paint over the image; note that where you paint with black, the blur disappears. Press X to swap the colors so that white is now the foreground color, then paint over areas where the blur is not visible to restore it. While painting, try various values: for instance, if you type **5**, you are painting with a 50 percent opacity; if you type **46**, you paint with a 46 percent opacity. Type **0** to return to 100 percent opacity. This is a technique that is worth experimenting with—try other filters on your own to explore painting on Filter effect masks to hide or reveal the effect of each filter.

Review

Questions

1　Name an example of how a color sampler can be used.

2　What color mode is typically used for color-correcting an image?

3　What is a neutral? How can you use it to color-correct an image?

4　How can you tell if an image has been corrected in Adobe Photoshop?

5　What is a DNG file?

Answers

1　It is common for the Color Sampler tool to be used inside the Curves panel, where it can be used to mark white, black, or gray points on the image. Using a Color Sampler makes it much easier to read the data from one particular point of the image from the Info panel.

2　There are many theories as to which color mode is the best working environment for color correction. Unless you are in a color-calibrated environment (using LAB), RGB should be the mode you choose to work in for color correction.

3　A neutral is a gray, or a shade of gray. You can often find a gray area in an image that can be used as a measuring tool to see if your colors are balanced. Some photographers like to introduce their own gray card in order to have a neutral against which to balance. They then crop the gray card out of the image when they are finished correcting the color balance.

4　By viewing the Histogram panel, you can tell if an image's tone curve has been adjusted. Even if you make simple curve adjustments, some degradation will occur in the tonal values of the image.

5　The DNG (Digital Negative) format is a non–proprietary, publicly documented, and widely supported format for storing raw camera data. The DNG format was developed to provide a standard format that all camera vendors would eventually support. You can also use DNG as an intermediate format for storing images that were originally captured using a proprietary camera raw format.

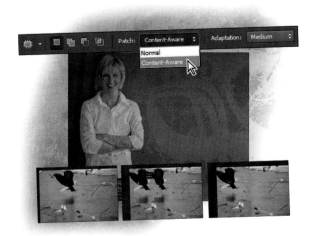

What you'll learn in this lesson:

- Using Content-Aware Scale
- Using Content-Aware Fill
- Using Content-Aware retouching
- Using Content-Aware Move

Using Content-Aware Tools in Photoshop

Over the last several versions, Photoshop has added incredible tools and features that are aware of your image content. By using these content-aware tools, you can ease the task of image retouching, re-sizing, and moving. Your changes will also appear less obvious than if you made them with the standard retouching tools.

Starting up

The content-aware tools available in Photoshop CC are not magic, but in many cases they work as though they were. In this lesson, you discover how you can take advantage of the content-aware tools to add that extra image space that you need, get rid of obstructing content, and more.

Before starting, make sure that your tools and panels are consistent by resetting your preferences. See "Resetting Adobe Photoshop CC preferences" in the Starting up section of this book. You will work with several files from the ps07lessons folder in this lesson. Make sure that you have loaded the pslessons folder onto your hard drive from the supplied DVD. For more information, see "Loading lesson files" in the Starting up section of this book.

See Lesson 7 in action!

Use the accompanying video to gain a better understanding of how to use some of the features shown in this lesson. You can find the video tutorial for this lesson on the included DVD.

Creating extra image area with the content-aware scale tool

The content-aware scale feature is quite handy when you need a bit more image area. Using this feature, you can realistically expand pixels in your image; you can also use it to protect areas of the image that have skin tone or are designated as being protected with the use of a saved selection. In this part of the lesson, you will open an image that needs to be expanded by approximately one inch. You will protect a part of the image first, using channels.

Opening the file

1   Choose File > Browse in Bridge. When Adobe Bridge is forward, navigate to the ps07lessons folder that you copied onto your hard drive.

2   Locate the image named **ps0701.psd** and double-click it to open it in Photoshop. You can also choose to right-click (Windows) or Ctrl+click (Mac OS), and when the shortcut menu appears, select Open with Adobe Photoshop CC. An image of a teacher in front of a chalkboard appears.

This image will be expanded on the right side to increase the image area.

3   Choose File > Save As. The Save As dialog box appears. Navigate to the ps07lessons folder. In the File name text field, type **ps0701_work**, choose Photoshop from the Format drop-down menu, and click Save. Leave the image open.

Viewing the on-screen ruler

Turn on the on-screen ruler before beginning this project. This will help you expand the image to the right amount later in this lesson.

1   Press Ctrl+R (Windows) or Command+R (Mac OS) to turn on the rulers. You can also choose View > Rulers from the menu bar.

Keep in mind that this is a toggle menu item, meaning that if a check mark is on the left of Ruler you already have them visible, and by selecting Ruler again, they go away.

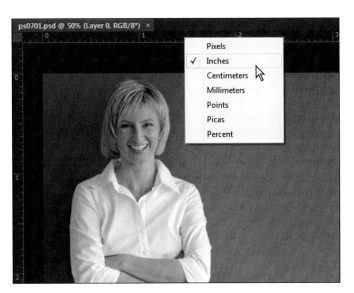

Change the unit of measurement to Inches.

2   This lesson uses inches as the unit of measure. To make sure that you have the ruler set for inches, right-click (Windows) or Ctrl+click (Mac OS) the ruler that appears at the top of the image area, and then select inches from the context menu that appears. You can also change your measurement rules by selecting Edit > Preferences > Units and Rulers (Windows) or Photoshop > Preferences > Units and Rulers, and then select Inches from the Rulers drop-down menu.

Converting the Background into a layer

Just as with many other advanced features in Photoshop, you need to convert the Background into a layer to take advantage of the content-aware scale feature.

1   If the Layers panel is not open, choose Window > Layers to show it now. You see the Background.

2   Press and hold the Alt (Windows) or Option (Mac OS) key, and then double-click the word Background in the Layers panel; Background is converted into Layer 0.

Protecting the teacher

You will now use the Quick Selection tool to make a selection of the teacher and then save that selection. This saved selection will be used later in this lesson to keep her from being affected by the scale.

1   Select the Quick Selection tool (image) and start painting directly on the teacher in the image; this starts to create a selection. You can continue to paint on the teacher until she is entirely selected. If you accidently select outside the teacher, press and hold the Alt (Windows) or Option (Mac OS) key. Keep in mind that you are not creating a silhouette from this selection, so it does not have to be perfect.

Start painting directly on the teacher in the image.

Remember that you can press the right bracket] or left bracket [to increase or decrease the size of the Quick Selection tool when needed.

2 With the selection still active, choose Select > Save Selection. Type **teacher** into the File name text field and click OK.

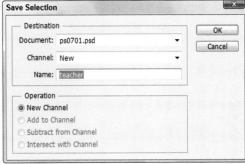

The teacher is selected.   *Saving the selection as a channel.*

3 Choose Select > Deselect, or use the keyboard shortcut Ctrl+D (Windows) or Command+D (Mac OS).

Scaling the background

You will now use the Content-Aware Scale feature and protect your saved selection.

1 Confirm that you do not have anything selected in your image, and then select Edit > Content-Aware Scale; transform handles appear, but do not make any changes yet.

2 Look for a Protect drop-down menu in the Options bar across the top of the work area and select your saved selection, which you named teacher.

Select to protect your saved selection.

Note that an alternate method of protecting people from being scaled is available. Protect skin tones (🧍) is a button that is available in the Options bar, but you will use your saved selection instead.

3 If necessary, press Ctrl+ – (minus sign) or Command+ – (minus sign) two times so you can see about an inch of additional workspace around your image.

4 Grab the right middle handle and start stretching your image to the right. Watch the ruler to see a guide appear as you drag. Release the handle when you are approximately at the 5″ mark on the ruler.

Stretch to about the 5″ mark.

5 Press Return, or click the Commit check box (✔) in the upper right of the Options bar. You will not see your expanded image until after the next step.

6 Choose Image > Reveal all to see your expanded image.

Keep in mind that this example works well for auto-scaling; in fact, many images do, but don't expect miracles. If you push the image too small, or expand it too much, you will see some degradation of the image.

7 Choose File > Save. Keep the file open for the next exercise.

Content-Aware Fill

There are times when you need to eliminate objects entirely from your image, and this is when the Content-Aware Fill feature can help. In this part of the lesson, you will remove the teacher entirely so that you are left only with the blackboard.

1 Make sure that you still have the **ps0701_work** image open and then select the Rectangular Marquee tool (▫).

2 Make a rectangular selection of the teacher, encompassing the entire teacher.

3   Select Edit > Fill, or press the keyboard shortcut Shift+Delete. This opens the Fill dialog box.

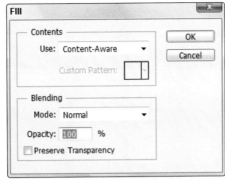

Select the teacher.   *Choose Edit > Fill.*

4   If Content-Aware is not selected in the Use drop-down menu, choose it now, and then click OK. The teacher is replaced seamlessly with the blackboard. If you see a seam or other artifacts, press Ctrl+Z (Windows) or Command+Z (Mac OS) to undo, and then repeat steps 2 and 3, making sure that your selection of the teacher extends beyond her body.

The content is replaced with the blackboard you copied.

5   Choose File > Save, and then File > Close to close this file.

Content-Aware Move

Another content-aware feature that you will find useful is the Content-Aware Move feature. Using this feature, you can nudge or entirely move a selection in an image from one location to another. Photoshop will try to seamlessly replace the original location of your selection with the content that is surrounding it, as well as feather and blend your selection in its new location. As is always the case, this does not work well with every type of image, but it can be handy when it does work.

1   Choose File > Browse in Bridge. When Adobe Bridge is forward, navigate to the ps07lessons folder.

2   Locate the image named **ps0702.psd** and double-click it to open it in Photoshop. You can also choose to right-click (Windows) or Ctrl+click (Mac OS), and from the shortcut menu that appears, select Open with Adobe Photoshop CC. An image of an eagle grabbing fish off the ice appears.

You will reposition the eagle in this image.

3   Choose File > Save As. The Save As dialog box appears. Navigate to the ps07lessons folder. In the File name text field, type **ps0702_work**, choose Photoshop from the Format drop-down menu, and click Save. Leave the image open.

4   Click the Spot Healing Brush tool (✐) in the Tools panel and select the hidden Content-Aware Move tool (✖).

Select the hidden Content-Aware Move tool.

5   Using the Content-Aware tool, click and drag to encompass the eagle, the fish, and the eagle's shadow within a selection. Make sure you complete the selection by surrounding the entire eagle selection.

6   Using the Content-Aware tool, click and drag the eagle to the upper-left corner of the image and release to see the result.

You can change the Content-Aware Move tool mode to Extend in the Options bar. Extend allows you to extend or contract objects such as hair, trees, and more.

Click and drag using the Content-Aware tool to make a selection.   *Click and drag the eagle to the upper-left corner of the image.*   *Release for the result.*

7   Choose File > Save to save the file. Keep the file open for the next part of the lesson.

If you are not happy with the results in your images, change the adaptation from strict to very loose in the Adaption drop-down menu that appears in the Content-Aware Move Options bar.

Content–Aware retouching

In Lesson 5, "Painting and Retouching," you discovered how to retouch using the Content-Aware Spot Healing Brush tool. In this lesson, you will review the Content-Aware Patch tool and how it takes the surrounding content into consideration before filling your selected area. You'll start with the same eagle image that you have been working on, retouch over any leftover shadow, and eliminate some of the birds in the image.

1   Make sure that you have the **ps0701_work.psd** image still open from the last part of this lesson.

2   Locate the hidden Patch tool. Click and hold the Content-Aware Move tool (✖) that you just used and select the Patch tool.

3   In the Options bar, click and hold the Patch mode drop-down menu and select Content–Aware.

Leave the Adaptation at Medium. This determines how closely the patch reflects the original image.

Change the Patch tool mode to Content-Aware.

4   Using the Patch tool, click and drag to surround the two birds on the left side of the image, as well as any leftover shadow from the previous position of the eagle.

Click and drag using the Patch tool to make a selection of the two birds and any left-over shadow.

5   With the Patch tool still active, click and drag the selected area over to a section in your image where you see only the icy water; try to stay away from dragging the patch over a spot that has birds in it, and then release. Your source selection is instantly replaced with the destination of the Patch tool selection.

If this does not work the first time for you, press Undo and try to select a smaller area to replace.

If you are working on a layered image, you can check Sample All Layers to have the Patch tool recognize all the layers in your image instead of just the active layer.

6   Choose File > Save and then Choose File > Close.

Self study

Try the following exercises on your own.

Content-Aware Moving

1   Open the file named **ps0703.psd** that is located in your ps07lessons folder.

2   Choose File > Save As. The Save As dialog box appears. Navigate to the ps07lessons folder on your hard drive. In the File name text field, type **ps0703a**, and then choose Photoshop from the Format drop-down menu, and click Save.

3   Use the appropriate content-aware feature to move the flowers to the right side of the image.

4   Choose to Save and close this file.

Content-Aware Retouching

1   Open the file named **ps0703.psd** that is located in your ps07lessons folder.

2   Choose File > Save As. The Save As dialog box appears. Navigate to the ps07lessons folder on your hard drive. In the File name text field, type **ps0703b**, choose Photoshop from the Format drop-down menu, and click Save.

3   Use the appropriate content-aware feature to eliminate the flowers on the right.

Review

Questions

1   What is the difference between regular fill and Content-Aware fill?

2   What is the best tool to replace a large selection of an image with another section?

3   If the Content-Aware Move tool leaves pixel remnants behind after a move, what can you do?

Answers

1   The difference between regular Fill and Content-Aware Fill is that the Content-Aware Fill is not an exact replication of the content. When you use the Content-Aware Fill, the selected area automatically fills with matching elements from the existing background.

2   The Patch tool (set to Content-Aware) is the best tool to make selective changes with large patches of images. The Patch tool differs from a regular Fill, because you can designate the source of the content for your replacement.

3   If your Content-Aware Move leaves pixel remnants of the original content, you should undo the last step, and then expand your selection of the content. You can do this with Select > Modify > Expand, or you can manually select outside the content. Then try the move again.

What you'll learn in this lesson:

- Starting to create layers
- Selecting and moving layers
- Using layer masks
- Creating compositions
- Understanding clipping masks

Introduction to Photoshop Layers

Once you discover how to use layers, you can expand your capabilities to create incredible compositions, repair images, and easily apply effects.

Starting up

Before starting, make sure that your tools and panels are consistent by resetting your preferences. See "Resetting Adobe Photoshop CC preferences" in the Starting up section of this book.

You will work with several files from the ps08lessons folder in this lesson. Make sure that you have loaded the pslessons folder onto your hard drive from the supplied DVD. See "Loading lesson files" in the Starting up section of this book.

See Lesson 8 in action!

Use the accompanying video to gain a better understanding of how to use some of the features shown in this lesson. You can find the video tutorial for this lesson on the included DVD.

Discovering layers

Think of layers as clear sheets of film, each containing its own image content. Layers can be stacked on top of each other, and you can see through the transparent area of each layer to view the content on the layers below. Each layer is independent of the others and can have its contents changed without affecting the others. You can reorder layers to create different stacking orders, and change the blending modes on the layers to create interesting overlays. Once you have mastered layers, you can create composites and repair image data like never before.

A new default image starts with only a background layer. The number of additional layers, layer effects, and layer sets that you can add to an image is limited only by your computer's memory. In this lesson, you'll find out how to take advantage of layers to create interesting composites and make non-destructive changes to your images.

Getting a handle on layers

In the first part of the lesson, you will work with the most fundamental concepts of using layers. Even if you are using layers already, it is a good idea to run through this section. Due to the fast pace of production, many users skip right into more advanced layer features without having the opportunity to learn basic layer features that can save them time and aggravation.

Creating a new blank file

In this lesson, you'll create a blank file and add layers to it one at a time.

1   Choose File > New. The New dialog box appears.

2   In the New dialog box, choose Default Photoshop Size from the Preset drop-down menu.

3   Choose Transparent from the Background Contents drop-down menu, and click OK. By selecting Transparent, your new document starts with one layer instead of the default, opaque, Background layer.

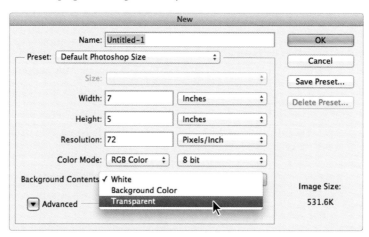

Create a new document with a transparent layer.

4 You will now save the file. Choose File > Save As and navigate to the ps08lessons folder. In the File name text field, type **mylayers**. Choose Photoshop from the Format drop-down menu and click Save. If the Photoshop Format Options dialog box appears, click OK.

To help you work with layers, Photoshop provides a panel specific to layers. In addition to showing thumbnail previews of layer content, the Layers panel allows you to select specific layers, turn their visibility on and off, apply special effects, and change the order in which they are stacked.

5 If the Layers panel is not visible, choose Window > Layers. Click the Layers tab and drag it out of the docking area for this lesson so that you can more closely follow the changes you are making.

6 If the Swatches panel is not visible, choose Window > Swatches. Click and drag the Swatches tab to take it out of the docking area.

Click on the panel tabs and drag the Swatches and Layers panels out of the docking area.

7 Select the Rectangular Marquee tool (□) and click and drag; to constrain the marquee selection to a square, press and hold the Shift key as you drag. Release the mouse when you have created a large, square marquee. Exact size is not important for this step.

8 Click any red color in the Swatches panel. In this example, CMYK Red is used.

9 Choose Edit > Fill, or use the keyboard shortcut Shift+Backspace (Windows) or Shift+Delete (Mac OS) to open the Fill dialog box.

10   In the Use drop-down menu, select Foreground Color. Leave the other settings at their default and click OK.

Fill with your foreground color.   The result.

You can press Alt+Backspace (Windows) or Option+Delete (Mac OS) to automatically fill with your foreground color without opening the Fill dialog box. Keep in mind that either the Backspace or Delete key can be used for this shortcut.

11   Choose Select > Deselect to turn off the selection marquee, or use the keyboard shortcut Ctrl+D (Windows) or Command+D (Mac OS).

12   Choose File > Save.

Naming your layer

You will find that as you increase your use of layers, your Photoshop image can become quite complicated and confusing. Layers are limited only by the amount of memory you have in your computer, so you could work with 100-layer images. To help you stay organized, and therefore more productive, be sure to name your layers appropriately.

1   Double-click the layer name, Layer 1. The text becomes highlighted and the insertion cursor appears. You can now type **red square**, and then press the Enter (Windows) or the Return (Mac OS) key, to provide this layer with a descriptive name.

2   You can also name a layer before you create it. Press and hold the Alt (Windows) or Option (Mac OS) key and click the Create a New Layer button (ﷲ) at the bottom of the Layers panel. The New Layer dialog box appears.

As a default, new layers appear on top of the active layer. Use Ctrl+Alt (Windows) or Command+Option (Mac OS) to open the New Layer dialog box and add the new layer underneath the active layer.

3 In the File name text field, type **yellow circle**, since you are about to create a yellow circle on this layer.

4 For organizational purposes, you can change the color of the layer in the Layers panel, which can help you locate important layers more quickly. For the sake of being color-coordinated, choose Yellow from the Color drop-down menu and click OK. A new layer named yellow circle is created. The Layer Visibility icon in the Layers panel has a yellow background. This background does not affect the actual contents of your layer.

New Layer	
Name: yellow circle	OK
☐ Use Previous Layer to Create Clipping Mask	Cancel
Color: ☒ None ⬍	
Mode: Normal ⬍ Opacity: 100 ▾ %	
☐ (No neutral color exists for Normal mode.)	

Press and hold the Alt/Option key when creating a new layer so that you can name it right away.

Now you will put the yellow circle on this layer.

5 Click and hold the Rectangular Marquee tool (▭), then choose the hidden Elliptical Marquee tool (○).

You can also cycle through the marquee selection tools by pressing Shift+M.

6 Click and drag while holding the Shift key down to create a circle selection in your image area.

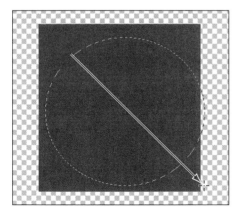

Click and drag while holding the Shift key to create a circle selection.

7 Position your cursor over the Swatches panel and click to choose any yellow color. In this example, CMYK Yellow is selected.

8   Use the keyboard shortcut Alt+Backspace (Windows) or Option+Delete (Mac OS) to quickly fill the selection with yellow.

9   Choose Select > Deselect, or use the keyboard shortcut Ctrl+D (Windows) or Command+D (Mac OS).

   You will now create a third layer for this file. This time, you'll use the Layers panel menu.

10 Click and hold the Layers panel menu and choose New > Layer. The New Layer dialog box appears.

If you prefer keyboard shortcuts, you can press Ctrl+Shift+N (Windows) or Command+Shift+N (Mac OS) to create a new layer.

11 Type **green square** in the File name text field and choose Green from the Color drop-down menu. Click OK; a new layer is created.

12 Click and hold the Elliptical Marquee tool to select the hidden Rectangular Marquee tool. Press and hold the Shift key, then click and drag a small square selection on your document.

13 Position your cursor over the Swatches panel and click to choose any green color from the panel. In this example, CMYK Green is selected.

14 Use the keyboard shortcut Alt+Backspace (Windows) or Option+Delete (Mac OS) to quickly fill the selection with green.

15 Choose Select > Deselect, or use the keyboard shortcut Ctrl+D (Windows) or Command+D (Mac OS).

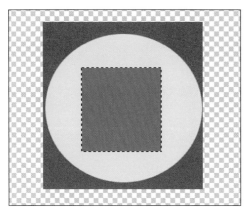

The document now has three layers.

16 Choose File > Save. Keep the **mylayers.psd** file open for the next part of this lesson.

Selecting layers

As basic as it may seem, selecting the appropriate layer can be difficult. Follow this exercise to see how important it is to be aware of layers by keeping track of which layer is active.

1   You should still have the **mylayers.psd** file open from the last exercise. If not, access the file in the ps08lessons folder and select the green square layer in the Layers panel.

2   Select the Move tool (✛) and click and drag to reposition the green square on the green square layer. Note that only the green square moves. This is because layers that are active are the only layers that are affected.

3   With the Move tool still selected, select the yellow circle layer in the Layers panel and then click and drag the yellow circle in your image file. The yellow circle moves.

4   Now, select the red square layer in the Layers panel.

5   Choose Filter > Blur > Gaussian Blur. The Gaussian Blur dialog box appears.

6   In the Gaussian Blur dialog box, type **7** in the Radius text field, then click OK.

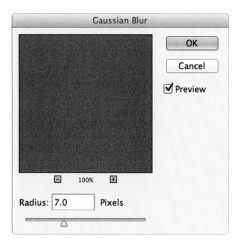
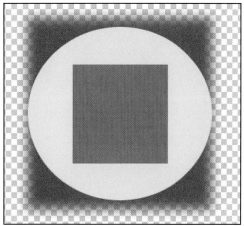

Apply a filter.   *The result.*

7   Choose File > Save. Keep the file open for the next part of the lesson.

Tips for selecting layers

There are several methods you can use to make sure that you are activating certain layers and changing the properties on the specific layer you want to modify.

1   You should still have the **mylayers.psd** file open from the last exercise. If it is not, access the file in the ps08lessons folder and select the red square layer in the Layers panel.

2   Make sure that the Move tool (✛) is selected, then press and hold the Ctrl (Windows) or Command (Mac OS) key and select the yellow circle in the image file. Notice that the yellow circle layer is automatically selected.

3   Now, press and hold the Ctrl (Windows) or Command (Mac OS) key and select the green square in the image file. The green square layer is selected. By pressing and holding the Ctrl or Command key, you turn on an auto-select feature that automatically selects the layer that contains the pixels you have clicked on.

4   Make sure that the Move tool is still selected, and right-click (Windows) or Ctrl+click (Mac OS) on the green square. Note that when you access the context tools, overlapping layers appear in a list, providing you with the opportunity to select the layer in the menu that appears. Select the green square layer.

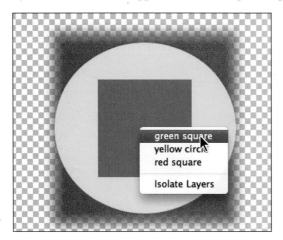

Select a layer using contextual tools.

5   Right-click (Windows) or Ctrl+click (Mac OS) on an area of the image file that contains only the red square pixels to see that only one layer name appears for you to choose from. Choose red square.

Moving layers

Layers appear in the same stacking order in which they appear in the Layers panel. For instance, in the file you have been working on in this lesson, the green square was created last and is at the top of the stacking order, essentially covering up the yellow circle and red square wherever it is positioned.

By moving the position of a layer, you can change the way an image looks, which allows you to experiment with different image compositions.

1   With the **mylayers.psd** file still open, click and drag the green square layer in the Layers panel below the red square layer. Release the mouse button when you see a light bar appear underneath the red square layer. The dark line indicates the location of the layer that you are dragging. Notice that the green square might not be visible at this time because it is underneath the red square, and thus hidden.

Click and drag to reorder layers.

2   You might find it easier to use keyboard commands to move the layers' positions in the stacking order. Select the green square layer and press Ctrl+] (right bracket) (Windows) or Command+] (right bracket) (Mac OS) to move it up one level in the stacking order. Press this keyboard combination again to move the green square layer back to the top of the stacking order.

3   Select the yellow circle layer and press Ctrl+[(left bracket) (Windows) or Command+[(left bracket) (Mac OS) to put the yellow circle one level down in the stacking order, essentially placing it behind the red square. Press Ctrl+] (right bracket) (Windows) or Command+] (right bracket) (Mac OS) to move it back up one level in the layer stacking order.

The image layers should now be back in the same order as when the image was originally created: red square on the bottom, yellow circle in the middle, and green square on the top.

4   Choose File > Save. Keep the file open for the next part of this lesson.

Changing the visibility of a layer

One of the benefits of using layers is that you can hide the layers that contain pixel data on which you are not currently working. By hiding layers, you can focus on the image editing at hand, keeping distractions to a minimum.

1   With the **mylayers.psd** file still open, select the Visibility icon (👁) to the left of the red square layer. The red square disappears.

Turn the visibility of a layer off and on by selecting the Visibility icon.

2   Click again on the spot where the Visibility icon previously appeared. The red square layer is visible again.

3   This time, press and hold the Alt (Windows) or Option (Mac OS) key, and click the same Visibility icon. By using the Alt/Option modifier, you can hide all layers except the one you clicked.

4   Alt/Option+click the same Visibility icon to make all the layers visible again.

Using masks in a layer

There is one last feature fundamental to understand before you delve further into layers: the layer mask feature. Without the mask feature, making realistic composites or blending one image smoothly into another would be much more difficult.

1   With the **mylayers.psd** file still open, choose the red square layer in the Layers panel.

2   Click the Add Layer Mask button (⬛) at the bottom of the Layers panel. A blank mask is added to the right of the red square layer.

Adding a layer mask.

3   To make sure your foreground and background colors are set to the default black and white, press **D** on your keyboard.

4   Select the Gradient tool (⬛) from the Tools panel, and make sure that the Linear Gradient option is selected in the Options bar.

5   Confirm that you have the layer mask selected by clicking it once in the Layers panel.

6   Click and drag across the red square in the image from the left side of the square to the right. Note that some of the red square becomes transparent, while some remains visible. Click and drag with the Gradient tool as many times as you like. Note that in the Layers panel, wherever black appears in the mask thumbnail, the red square is transparent, as the mask is essentially hiding the red square from view.

   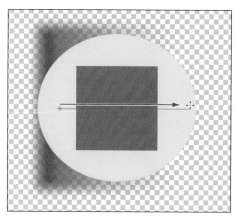

Select the layer mask.   *Click and drag using the Gradient tool across the image.*

7   Choose File > Save. Keep this file open for the next part of this lesson.

Preserve transparency

The last step in this practice file will be to apply transformations to your layers. Transformations include scaling, rotating, and distorting a layer. To help illustrate how transformations work, you will first duplicate a layer and link it to the original.

1   With the **mylayers.psd** file still open, select the green square layer.

2   Select the Move tool (⊕), and then press and hold the Alt (Windows) or Option (Mac OS) key and position the cursor over the green square in the image. You will see a double-arrow cursor (▸). While still pressing and holding the Alt/Option key, click and drag the green square to the right. A duplicate of the layer is created; release the mouse to see that a green square copy layer has been added to the Layers panel.

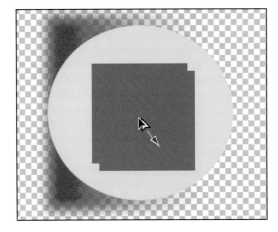

Duplicate a layer using the Alt/Option key.

3   Double-click the layer named green square; when the text is highlighted, type the name **green square shadow**.

4   Delete the word copy from the topmost layer named green square copy.

5   Click the green square shadow layer to select it. You'll now take advantage of a feature that allows you to fill without making a selection. Choose Edit > Fill, or use the keyboard shortcut Shift+Backspace (Windows) or Shift+Delete (Mac OS). The Fill dialog box appears.

6 In the Fill dialog box, choose Black from the Use drop-down menu. Leave the Mode (in the Blending section) set to Normal and Opacity set to 100 percent, check Preserve Transparency, and click OK.

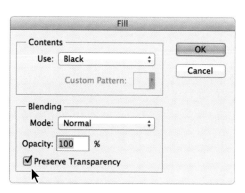 

Preserve Transparency maintains the transparent sections of a layer.   *The result.*

Notice that because you chose to preserve the transparency, only the green pixels are changed to black and the rest of the layer (the transparent part) remains transparent. You'll use this feature later in this lesson when creating a composition from several images.

7 With the green square shadow layer still active, select Filter > Blur > Gaussian Blur. The Gaussian Blur dialog box appears.

8 In the Gaussian Blur dialog box, type **8** in the Radius text field, and click OK.

9 Using the Move tool (✛), reposition the green shadow layer so that it appears slightly off to the lower right of the green square layer, creating the look of a shadow.

10 Type **8**. When you have a layer selected and the Move tool active, you can type a numeric value to instantly change the opacity. By typing 8, you have changed the opacity of the green square shadow to 80 percent.

In this section, you will link the green square layer and green square shadow layer together. This allows you to move them simultaneously and also to apply transformations to both layers at the same time.

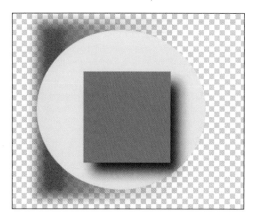

Use the Move tool to reposition the shadow layer.

11 Select the green square layer, then Shift+click the green square shadow layer. Both are now selected.

12 Select the Link Layers button (⊖⊖) at the bottom of the Layers panel. The Link icon appears to the right of the layer names, indicating that they are linked to each other.

Keep layers together by linking them.

13 Select the Move tool, and click and drag the green square to another location. Notice that the shadow also moves. Move the squares back to the center of the image.

14 Choose Edit > Free Transform, or use the keyboard shortcut Ctrl+T (Windows) or Command+T (Mac OS). A bounding box appears around the green square and its shadow.

15 Click the lower-right corner handle and drag it to enlarge the squares. Release the mouse when you've resized them to your liking. No particular size is necessary.

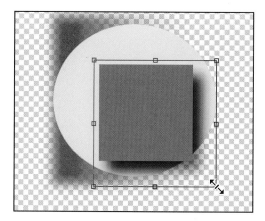

Click and drag the bounding box to scale the layer contents.

16 Press the Esc key (in the upper-left corner of your keyboard) to cancel the transformation.

17 Now, choose Edit > Free Transform again, but this time press and hold the Shift key while dragging the lower-right corner of the bounding box toward the lower-right corner of your image. Pressing and holding the Shift key keeps the layer contents proportional as you scale. Release the mouse when you're done with the transformation.

18 You can also enter exact scale amounts by using the Options bar. Type **150** in the W (Width) text field, and then click the Maintain Aspect Ratio button (∞). The layer contents are scaled to exactly 150 percent. Select the check box in the Options bar to confirm this transformation.

19 Choose File > Save, and then File > Close to close this practice file.

Creating a composition

Now you will have the opportunity to put your practice to work by creating a composition with images and type.

1   Choose File > Browse in Bridge and navigate to the ps08lessons folder inside the pslessons folder on your computer.

2   Double-click the file **ps0801_done.psd** to see the composition that you will create. You can keep this file open for reference, or choose File > Close.

The completed lesson file.

3   Return to Bridge and double-click **ps0801.psd** to open it in Photoshop. An image of a blue sky with clouds appears.

4   Choose File > Save As. In the Save As dialog box, navigate to the ps08lessons folder and type **ps0801_work** into the File name text field; leave the format as Photoshop and click Save.

Moving images in from other documents

You'll start this composition by opening another file and dragging it into this file. Be aware that when moving one document into another, an image's resolution plays an important part in how that image appears proportionally in the destination file. For instance, if a 72-ppi image is moved into a 300-ppi image, it becomes relatively smaller, as the 72-ppi image takes up much less pixel space in the 300-ppi image. On the other hand, if you move a 300-ppi image into a 72-ppi image, it takes up a larger space. If you plan to create composites of multiple images, it is best to choose Image > Image Size and adjust the pixel resolutions of the images before combining them. In this section, you will learn how to check the resolution of your images before combining them into one document.

1   With the **ps0801_work.psd** file open, choose Image > Image Size. The Image Size dialog box appears. Notice that this image's resolution is 300 ppi. Click OK.

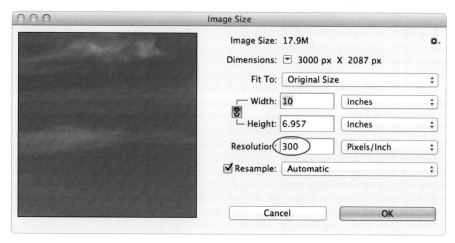

The image resolution of this file is 300 ppi.

2   Choose File > Browse in Bridge and navigate to the ps08lessons folder inside the pslessons folder on your computer.

3   Double-click **ps0802.psd** to open it in Photoshop. An image of a boy jumping appears. For this image, you will check the resolution without opening the Image Size dialog box.

4   Click and hold the document size box to see a pop-up window appear in the lower-left corner of the workspace. This information provides you with dimension and resolution information. Note that this image is also 300 ppi. Release the mouse button to dismiss the pop-up window.

Check the resolution in the document window.

5   Select Window > Arrange > 2-up Vertical. This positions the **ps0801_work.psd** and **ps0802.psd** documents so that you can see them both at the same time.

6   Select the Move tool (⊹).

7 Press and hold the Shift key, and click and drag the **ps0802.psd** image into the **ps0801_work.psd**. Holding the Shift key assures you that the layer is being placed in the exact center of the document into which it is being dragged. Release the mouse when a border appears around the **ps0801_work.psd** image.

You don't have to see both images at the same time to drag and center one image into another image. You can press and hold the Shift key while using the Move tool to click and drag the image over. When you drag an image to the tab of another file, that file comes forward. But don't release; drag your copied image into the image area, and then release.

8 Choose File > Save. Keep the file open for the next part of this lesson.

9 Click the tab for the **ps0802.psd** file, and then click the X in the tab or choose File > Close. You can also use the keyboard shortcut Ctrl+W (Windows) or Command+W (Mac OS) to close the file. If you are asked to save the file, choose No.

Creating a layer mask

You just created the first layer in this document. It is important to keep your layers organized as you work; the Layers panel can become cumbersome when additional layers are created without being properly named.

1 Double-click the word Layer 1 in the Layers panel. When the Layer 1 text becomes highlighted, type **boy**.

Now you'll select the boy and create a layer mask to cover the background sky.

2 Select the boy layer in the Layers panel to make sure it is the active layer, and then select the Quick Selection tool (✍). With the Quick Selection tool, start brushing over the image of the boy. A selection is created as you brush. If you accidently select the area outside the jumping boy, press and hold the Alt (Windows) or Option (Mac OS) key and brush over that area again to delete it from the selection.

Because you will be turning your selection into a mask, you do not have to be precise. You can edit the selection later if necessary.

Create a selection using the Quick Selection tool.

3   With the selection still active, select the Add Layer Mask button (■) at the bottom of the Layers panel. A mask is created, revealing only your selection of the jumping boy.

Select the Add Layer Mask button.   *The result.*

Editing the layer mask

Your mask may not be perfect, but you can easily edit it using your painting tools. In the example shown here, the hand was not correctly selected with the Quick Selection tool and therefore created an inaccurate mask. Zoom into the image and locate a section where your selection may not be precise; it is more than likely to be around the boy's hands.

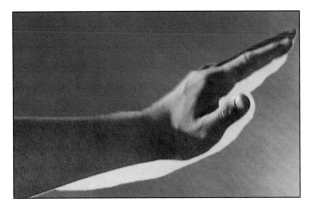

The mask needs to be adjusted in this section.

1   Select the layer mask thumbnail that is to the right of the boy layer's thumbnail in the Layers panel.

Select the layer mask thumbnail.

2   Press **D** on your keyboard to select the default foreground and background colors of black and white. Note that when working on a mask, painting with white reveals the image, while painting with black hides it.

3   Press **X** on your keyboard, and note that by pressing X, you are swapping the foreground and background colors in the Tools panel. Make sure that black is the foreground color.

4   Select the Brush tool and position the cursor over an area of the image where the mask is a bit inaccurate. You see a circle representing the brush size.

If you have Caps Lock pressed, you will not see the brush size preview.

If the brush size is too big or too small for the area of the mask that needs to be retouched, adjust the size before you start painting.

5   Press the **]** (right bracket) key to make the brush size larger, or the **[** (left bracket) key to make the brush size smaller.

6   Use the Opacity slider in the Options bar to change the opacity back to 100, or press **0** (zero). Pressing 0 (zero) is the keyboard shortcut for returning your brush opacity to 100%.

7   Start painting the areas of the mask that were not accurate; in this case, perhaps where some of the sky on the boy layer still appears. Experiment even further by painting over the entire hand. The hand disappears.

8   Press **X** on your keyboard to bring white to the foreground, and paint over the location where the hand was to reveal it again. You are essentially fine-tuning your mask by painting directly on it.

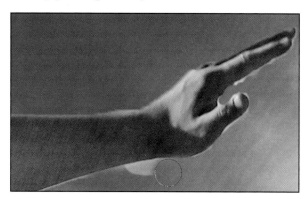

Painting the mask.

9   If you find that your brush should have a harder edge, press Shift+] (right bracket). For a softer edge press Shift+[(left bracket).

The benefit of working with a layer mask is that you can fine-tune and edit it as many times as you want without permanently altering the image. This gives you a lot of freedom and control, and allows you to make more accurate selections. This type of image editing is referred to as nondestructive.

10   When you are finished editing your selection, press Ctrl+0 (zero) (Windows) or Command+0 (zero) (Mac OS) to return to the Fit in Screen view. Then, to deselect the layer mask thumbnail, select the boy layer thumbnail in the Layers panel.

Cloning layers

You'll now clone (or duplicate) the boy layer two times. You'll then apply filters and adjust the opacity of the new layers.

1   Select the boy layer thumbnail in the Layers panel to ensure that it is the active layer. Select the Move tool (⊹) and reposition the boy so that his feet touch the bottom of the image.

Click and drag the boy layer downward.

2   With the Move tool still selected, press and hold the Alt (Windows) or Option (Mac OS) key while dragging the jumping boy image up toward the middle of the image. By pressing and holding the Alt/Option key, you are cloning the layer. Don't worry about a precise location for the cloned layer, as you'll adjust its position later. Release the mouse before releasing the Alt/Option key.

Clone the layer of the boy jumping.

3   Press and hold the Alt (Windows) or Option (Mac OS) key once again and drag the newly created layer upward to clone it. Position this new layer at the top of the image. There are now three layers with the boy jumping.

4   In the Layers panel, double-click the layer named *boy copy*. When the text becomes highlighted, type **boy middle** to change the layer name.

5 Double-click the layer named boy copy 2. When the text becomes highlighted, type **boy top** to change the layer name.

You now have three jumping boy layers.

6 Choose File > Save to save this file. Keep the file open for the next part of this lesson.

Aligning and distributing layers

The layers may not be evenly spaced or aligned with each other. This can be adjusted easily by using the Align and Distribute features in Photoshop.

1 Select the boy layer and then Ctrl+click (Windows) or Command+click (Mac OS) on the boy middle and boy top layers. All three layers become selected.

Note that when you have two or more layers selected, there are additional options in the Options bar to align and distribute your layers.

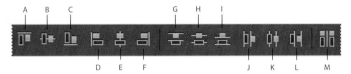

A. Align top edges. B. Align vertical centers. C. Align bottom edges. D. Align left edges.
E. Align horizontal centers. F. Align right edges. G. Distribute top edges.
H. Distribute vertical centers. I. Distribute bottom edges. J. Distribute left edges.
K. Distribute horizontal centers. L. Distribute right edges. M. Auto-Align Layers.

2 Choose the Align Horizontal Centers button (≜) and then the Distribute Vertical Centers button (≜). You might or might not see a dramatic adjustment here; it depends on how you positioned the layers when you created them.

3 Choose File > Save. Keep the file open for the next part of this lesson.

Applying filters to layers

Now you'll apply a filter to the boy and boy middle layers and then adjust their opacity.

1 Select the boy middle layer in the Layers panel.

2 Choose Filter > Blur > Motion Blur. The Motion Blur dialog box appears.

3 Type **–90** in the Angle text field, drag the distance slider to 150, and then click OK. You have created a blur that makes it look like the boy is jumping up.

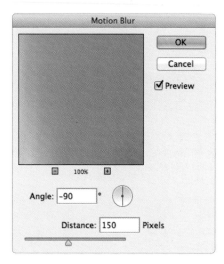

Apply the motion blur.   *Result.*

4 Choose the boy layer in the Layers panel and press Ctrl+F (Windows) or Command+F (Mac OS). This applies the last-used filter to this layer.

You will now adjust the opacity on these layers.

5 With the boy layer still selected, click the arrow to the right of Opacity in the Layers panel. A slider appears. Click and drag the slider to the 20 percent mark.

Drag the opacity slider.

6 Make sure that the Move tool (✛) is active, and select the boy middle layer. This time, you'll change the opacity using a keyboard shortcut. Type **5**; the layer opacity is instantly changed to 50 percent.

The layers after the opacity has been adjusted.

*While the Move tool is active, you can type in any value to set the opacity on a selected layer. For instance, typing **23** would make the layer 23 percent opaque, and **70** would make the layer 70 percent opaque. Type **0** (zero) to return to 100 percent opacity.*

7 Choose File > Save to save this file. Keep the file open for the next part of this lesson.

Creating a type layer

You are now going to add a text layer to this document and apply a warp, as well as a layer style.

1 In the Layers panel, select the boy top layer to make it active. The new type layer will appear directly above the active layer.

2 Select the Type tool (T) and set the following options in the Options bar:

From the font family drop-down menu, choose Myriad Pro. From the font style drop-down menu, choose Black. If you do not have Black, choose Bold.

Type **200** in the font size text field.

A. *Presets.* **B.** *Text orientation.* **C.** *Font family.* **D.** *Font style.* **E.** *Font size.* **F.** *Anti-aliasing.* **G.** *Left-align text.* **H.** *Center text.* **I.** *Right-align text.* **J.** *Text color.* **K.** *Warp text.* **L.** *Character and Paragraph panels.*

3   Now, click once on the Text color box in the Options bar. The Color Picker dialog box appears, with a Select text color pane.

4   You can either enter a color value in this window or click a color in the color preview pane. In this example, you will click a color. Position your cursor over an area in the image that has light clouds, and click. This samples that color, and applies it to the text. Click OK to close the Color Picker.

Sample a color from your image.

You are now ready to type.

5   Click once on the image near the boy's sneaker on the left side of the image. Exact position is not important, as it can be adjusted later.

6   Type **JUMP**, then press and hold the Ctrl (Windows) or Command (Mac OS) key and drag the word Jump to approximately the bottom center of the image. By pressing and holding the Ctrl/Command key, you do not have to exit the text entry mode to reposition the text.

Reposition the text using the Ctrl or Command key.

7   Select the Create Warped Text button (⌁) in the Options bar. The Warp Text dialog box appears. Select Arc Upper from the Style drop-down menu. If you like, experiment with the other style selections, but return to Arc Upper when finished. Click OK. The text is warped.

Warping the text.

8   Click the check mark (✔) in the Options bar to confirm your text entry.

9 In the Layers panel, click and drag the Opacity slider to about 70 percent, or type **70** into the Opacity text field.

10 Choose File > Save and keep the file open for the next part of this lesson.

Applying a layer style

Layer styles allow you to apply interesting effects to layers, such as drop shadows, embossing, and outer glows, to name a few. In this section, you will add a drop shadow to your text layer.

1 Select the text layer to make sure that the layer is active.

2 Click and hold the Add a Layer Style button (*fx*) at the bottom of the Layers panel. Choose Drop Shadow from the menu; the Layer Style dialog box appears.

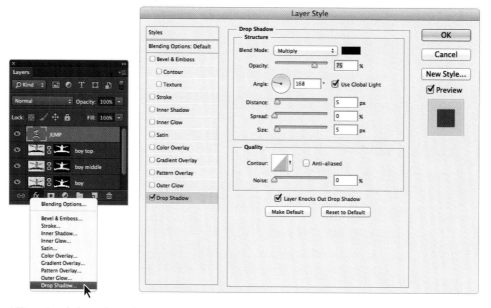

Adding a drop shadow to the text layer.

At some point, you should experiment with all the layer style options listed in the column on the left, but for now you'll work with the drop shadow options.

3 With the Layer Styles dialog box open, click and drag the shadow (in the image window) to reposition it. You can also manually enter values. In this example, the shadow is set to an angle of **160**, the distance at **70**, and the size at **30**. Click OK; the drop shadow is applied.

Creating a clipping mask

You will now create a clipping mask to complete this image. A clipping mask allows you to use the content of one layer to mask the layers above it. In this example, you will create a shape on a vector layer and position it under what is now the background. You will then clip through several layers, masking them within that original vector layer. Although this might sound confusing, it really isn't once you have seen the clipping mask feature in action.

1   First, you need to convert the Background to a layer so you can change its stacking order in the Layers panel.

2   Press and hold the Alt (Windows) or Option (Mac OS) key and double-click the Background layer in the Layers panel. It is automatically converted to Layer 0.

3   Double-click the Layer 0 name, and when the text becomes highlighted, type **sky**.

4   Click and hold the Rectangle tool (▢) and select the hidden Rounded Rectangle tool (▢). In the Options bar, make sure that Shape is selected in the Pick tool mode drop-down menu, and then type **1 in** (inch) in the Radius text field. This value is for the curved corners of the rounded rectangle you are creating.

5   Click and drag from the boy's thumb on the left side of the image down to the bottom of the letter "P" in JUMP. The shape is created; don't worry about the color.

Set the shape options, then click and drag to create the shape layer.

6   In the Layers panel, click and drag the Rounded Rectangle 1 so that it is beneath the sky layer.

7   Press and hold the Alt (Windows) or Option (Mac OS) key, and position your cursor over the line that separates the Rounded Rectangle 1 layer from the sky layer. When you see the Clipping Mask icon (⬇□) appear, click with the mouse. The sky layer is clipped inside the shape layer.

Alt/Option+click in between the layers.   The result.

8   Now, position your cursor on the line separating the sky layer from the boy layer, and Alt/Option+click the line. The clipping now extends up into the boy layer.

9   Position the cursor on the line separating the boy layer from the boy middle layer, and Alt/Option+click again. The clipping mask is now extended to the boy middle layer.

10   Select the Move tool (⊹) and the Rounded Rectangle 1 layer. Click and drag to reposition the layer to see how the sky, boy, and boy middle layers are clipped inside the shape.

You will now trim the layers to eliminate areas you don't need.

11   Choose Image > Trim; the Trim dialog box appears. Leave the settings at the default and click OK. The image is trimmed down to the smallest possible size, without cropping out any image data.

Filtering your layers

A handy layer feature is the ability to filter layers. By filtering layers, you can easily locate layers based upon attributes such as the kind of layer, the blending mode used, name, and more.

1   To experiment with the filter, click the Filter for type layers button (T) to the right of the Pick a file type drop-down menu.

2   Click the Filter for type layers button; only the selected type of layer appears. Note that when you click Kind, you can choose from other attributes, such as Name, Effect, Mode, Attribute, and Color.

You can filter the layers that appear in the Layers panel.

A. *Filter for pixel layers.*
B. *Filter for adjustment layers.*
C. *Filter for type layers.*
D. *Filter for shape layers.*
E. *Filter for smart objects.*
F. *Turn layer filtering on/off.*

3   Choose File > Save, and then File > Close.

Self study

Layers are fun to build and use when creating professional composites. Included in the ps08lessons folder are several images (**boyguitar.psd**, **girlguitar.psd**, **pianokeys.psd**, and **sheetmusic.psd**) that you can use in any way that you want to create a composite. Experiment with these sample files to create new layers, layer masks, and clipping masks. Take the composition further by adding text and warping it.

Review

Questions

1   List at least three ways that you can create a layer in a document.

2   Why should you be concerned about resolution when compositing several images?

3   What is the difference between the Background layer and a regular layer?

Answers

1   You can create new layers in a document using several methods:

   a. Create a new blank layer using the Create a New Layer button (⊟) in the Layers panel. You can also choose Layers > New > Layer or select New Layer from the Layers panel menu.

   b. Create a new layer by clicking and dragging content from one image to another.

   c. Create a text layer; when you add text, a new text layer is automatically created.

   d. Create a shape. If the Shape tool is selected and the Options bar is set to Shape tool, a new Shape layer is automatically created.

2   When combining images from several different sources, it is important for the pixel dimensions or resolutions to be similar, or the images will not be proportional to each other and may not work well as a composite.

3   The Background layer is different from a regular layer in that it does not support layer features. It cannot be moved in the stacking order, repositioned, transformed, or have its blending mode or opacity changed.

What you'll learn in this lesson:

- Combining images
- Removing backgrounds
- Creating advanced selections and masks
- Organizing and grouping layers

Removing Backgrounds to Create Layered Compositions

In this lesson, you'll learn how to combine images and will be introduced to several methods to help you remove backgrounds from images. You'll also learn about file formats and options for saving your files for use on the Web or in print.

Starting up

Before starting, make sure that your tools and panels are consistent by resetting your preferences. For more information, see "Resetting Adobe Photoshop CC preferences" in the Starting up section of this book.

You will work with several files from the ps09lessons folder in this lesson. Make sure that you have loaded the pslessons folder onto your hard drive from the supplied DVD. See "Loading lesson files" in the Starting up section of this book.

In this lesson, you'll use multiple images to create a composite image that you will then save for both print and online use. While this lesson covers some basic information about working with files for online distribution, you can learn even more about saving files for the web in Lesson 13, "Creating Images for Web, Video, and Interactive Use."

See Lesson 9 in action!

Use the accompanying video to gain a better understanding of how to use some of the features shown in this lesson. You can find the video tutorial for this lesson on the included DVD.

A look at the finished project

In this lesson, you will develop a composite using several images, while addressing issues such as resolution, resizing, and choosing the right file format.

To see the finished document:

1   Choose File > Open, or File > Browse in Bridge, and navigate to the pslessons folder on your hard drive and open the ps09lessons folder.

2   Double-click the **ps0901_done.psd** file that is located in the ps09lessons folder; the completed image is displayed in Photoshop.

The completed lesson file.

3   Make sure that the Layers panel is active by choosing Window > Layers.

4   Click the visibility icon (👁) to the left of the dog layer to hide the layer. Click the box where the visibility icon used to be to make the layer visible again.

As mentioned in the previous lesson, layers allow you to combine different elements into a single file while retaining the ability to move and modify each layer independently of the others. Layers appear in the same stacking order that you see in the Layers panel; this is why the dog is on top of the image of the sky and the doghouse. In this lesson, you'll use some of the skills you discovered in Lesson 8, "Introduction to Photoshop Layers", to create multiple layers in Photoshop just as the ones in this finished file.

5   You can keep this file open for reference, or choose File > Close to close the file. If a Photoshop warning box appears, choose Don't Save.

Opening existing image files

Now you will assemble all the images that are part of the final combined image.

1   Choose File > Browse in Bridge and navigate to the ps09lessons folder you copied onto your system.

2   From the ps09lessons folder, select the file of the grass and sky named **ps0901.psd**. Press and hold the Ctrl key (Windows) or Command key (Mac OS), and also select the file of the dog named **ps0902.psd**. Pressing and holding the Ctrl or Command key allows you to select multiple files.

3   Choose Tools > Photoshop > Load Files in Photoshop Layers. By taking advantage of this feature, you can load two of more files into one new Photoshop file easily. The file opens as a new untitled file. The size is determined by the size of the largest file, and contains as many layers as image files you selected. In this case, a new untitled file with two named layers is created.

Load selected files into a new layered Photoshop file using Bridge.

4   Save the file by selecting File > Save As to save this file. When the Save As dialog box appears, navigate to the ps09lessons folder and type **ps0901_work** in the File name text field. Choose Photoshop from the format drop-down menu and click Save. If the Photoshop Format Options dialog box appears, click OK.

If you receive an Embedded Profile Mismatch warning when opening the images, it might be that you have forgotten to reset your preferences using the instructions on page 3. If you receive the warning, choose the Use Embedded Profile option, and then click OK.

Understanding document settings

In this section, you will move another image file into this file. Before you combine the images, you need to be familiar with each document's unique attributes, such as size, resolution, and color mode. Moving layers between documents that have different resolutions may create unexpected results, such as causing the images to appear out of proportion.

Viewing an image's size and resolution

1   With your image file of the grass and dog still open, press Alt (Windows) or Option (Mac OS) and click the file information area in the status bar, located in the lower-left corner of the document window. The pixel dimensions of the image are displayed as 1,000 pixels wide by 839 pixels tall and the Resolution is 300 pixels/inch.

Image size and resolution information.

2   Choose File > Open, or File > Browse in Bridge. From the ps09lessons folder, open the image of the doghouse named **ps0903.psd**. You will check the image size of this image using one of the menu items at the top of the Photoshop workspace.

3   Choose Image > Image Size; the Image Size dialog box appears.

The Image Size dialog box shows Width and Height in increments that you choose. For this lesson, you will use Pixels. If Pixels is not selected, click and hold the Width increments drop-down menu and select Pixels.

The increments that you choose to measure by typically relate to whether you are creating on-screen images, or images that will be printed on various devices.

The most important factors for size and resolution of on-screen images are the pixel dimensions and the pixels per inch (ppi). If you are creating an image for print (in the U.S.), you should change your increments to the print measurement that you prefer and also reference the Resolution. Typically, for high-quality printing, you would need your image to be close to actual print size and at least 266 ppi in resolution.

4   The image size of the doghouse is 1,242 pixels by 1,546 pixels. At this size, the doghouse image is much larger than the other two images. This would be apparent if you were to combine the two files.

5   In the Image Size dialog box, make sure that there is a constrained closed chain (🔗) to the left of Width and Height text fields. Also, make sure the Resample Image is set to Automatic.

6   If the Width and Height increments are not set to Pixels, select Pixels from the increment drop-down menu now.

7   Type **700** pixels for height in the Pixel Dimensions portion at the top half of the dialog box. Click OK to apply the transformation and click OK to close the Image Size dialog box.

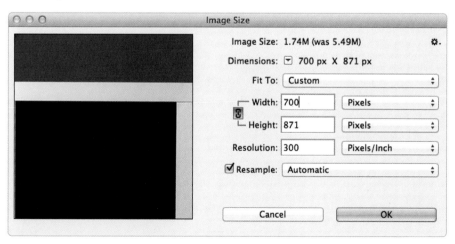

Change the Width to 700 Pixels.

8   The doghouse should now fit nicely with the dog in the other image.

Combining the images

For this project, you'll drag and drop the image of the doghouse into the image with the dog and grass and sky.

Using Duplicate to move a layer

In this next section of the lesson, you will move one layer to another using the Duplicate Layer feature. Keep in mind that when you add new layers to your documents, the new layers typically appear on top of the active layer.

1   Return to the **ps0901_work** file by clicking the tab at the top of the workspace, and then locate the Layers panel. If you don't see it, choose Windows > Layers. Note the stacking order of your image files. The dog image should be at the top of the stack; if it is not, drag it to the top of the stack now. Click the bottom layer (**ps0901.psd**) to make it the active layer.

2   Click the tab of the doghouse image, **ps0903.psd**, to make that image come forward as the active file.

3   In the Layers panel, press and hold the Alt (Windows) or Option (Mac OS) and double-click the Background layer to turn it into a layer, now named Layer 0.

4   Right-click (Windows) or Ctrl+Click (Mac OS) the new Layer 0. When the context menu appears, select Duplicate Layer; a Duplicate Layer dialog box appears.

5   Type **doghouse** in the As section of the Duplicate Layer dialog box. This will be the name of your newly duplicated layer.

6   In the Destination section, choose the **ps0901_work** file from the drop-down menu, and then click OK.

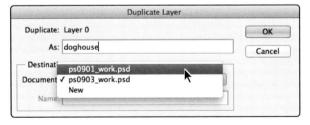

You can choose to duplicate selected layers into other open images.

You can select to move one or more layers from one file to another using the Duplicate Layer feature. You can also use Duplicate layer to copy selected layers to a brand new file.

7   Choose File > Close to close the **ps0903.psd** file. Do not save any changes.

8   If you take a look at your **ps0901_work** file, you see that the doghouse layer has been added in-between the layer of the grassy hill (**ps0901.psd**) and the dog (**ps0902.psd**).

The image of the doghouse is now inbetween the other two layers.

9   Since you will be adding one more layer to the top of this composite, click the dog layer (**ps0902.psd**) to make that the active layer.

Dragging and dropping to copy one image to another

In this section, you'll drag and drop one image into another.

1   Choose File > Browse in Bridge and double-click the image named **ps0904.psd** to open the image of the tennis ball.

2   Select the Move tool (⊹), and then click the image of the tennis ball; do not make a selection.

3   Click in the middle of the tennis ball image and drag it up to the tab at the top of the work area that is labeled ps0901_work. When your cursor is positioned over the tab, the ps0901_work image comes forward: DO NOT release the mouse. Continue dragging down into the image area of your dog composite work file and then release. The tennis ball picture is placed into the dog composite as a new layer. If you receive a message that you cannot use the move tool because the layer is locked, you did not wait until the ps0901_work.psd image came forward before releasing the mouse.

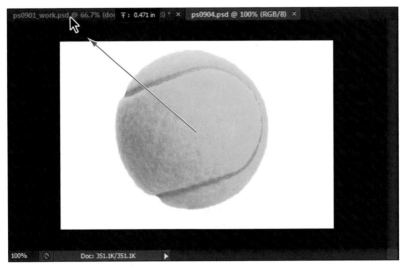

Click and drag the tennis ball image up to the ps0901_work tab.

4   Change the name of the new tennis ball layer by double-clicking the default name of Layer 1 (in the Layers panel), and changing it to **tennis ball**.

5   Select the tab of **ps0904.psd** and choose File > Close to close the file containing the picture of the tennis ball. Do not save any changes to the file.

6 With the composite image of the sky, dog, doghouse, and tennis ball active, choose View > Fit on Screen, or use the keyboard shortcut Ctrl+0 (zero) (Windows) or Command+0 (zero) (Mac OS). This fits the entire image into your document window. You can also see that you have four layers in this document.

The images as layers inside the same image file.

7 Choose File > Save to save this file, but keep it open for the next part of this lesson.

Transforming and editing combined images

Although you have combined four images together, they still require some work. The white background remains in three of the layers, and the layers are not in the proper proportion to each other.

In this section, you will do the following:

- Change the size of a layer.
- View the stacking order of the layers.
- Name the layers to organize them.
- Remove the background from the copied images.
- Refine the edges of the combined images.

Changing the size of a layer

You can make size adjustments to layers and the objects that reside on the layers. Here, you will adjust the size and position of the placed images.

1   Make sure the Layers panel is visible. If you do not see the Layers panel, choose Window > Layers.

3   Select the tennis ball layer in the Layers panel, choose Edit > Free Transform, or use the keyboard shortcut Ctrl+T (Windows) or Command+T (Mac OS). Handles appear around the edges of the tennis ball. If you do not see handles, press Ctrl+0 (zero) (Windows) or Command+0 (zero) (Mac OS) to fit the image into the window.

4   Press and hold the Shift key (Windows and Mac OS), and then click and drag any one of the handles on the outside corner edges of the tennis ball toward the center. The image size is reduced.

Notice that the scale percentages in the Options bar change as you scale the image. Reduce the size of the tennis image to approximately 50 percent of its original size.

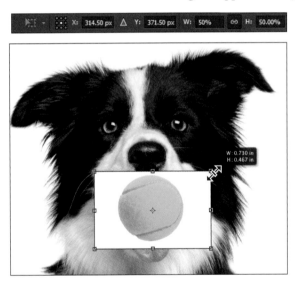

Scale the tennis ball layer to approximately 50%.

Pressing and holding the Shift key maintains the proportions as you scale, while the Alt or Option key scales the image toward its center.

5   In the Options bar, click the Commit Transform button (✓) located on the right side, or press Enter (Windows) or Return (Mac OS) to accept the changes.

Removing a background

Photoshop makes it easy to remove the background of an image. Here, you'll use a method that works well with solid backgrounds, such as the white behind the tennis ball. You won't use this method on the dog or doghouse, as they need a more precise selection method.

1   Make sure that the tennis ball layer is active in the Layers panel.

2   In the Tools panel, click the Eraser tool to select the hidden Magic Eraser tool (✎). The Magic Eraser tool automatically erases the color that you click in an image. The range of color that it selects is based upon the Tolerance that you set in the Options bar. The range can go from 0 (selecting very little of a particular color) to 255 (selecting all pixels). In this example, you will leave the tolerance set at 32.

3   Position the Magic Eraser tool over the white area behind the tennis ball, and click once to remove the white background.

Use the Magic Eraser tool to remove the background behind the tennis ball.

Refining the edges of layers

When moving, copying, pasting, or even using the Magic Eraser tool, you might see some artifacting around the edge of your layer content. The Photoshop anti-aliasing feature that allows for smooth gradations in tonal value can sometimes cause stray background pixels to remain and create an unwanted hard edge. You can use a simple technique called defringing to clean up those edges. To defringe, select the layer you want to clean up in the Layers panel, and then choose Layer > Matting > Defringe. In the Defringe dialog box, maintain the default setting of 1 pixel, and then click OK. The Defringe command blends the edges of the layer into the background, making it appear more natural.

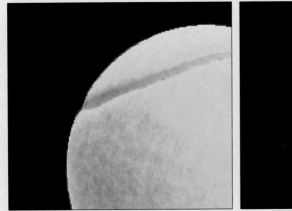 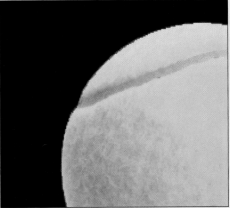

The tennis ball before it is defringed.   *The tennis ball after it is defringed.*

Creating a vector mask

In this next part of the lesson, you have an opportunity to eliminate the white background of your doghouse layer using the Pen tool. You discovered how to use the Pen tool in Lesson 4, "Making Selective Changes in Photoshop CC;" you will now have an opportunity to practice using the Pen as well as creating a mask from your vector path.

Creating your path

Before starting, you need to turn off the visibility of the tennis ball and dog layer (**ps0902.psd**).

1   Click the eye icon (👁) to the left of the tennis ball layer and the **ps0902.psd** layer. These are temporarily hidden.

2   Select the doghouse layer in the Layers panel to activate it.

Turn off the visibility of the top two layers
and select the doghouse layer.

3   Select the Zoom tool and then make sure to turn Scrubby Zoom off using the check
box in the Magnifier options bar across the top.

4   Using the Zoom tool, click and drag to create a zoom area of the upper-left part of the
roof. If you did not zoom correctly, press Ctrl+0 (zero) (Windows) or Command+0
(zero) (Mac OS) to fit the image into your present window. Then try zooming again.

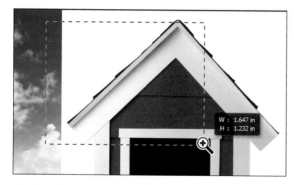

Zoom into the image to see the roof better.

You are zoomed in so you can create a more accurate path. Keep in mind that when
you are this zoomed in, you can press and hold the spacebar and click and drag to
reposition your image at any time.

Starting your pen path

At the end of Lesson 4, "Making Selective Changes in Photoshop CC," you discovered how to start using the Pen tool. In this section of the lesson, you have an opportunity to practice a bit more. You will use the pen path to make a vector mask and eliminate the white background. The benefit to using a vector mask is that it provides a very clean, precise mask, and can also be edited after the mask has been created. (For additional practice using the Pen tool, see Lesson 11, "Working with the Pen tool.")

1   Select the Pen tool and position your cursor over the top of the roof; you see an asterisk indicating that you are about to start a new path.

An asterisk indicates that you are beginning a new path.

2   Click and drag down to create a directional line that runs along about an eighth of an inch, or a small amount and then release. You have created a directional line that will determine how your actual path will be created.

3   Continue clicking and following the roof. Clicking and dragging a little is
    recommended to help create a smooth path. The only time you don't want to click
    and drag is on a corner, where you will click and release before moving on to create
    the next path.

Click and drag with the Pen tool, except when creating a corner point.

4   Continue to create your path. After the roof, the path becomes much easier as you
    need to only click from one point to another to create straight connecting paths.

Click from one point to another for straight paths.

5   When you reach the point you started at, press and hold the Alt key (Windows) or Option key (Mac OS) to close the path. You will see a circle next to the cursor indicating that you are closing the path you started. Pressing and holding the Alt/ Option key is necessary because the first anchor point that you created was clicked and dragged, making it a curved anchor point. If you just click that curved anchor point without pressing and holding the Alt/Option key, it will react strangely and loop the last section of your path.

Make sure to press and hold Alt/Option when clicking the closing anchor point.

6   Choose Windows > Path to show the Paths panel and see your active path displayed in the panel. Click the path and drag it down to the dog-eared Create new path icon (⊐) at the bottom. You path is now saved as Path 1. You can use the Path panel to save, activate, delete, and add new paths.

Drag your Work Path to the Create new path icon to save it.

7   Click in the blank area of the Paths panel and notice that the path is now deactivated. You do not see the path line in your image area anymore. When you click Path 1 in the Paths panel, it returns. This is important to note because when you transform images with paths, you need to make sure to deactivate paths first, or else you will scale the path instead of the layer.

8   Confirm that your path is still active by clicking Path 1.

9   Choose File > Save, and keep the file open for the next part of this lesson.

Turning into vector mask

You will now take the path that you created around the doghouse and turn it into a mask, essentially eliminating the white background from this layer.

1   If the Layers panel is not visible, choose Window > Layers. When the Layers panel appears, make sure that you are on the doghouse layer.

2   With the pen path still active, press and hold the Control key (Windows) or Command key (Mac OS) and click the Add layer mask button (▣) at the bottom of the Layers panel. By pressing and holding the Ctrl/Command key, you immediately create a vector mask from your active pen path.

3   Select your Direct Selection tool (▷) that is hidden under your Path Selection tool (▶) in the Tools panel.

4   Click your path to see that you can reactive your pen path and edit the anchor points, even after making it a mask. If editing is necessary, use the Direction Selection tool to reposition anchor points and directional lines

Select the Direct Selection tool to edit the path.　　*Use the Direction Selection tool to reposition anchor points and directional lines.*

5   Save this file and keep it open for the next part of the lesson.

Using Refine Edge to select the dog

In this part of the lesson, you create a more advanced selection of the furry dog, and then create a pixel mask to eliminate the background.

Using the Quick Selection tool

The Quick Selection tool is always a great way to start a selection, especially if you plan on using the Refine Edge feature to improve the selection.

1   Press Ctrl+0 (zero) (Windows) or Command + 0 (zero) to make the image size fit your window. This way, you should be able to see the entire dog layer.

2   Turn on the visibility of the **ps0902.psd** layer of the dog, and then click the layer to make it active.

3   Select the Quick Selection (✐) tool from the Tools panel and start painting the dog. Remember to use the left ([) and right brackets (]) to enlarge or reduce the size of the Quick Selection tool. Also keep in mind that you can press and hold the Option/Alt key to deselect anything that is selected outside the dog.

Make a selection with the Quick Selection tool.

Refining a selection

In this next part of the lesson, you will take the quick selection that you made and improve the masking of the fine hairs in the fur.

1   Click the Refine Edge button in the Options bar. If you do not see Refine Edge, you might not have a Selection tool active. Make sure that you have the Quick Selection tool, or any selection marquee tool active, to see the Refine Edge option.

2   When the Refine Edge dialog box appears, press **F**. Pressing F cycles you through the different View Modes. Continue pressing F until you see the dog selection on a black background. Remember that the view is only to help you make a better selection.

3 In the Edge Detection section, select the check box for Smart Radius and then increase the radius to 5. You can do this by dragging the slider to the right, or by typing **5.0** into the Radius text field.

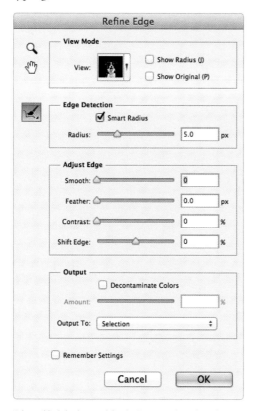

Select a black background for the View Mode and set the Smart Radius to 5.0.

Keep in mind that the Smart Radius automatically builds a selection based upon the edge that you have defined in your selection. By adding a pixel value to the Smart Radius, you set up parameters as to how far you want Photoshop to search for those edges.

You will now clean up some of the edges with the Refine Radius tool.

4   Click and hold the Refine Radius tool to make sure that it is selected.

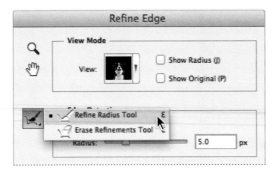

Select the Refine Radius tool.

5   If necessary, press Ctrl/Command++ (plus sign) to zoom into the image and get a better look at the edge selection.

6   Using the Edge Refine Radius tool (▨), start to paint over some of the edges that look like they contain some of the original white background in them.

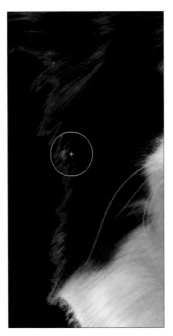

Start refining the edge where you still see the original background.

Don't forget that you can press the spacebar and push around the image on the screen instead of using the scrollbars.

7   If you refine the edge too much, you might lose some of the details of the fur. You can undo your refinement by clicking and holding the Refine Edge tool and selecting the Erase Refinements tool (). Through this method, you are painting back over the area that you refined too much.

8   In the Output section, choose to output to a Layer mask, and click OK.

9   If necessary, press Ctrl/Command+0 (zero) to fit the image into the window.

The dog with the new mask.

The layer mask as it appears in the Layers panel.

Adding the tennis ball to the composition

You will do a little magic in Photoshop to make it look like the dog is carrying the tennis ball in his mouth.

1   Turn on the visibility of the tennis ball layer by clicking the Indicates layer visibility square to the left of the layer name.

2   Position the ball so that it looks as though it would fit in the dog's mouth. Ignore the fact that it is actually on top of his nose.

Position the tennis ball in the dog's mouth.

3   Turn off the visibility of the tennis ball layer.

4   Select the dog layer (**ps0902.psd**) in the Layers panel.

5   Select the Quick Selection tool and click and drag to select the dog's nose and upper mouth.

Select the upper mouth and nose in the dog.

6   Click Refine Edge in the Options bar and select the Smart Radius check box.

7   Enter **5.0** into the Radius check box.

8 In the Output section, choose to Output to a New Layer with Layer Mask, and click OK.

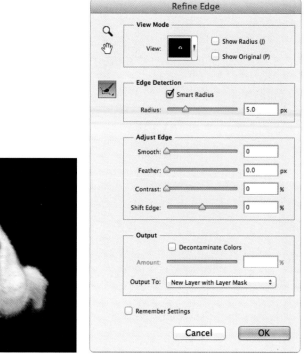

Refine the edge of your selection, and output to a new layer with a layer mask.

You have created a new layer, called ps0902.psd copy, which you see in the stacking order of your Layers panel. You will not see your layer in the actual image at this point because it blends in with the original dog layer.

9 In the Layers panel, double-click the layer name ps0902.psd copy to highlight it and change the name to **mouth**.

10 Turn on the visibility of the tennis ball layer.

11 Click and drag your new layer (named mouth) so that it is on top of the tennis ball layer in the Layers panel. Your tennis ball is sandwiched between the upper mouth and the layer that includes the entire dog.

The tennis ball is between the dog layers.

The stacking order in the Layers panel.

In the next part of this lesson, you will use a layer style to make the ball look like it is sitting in the mouth of the dog.

Using layer styles

In this next part of the lesson, you will use the Drop Shadow style to make the ball look like it is sitting in the mouth of the dog.

1 Select the tennis ball layer, and then click the Add a layer style button (*fx*) in the Layers panel.

2 Select Drop Shadow; the Layer Style dialog box appears.

3 In the Layer Style dialog box, make sure that only Drop Shadow is checked in the Styles column to the left, and then change these settings:

- Opacity: **50**%

- Angle: **90** degrees

- Distance: **5** px

- Spread: **0** (zero) %

- Size: **15** px

4 Click the arrow to the right of the contour picker. The tooltip indicates Click to open Contour picker; select the option named Gaussian. Click anywhere inside the Layer Style window to confirm the Gaussian contour selection, and then close the contour window.

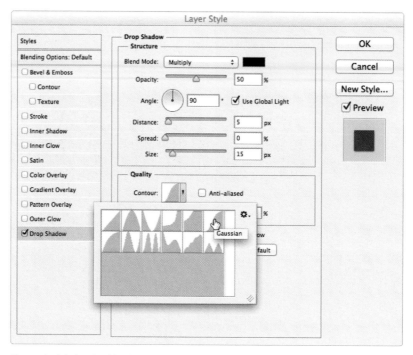

Change the default style of the drop shadow.

5 Select New Style. This is so you can use this combination of style attributes again.

6 When the New Style dialog box appears, type **shadow** into the File name text field, and then click OK.

Name your saved style.

7 Click OK to close the Layer Style dialog box. The style is applied to the tennis ball layer.

Reusing layer styles

You will now use the same style to create a shadow on the top of the tennis ball.

1   Select the mouth layer.

2   Choose Windows > Styles to open the Styles panel.

3   In the Styles panel, click and hold the panel menu that is located at the upper-right of the Styles menu and select Small List. You can now see all the styles listed by name.

4   Scroll to the bottom of the list and choose the shadow style that you saved earlier. The same drop shadow is applied to the upper part of the mouth.

Add layer styles to the image

The result.

5   Choose File > Save to save this file.

Grouping the layers

Now you will group the dog layers together. This will make it easier to reposition all the layers at once.

1   In the Layers panel, select the mouth layer, and then Ctrl/Command+click the tennis ball layer and the **ps0902.psd** layer; all three layers are now selected.

2   Press Ctrl+G (Windows) or Command+G (Mac OS) to group these layers together in one folder.

3   Double-click the Group 1 name and type **dog**.

4   Switch to the Move tool (⊹) and reposition the dog to be in the lower-left of the image; note that all the other layers in the group move together.

Move the dog group of layers to the lower-left.   *The final Layers panel.*

5   Choose File > Save to save the file. You can choose File > Close to close this file, or leave it open for the Self study section of this lesson.

Self study

For this section, you can continue using the **ps0901_work** file that you started earlier. You can also choose to open the **ps0901_done.psd** file to start from this point.

Adding shadows is an easy way to make your composite look more realistic. Since this section is a self-study, you will not be taken step-by-step throughout this exercise. Use what you have learned in this lesson to do the following tasks in the **ps0901_done** (or work) image.

- Create a new blank layer on top of the **ps0901.psd** layer in the Layers panel.
- Name the layer **shadow**.
- Change your Brush tool to a large soft brush and paint a shadow on the new layer.
- Play with either the opacity of the brush, or the opacity of the layer to create realistic shading under the dog house and on the grass.
- You can see the finished self-study by opening the file named **ps0901_self_study.psd** located in your ps09lessons folder.

The shadow added to the layered file.

The new shadow layer in the Layers panel.

Review

Questions

1 What is the benefit to using Bridge when opening multiple files into Photoshop?

2 Name two methods that you can use to move layers from one image file to another.

3 What are at least two benefits of using a layer style (Effects)?

Answers

1 By using Adobe Bridge, you can take advantage of Photoshop Tools, such as Tools > Photoshop > Load files into Photoshop Layers. This feature allows you to open multiple files into one layered image.

2 There are many ways to move layers from one file to another; here are just a few that you could use. To move layers from one image file to another, do any of the following:

- Right-click (Windows) or Ctrl+click (Mac OS) on the layer and choose Duplicate Layer. Choose the image file that you want to move the layer to, or choose to create a new file with the selected layer.

- Make sure the layers are selected in the Layers panel and then use the Move tool to click and drag the image on the canvas up to the tabbed name of the destination file.

- Make sure the layers are selected in the Layers panel and then choose to Copy, select the destination file, and choose Paste.

3 Some of the benefits to using a layer style include the following:

- The style can be changed or edited, at any time, by double-clicking the style in the Layers panel.

- You can re-use a combination of styles on multiple layers.

- You can easily delete, or turn on or off the visibility of the layer style at any time.

What you'll learn in this lesson:

- Changing color using an adjustment layer
- Filling with a pattern
- Using the black and white feature
- Applying layer blending options

Using Layer Styles and Adjustment Layers

Layers provide many creative possibilities, some more evident than others. In this lesson, you will build a layered file, and then you'll take it further by using features such as adjustment layers, layer effects, and clipping groups.

Starting up

Before starting, make sure that your tools and panels are consistent by resetting your preferences. For more information, see "Resetting Adobe Photoshop CC preferences" in the Starting up section of this book.

You will work with several files from the ps10lessons folder in this lesson. Make sure that you have loaded the pslessons folder onto your hard drive from the supplied DVD. See "Loading lesson files" in the Starting up section of this book.

See Lesson 10 in action!

Use the accompanying video to gain a better understanding of how to use some of the features shown in this lesson. You can find the video tutorial for this lesson on the included DVD.

If you have been following the lessons in order, you have already discovered that layers, in their simplest form, offer Photoshop users an amazing amount of flexibility to create and modify images. The more advanced features of layers offer even more options, many of which you can exploit in various ways while keeping the original image information intact.

Making color changes using adjustment layers

Changing the color of an object in Adobe Photoshop is common practice, but how do you make it look realistic, and how can you recover the image if you make a mistake? What if you want to see three or four different variations? All these tasks can be completed easily and efficiently using adjustment layers. In this section, you'll change the color of a jacket on a model, and then, using the same adjustment layer, change it again multiple times.

1 Choose File > Browse in Bridge to open Adobe Bridge.

2 Navigate to the ps10lessons folder inside the pslessons folder you have created on your computer and double-click **ps1001.psd** to open it in Photoshop. An image of a girl wearing a blue jacket appears.

   You will take the original jacket and change the color of it. You will also add a pattern to the jacket, using an adjustment layer.

The original image.   *A solid color adjustment.*   *A pattern adjustment.*

3 Choose File > Save As. In the File name text field, type **ps1001_work**, and then navigate to the ps10lessons folder. Choose Photoshop from the format drop-down menu and click Save.

The first thing that you will make is a selection with the Quick Selection tool.

4   Select the Quick Selection tool (✐), then click and drag the jacket. If you miss some of the jacket, just paint a stroke over it to add it to the selection. If your selection goes too far, press and hold the Alt (Windows) or Option (Mac OS) key and click the part of the selection that you want to deactivate.

You can also increase or decrease your Quick Selection tool size by pressing the [(left bracket) or] (right bracket) keys.

*Paint the jacket with the Quick Selection
tool to make a selection.*

5   If the Layers panel is not visible, choose Window > Layers.

6   Click and hold the Create new fill or adjustment layer button (◗) at the bottom of the Layers panel.

7   Select Hue/Saturation from the pop-up menu. The Properties panel appears with the Hue/Saturation options visible.

Hue refers to the color. By changing the hue, you can essentially change the color of an object without taking away any of the shading properties, which are normally created from the neutral gray value.

8   Select the Colorize check box and click and drag the Hue slider to the right to about the 70 point, or type **70** in the Hue text field.

In the next step, you will bring the saturation down a bit so the green you are creating is less bright.

9   Click and drag the Saturation slider to the left to about the 20 point, or type **20** into the Saturation text field.

Change the color and saturation
using the Hue/Saturation sliders.

The jacket is now green, but your selection might not be as accurate as you would like. In the next section, you will use your painting tools to refine the mask attached to the adjustment layer. A benefit of adjustment layers is that you can use them to paint masks at any point in the process to modify your selection.

10 Choose File > Save. If the Format Options dialog box appears, click OK.

If you inadvertently close any images while working on a project, you can quickly reopen them by choosing File > Open Recent, and selecting the file from the drop-down menu.

Painting on the adjustment layer mask

If you take a look at the Layers panel you just created, you see a Hue/Saturation adjustment layer that has a mask thumbnail to the right of the layer thumbnail. You can activate this mask separately, and then use painting tools to refine it.

1   Alt+click (Windows) or Option+click (Mac OS) the adjustment mask thumbnail to the right of the Hue/Saturation thumbnail in the Layers panel.

The mask appears. You are not doing anything to the mask at this time, but you should take a look at what the actual mask looks like. Notice that where there is white, the hue and saturation changes take place. Where the mask is black, the changes are not occurring. Using the painting tools in Photoshop, you can edit a mask by painting black and white and even varying opacities to control the results of the adjustment layer.

Where the mask is white, the Hue/Saturation change is occurring.

2   To return to the normal layer view, click once on the word *Background* in the Layers panel.

You will now make changes to the adjustment mask thumbnail.

3   Click once on the adjustment mask thumbnail (to the right of the Hue/Saturation adjustment layer thumbnail).

*Paint on the adjustment layer's mask
to refine your selection.*

4   Now, select the Brush tool (✐), and press **D** on your keyboard to set the colors to the default of black and white. Note that when in a mask, white is the foreground color and black is the background color.

5   Adjust your brush size as needed to paint the areas in the mask that might not have been selected, and thus not affected, when you created the adjustment layer.

Refine Edge (covered in Lesson 4, "Making Selective Changes in Photoshop CC,") is actually the best method to use to select hair, but for this exercise, you will use the Brush tool to help you understand the process of painting your selection on a mask.

Paint the areas that you might have missed with your original selection.

You can make your brush size larger by pressing the] (right bracket) key and smaller by pressing [(left bracket) key. Make your brush harder by pressing Shift+] and softer by pressing Shift+[.

6   Press **X** on your keyboard to swap the foreground and background colors. Black is now the foreground color.

7   Now, find a section of your image—perhaps the hand tucked in underneath the elbow—that has the Hue/Saturation change applied to it in error.

You will paint this area with the black paint brush, with the mask active, to block the change from occurring there.

It is very easy to deselect the mask and paint on your actual image. Avoid this by clicking once on the Layer mask thumbnail.

8   Adjust your paint brush to the right size and softness, and paint over the hand to reveal the actual flesh color.

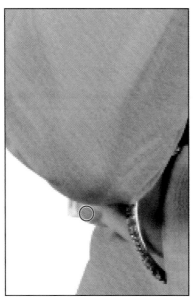

Eliminate the areas that you might have included, in error, in the original selection.

If you did such an accurate selection that you have no areas to repair, paint an area somewhere on your image anyway, just to see the effects of painting black on the mask. When you are done experimenting, press **X** *to swap back to the white foreground color and repair the mask, as necessary.*

Adjusting the Hue/Saturation layer

Now that you have created an accurate mask, the next few steps will be rather simple. Perhaps your client has suggested that you use a more vibrant violet for the blazer. In this section, you will apply more color to the blazer, and also edit the existing hue and saturation.

1   Click once on the adjustment layer thumbnail to reopen the Hue/Saturation information in the Properties panel.

Click the adjustment layer thumbnail to change the settings.

2   On the Properties panel, click and drag the Hue slider to the right to about the 260 point, or type **260** into the Hue text field.

3   Click and drag the Saturation slider to the right to about the 40 point, or type **40** into the Saturation text field.

The green is now changed to a violet.

Readjusting the Hue and Saturation.

You can reopen the Hue/Saturation adjustment layer as many times as you want.

4   Choose File > Save, and keep the image open for the next section.

Adding a pattern fill layer

You can add a pattern and apply it to an image using a fill layer. This gives you the ability to scale the pattern, as well as adjust the opacity and blending modes. In this section, you will create a simple pattern that will be scaled and applied to the image using a new fill layer.

Defining the pattern

You can create a pattern in Photoshop out of any pixel information that you can select with the Rectangular Marquee. In this section, you will use the entire image area as the pattern, but you could also activate a smaller portion of an image and define it as a pattern.

1   Leave the **ps1001_work.psd** file open, and open an additional image. Choose File > Browse in Bridge to open Adobe Bridge.

2   If you are not already there, navigate to the ps10lessons folder inside the pslessons folder you created on your computer and double-click the file named **ps1002.psd**. An image of an ornate pattern appears.

Define a pattern from an entire image, or just a rectangular selection.

Because you are using the entire image to create the pattern, you do not need to select anything.

3   Choose Edit > Define Pattern. The Pattern Name dialog box appears. Type **ornate** in the File name text field, and click OK.

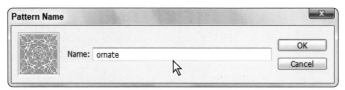

Defining a pattern for future use.

4   Choose File > Close to close the image without making any changes.

Applying the pattern

You will now apply the pattern to the jacket using a new fill layer.

1   You spent a fair amount of time perfecting your mask, and you certainly don't want to have to do that again. Press and hold the Ctrl (Windows) or Command (Mac OS) key and click the Layer mask thumbnail of your adjustment layer. The mask is activated as a selection.

You can Ctrl/Command+click any layer or mask to activate its contents as a selection.

2   Now that you have an active selection of the woman's blazer, click and hold the Create New Fill or Adjustment Layer button (●) at the bottom of the Layers panel, and choose Pattern. The Pattern Fill dialog box appears.

Your new pattern swatch should be visible. If it is not, click the downward arrow to the right of the visible swatch to select a different pattern.

Select the Pattern Fill layer.

The Pattern Fill dialog box appears.

The result.

The result may be a little unexpected at first, as no scaling or blending mode has been applied to this fill pattern yet.

3   With the Pattern Fill dialog box still open, use the Scale slider to set the scale of the pattern to 25 percent, or type **25** into the Scale text field, and click OK.

4   With your new Fill layer still selected, click and hold Normal in the blending mode drop-down menu on the Layers panel, and choose Multiply.

Select the blending mode.   The result.

You can experiment with other blending modes to see how they affect the final rendering of the pattern.

If you select your Move tool, and then select a blending mode from the Set the blending mode drop-down menu, you can press Shift+↓ (down arrow) to move down the list of different blending options. Press Shift+↑ (up arrow) to move up the list of blending options.

5   Choose File > Save and then File > Close to close this image.

Using the Black & White adjustment layer

Changing color images to grayscale is easy—you just switch the color mode using Image > Mode > Grayscale, right? Not if you want to achieve the best possible conversion from color to black and white. In this section, you will learn how to use the Black & White adjustment layer.

1   Choose File > Browse in Bridge to open Adobe Bridge.

2   Navigate to the ps10lessons folder inside the pslessons folder you created on your computer and double-click the file named **ps1003.psd**. A cityscape appears.

You will convert this cityscape image to grayscale.

3   Choose File > Save As; the Save As dialog box appears. Navigate to the ps10lessons folder. In the File name text field, type **ps1003_work** and select Photoshop from the Format drop-down menu. Click Save.

4   Click the Create New Fill or Adjustment Layer button (⬤) at the bottom of the Layers panel and select Black & White. The Black and White settings become active in the Properties panel.

This window may appear very confusing at first. Without some assistance, it would be difficult to decipher which color adjustments are going to affect the image and where. Fortunately, Adobe has created some helpful features to make a better conversion easier for users.

5   Click the pointing Finger icon (👆) in the Properties panel to make that option active.

6   Click and hold the sky in the image; a pointing finger with a double arrow (👆) appears. The color that would make changes to that part of the image (the sky) is affected.

7 Continue pressing and holding on the sky image and drag to the right; notice that you automatically lightened the blues in the sky. Click and drag to the left to make the conversion darker.

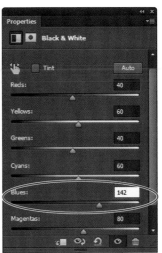

Click and drag in the sky area to automatically adjust the color.

8 Now, click the darker streaming car lights in the image; the Reds are highlighted. Click and drag to the right to lighten them. You can just make visual adjustments for this image, but if you want to maintain certain values, open the Window > Info panel.

Click and drag on the car lights to lighten the conversion.

9 You can turn the visibility of this adjustment layer off and on by clicking the Visibility icon (👁) to the left of the Black & White 1 adjustment layer.

10 Choose File > Save. Keep the file open for the next section of this lesson.

Adding a tint

In this section, you will add a tint to your image. A tint of color can be added to an RGB image to create a nice effect.

The Black & White adjustment layer is disabled in CMYK mode.

1   Double-click the Black & White 1 layer thumbnail (⬤) icon (to the left of the Black & White 1 name and mask) in the Layer's panel. This activates the Black & White settings in the Properties panel.

2   Select the *Tint* check box.

You can click the color box to the right of the Tint check box to assign a color from the color libraries.

Apply a tint of color.   *The result.*

3   Click once on the Color box to the right of the *Tint* check box; the Color Picker (Tint Color) dialog box appears.

4   Click the Color Libraries button; the Color Libraries dialog box appears. From the Book drop-down menu, select Pantone+ Solid Coated, if it is not already selected.

5   Type **642** quickly, without pausing between typing the numbers. There is no text field in this dialog box; by typing a Pantone number, you can easily locate it in the list of colors. Type too slowly and you could have an inaccurate color selection. You can try it again if Pantone 642 C is not selected. Click OK to close the Color Libraries dialog box. The color tint is assigned Pantone 642 C.

6   Choose File > Save. Leave the file open for the next section of this lesson.

Applying a gradient to the adjustment layer

The next step is a simple one that adds an interesting blending technique for using adjustment layers. By applying a gradient to the mask, you can blend the Black & White effect into a color image.

1   Press **D** on your keyboard to make sure that you are back to the default foreground and background colors of black and white.

2   Click once on the Black & White adjustment layer mask thumbnail to select it.

3   Select the Gradient tool (▬), and type **0**. By typing **0**, you are assigning 100 percent opacity to the gradient.

4   Click and drag from the left side of the image to the right. A gradient is created in the same direction and angle as the line you draw.

When you release the Gradient tool, there is a blend from the black-and-white adjustment to the original color image. If you don't like the angle or transition, you can re-drag the gradient as many times as you want. Click and drag a short line for a shorter gradient transition, or click and drag a longer line for a more gradual transition.

If your colors are opposite to the ones in this example, your foreground and background colors could be reversed. Press **X** to reverse your colors and try again.

Click and drag with the Gradient tool to create a gradient mask.   *The layer mask.*

The Gradient tool can create straight-line, radial, angle, reflected, and diamond blends. Select the type of gradient from the Options bar across the top of the Photoshop work area. If you want to drag a straight gradient line, press and hold the Shift key while dragging to constrain the gradient to a 0-degree, 45-degree, or 90-degree angle.

5   Choose File > Save. Keep the file open for the next part of this lesson.

Layer styles

By using layer styles, such as shadows, glows, and bevels, you can change the appearance of images on layers. Layer styles are linked to the layer that is selected when the style is applied, but you can also copy and paste them to other layers. You can also save combinations of styles as a custom style to be applied to other layers.

Creating the text layer

In this section, you will create a text layer and apply a combination of effects to it. Then you will save the combined effects as a new style to apply to another layer. You should still have the file **ps1003_work.psd** open from the last lesson.

1   Select the Type tool (T) and click anywhere on the image. Type **City Lights**.

2   Press Ctrl+A (Windows) or Command+A (Mac OS) to select all the text. Alternatively, you can choose Select > All from the menu bar.

Get ready for a three-key command. It might seem awkward if you haven't used this combination before, but it is used in many other Creative Cloud applications to resize text visually, and it is a huge time-saver.

3   Press and hold Ctrl+Shift+> (greater than) (Windows) or Command+Shift+> (Mac OS), and repeatedly press the > key. The text enlarges. You can change the combination to include the < (less than) key to reduce the size of the text. No particular size is needed.

4   In the Options bar, click the Center text button (▤) to center your text. If you need to adjust the position of the text, press and hold the Ctrl/Command key and click and drag the text to the center of the image area.

   If you would rather not use the key command, type **85** in the font size text field in the Options bar at the top of the Photoshop workspace.

   Next, you will find a typeface that you want to use. Again, no particular typeface is required for this exercise. Pick one that you like, but make sure that it is heavy enough to show bevel (edge) effects. The font in the example is Myriad Bold.

5   Make sure the Type tool is still active and the text is selected, by pressing Ctrl+A (Windows) or Command+A (Mac OS), or by choosing All from the Select menu.

6   Now, highlight the font family name in the Type tool Options bar at the top of the Photoshop workspace, and press the up arrow (↑) or down arrow (↓) keys to scroll through your list of font families.

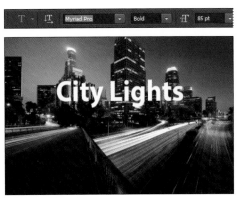

Select the text and then select the font name in the Options bar.

Press the down or up arrows to change the font selection. Your font selection might differ from this example.

If you would rather not use the font shortcut, you can select the font you want from the Font family drop-down menu in the Options bar.

If your Swatches panel is not visible, choose Window > Swatches to bring it forward.

7 With the text still selected, choose White from the Swatches panel. Click the Commit check mark (✔) in the far right of the Options bar to commit your type changes.

As mentioned earlier, do not leave the Type tool to select the Move tool and reposition the text. If you want to reposition your text, keep the Type tool selected and press and hold the Ctrl (Windows) or Command (Mac OS) key while dragging.

Applying the Outer Glow layer style

Now you will apply a combination of layer effects to the text layer you just created.

1 Click the text layer name City Lights, which is to the right of the Text layer indicator in the Layers panel, to make sure the layer is active.

2 Click the Add a layer style button (*fx*) at the bottom of the Layers panel, and select Outer Glow from the pop-up menu. The Layer Style dialog box appears. The default settings may be too subtle, so you will make some changes.

Select the Outer Glow style.

There are many options available for each layer style. As a default, certain blending modes and opacities, as well as spread size and contours (edges), are already determined. In the next step, you will change the contour and the size of the outer glow.

What is a layer style contour?

When you create custom styles, you can use contours to create unique edge effects and transitions. As you can see in the examples shown here, the same style can look very different:

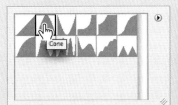 

The Cone contour.

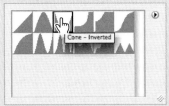 

The Cone-Inverted contour.

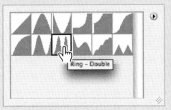 

The Ring-Double contour.

3 Select the arrow to the right of the Contour thumbnail in the Quality section of the Layer Style dialog box. The Contour Presets dialog box appears. Click the Half Round contour. Double-click the Half Round contour to close the dialog box.

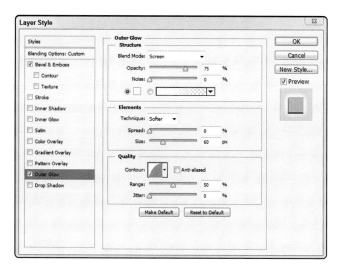

Select a preset contour for the Outer Glow style.

You can open the Contour Editor and create your own custom contours by clicking the Contour thumbnail instead of selecting the arrow to the right of the thumbnail.

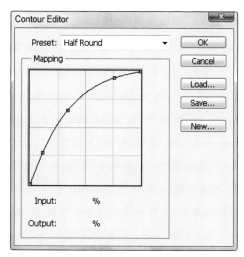

Editing a contour.

Now you will change the size of the outer glow.

4 In the Elements section of the Layer Style dialog box, drag the Size slider to the number 60, or type **60** into the Size text field. The glow becomes more apparent.

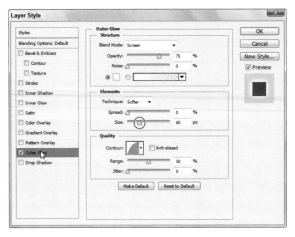

Drag the size slider to 60.   *The result.*

5 Keep the Layer Style dialog box open for the next step.

Applying the Bevel and Emboss layer style

You will now apply a second style. The Layer Style dialog box should still be open. If it is not, you can double-click the word Effects in the Layers panel. This reopens the Layer Styles dialog box.

1 Click Bevel and Emboss in the Styles list on the left side of the Layer Style dialog box. The Bevel and Emboss effect is applied, and the options appear on the right.

If you check a style, the options do not appear on the right. You must click a style name for its options to appear.

2 From the Style drop-down menu in the Structure section of the Layer Style dialog box, choose Emboss.

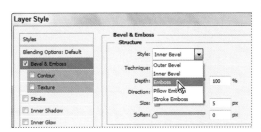

Experiment with the different Bevel and Emboss structures.   *The result.*

You can experiment with many bevel and embossing styles. You can change the Technique to be Smooth, Chisel Hard, Chisel Soft, or even direct the embossing to go down or up, using the Direction radio buttons. Experiment with these options; no particular settings are needed for this exercise.

Changing the shading

You will now change the shading. In the Shading section of the Bevel and Emboss Layer Style dialog box, there are several choices that relate to light, including the Angle, Gloss Contour (as discussed earlier), or Highlight and Shadow colors. In this section, you will change the angle of the light and the highlight color.

1   In the Shading section to the right of Angle, there is a Direction of light source slider. You can change the current light angle by clicking and dragging the marker indicating the current light angle. Click and drag the marker to see how it affects the embossing style.

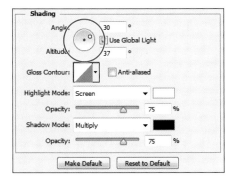

Click and drag inside the circle to change the direction of the light source.

Use Global light is selected as a default. This assures you that all other effects that rely on a light source use the same angle that you determine for this style.

2   Click and hold to select Normal from the Highlight Mode blending drop-down menu.

3   Now, click the white box to the right of Highlight Mode. This opens the Select highlight color picker and allows you to sample a color from your image, or create your own highlight color using the Color Picker. Choose any yellow-gold color; in this example, an RGB value of R: **215**, G: **155**, B: **12** is used. Click OK.

4 Click the Shadow color box, to the right of Shadow Mode, and change the color to blue. In this example, an RGB value of R: **30**, G: **15**, B: **176** is used.

Set a highlight color.   *Set a shadow color.*   *The resulting bevel and emboss.*

5 Click OK to close the Color Picker. Keep the Layer Style dialog box open for the final step in this project.

Changing the fill opacity

In addition to setting opacity, which affects layer styles as well as the contents of the layer, you can adjust the fill opacity. The fill opacity affects only the contents of the layer, keeping the opacity of any layer styles that have been applied at the original opacity. This is a very easy method to use to make text look like it is embossed on paper or engraved in stone.

1 Select the Blending Options Default. This is the top-most item underneath the Styles panel.

2 Click and drag the Fill Opacity slider to the left. In the example, it is dragged to the 20 percent point. Keep the Layer Style dialog box open for the next part of the lesson.

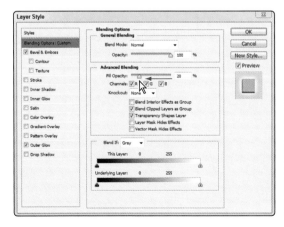

Changing the fill opacity does not affect the layer style opacity.   *The result as semi-transparent text.*

Saving the style

Now you will save the style you created.

1 With the Layer Styles dialog box still open, click the New Style button on the right side of the window. The New Style dialog box appears.

2 Type **my glow** in the File name text field, and click OK.

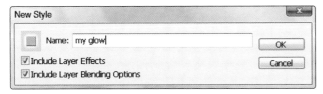

Saving a style from combined styles.

3 Click OK in the Layer Styles dialog box. The style is now added to the Styles panel.

Accessing the style

Now you will create a new shape layer and apply the saved my glow style to it.

1 Click and hold the Rectangle tool (■) to select the hidden Custom Shape tool (✿).

2 Make sure that Shape is selected in the Options bar at the top of the Photoshop workspace.

3 Click the arrow to the right of the Custom Shape picker in the Options bar, and double-click the Light Bulb 2 shape.

Select the Custom Shape tool.   *Confirm you are creating a layer shape.*   *Choose the Light Bulb 2 shape.*

4 Press **D** on your keyboard to make sure you are back to the default black-and-white foreground and background colors.

5 Press and hold the Shift key (to keep proportions correct), and click and drag in the image area to create the light bulb shape layer.

6 If any effects were automatically applied, delete them by clicking the Effects sublayer and dragging it to the Delete icon (🗑) in the lower-right corner of the Layers panel.

7 If the Styles panel is not visible, choose Window > Styles. The Styles panel appears. It is easier to find your saved style if you view the panel as a list, rather than as a thumbnail. You can change the view by selecting the panel menu and choosing Small List.

8 Scroll down if necessary, and then choose my glow.

Choose to view by Small List.   *Select your saved style, my glow.*

The same style is applied to the light bulb shape.

9 Choose File > Save, and then choose File > Close to close your file.

Self study

Adjustment layers only affect the layers beneath them, leaving any layers on top of them in the Layers panel unaffected. You can also press and hold your Alt (Windows) or Option (Mac OS) key and click a layer directly beneath the adjustment layer to clip the adjustment to just that layer, and not affect layers beneath the clipped layer.

1   To experiment with this concept, open the file named **ps1004.psd**.

2   Select the sky layer and create a Hue/Saturation adjustment layer for it.

3   Drag the Saturation slider all the way to the left, effectively creating an RGB grayscale image.

4   Click and drag the adjustment layer up through the layers in the Layers panel to see how the position of the adjustment layer affects the layers beneath.

Review

Questions

1   Name three reasons why you should use an adjustment layer to change color in Photoshop.

2   What can you do to make a pattern fill layer blend in more naturally with the image underneath?

3   What does Global Lighting mean?

Answers

1   Three reasons for using an adjustment layer to change color in Photoshop are:

   a. By using an adjustment layer, you keep the original image data intact.

   b. Using the Color Picker and a Color adjustment layer, you can choose a specific hue, which you can then change again repeatedly until you get the color you want.

   c. You can easily update or change the color by double-clicking the adjustment layer thumbnail.

2   You can experiment with several blending modes to create a more natural blend with a pattern fill layer. In the example in this lesson, Multiply was selected, but other modes, such as Darken and Lighten, can create interesting results as well.

3   Global Lighting helps to keep the light source consistent between layer styles. This way, the light source for a shadow is the same as for the bevel and emboss, helping the image lighting effects look more realistic.

What you'll learn in this lesson:

- Using the Pen tool
- Making a selection with the Pen tool
- Building a mask with the Pen tool

Working with the Pen Tool

Photoshop includes many vector tools that allow you to create precise scalable artwork, selections, and masks. In this lesson, you find out how to build custom shapes and paths using the Pen tool in Photoshop CC.

Starting up

Before starting, make sure that your tools and panels are consistent by resetting your preferences. For more information, see "Resetting Adobe Photoshop CC preferences" in the Starting up section of this book.

You will work with several files from the ps11lessons folder in this lesson. Make sure that you have loaded the pslessons folder onto your hard drive from the supplied DVD. For more instructions, see "Loading lesson files" in the Starting up section of this book.

See Lesson 11 in action!

Use the accompanying video to gain a better understanding of how to use some of the features shown in this lesson. You can find the video tutorial for this lesson on the included DVD.

Working with the Pen tool

The Pen tool is one of the most powerful tools in Photoshop; with it, you can create any line or shape that you need using anchor points that can be rounded, smooth, sharp, or angular. If you are familiar with Adobe Illustrator, you know the power of the Pen and how it helps you to create precise illustrations, logo designs, and more. In addition to creating precise selections, you can edit your path using tools such as the hidden Pen tool features and the Direct Selection tool. The Pen tool in Photoshop is generally used for creating custom shapes and masks. In this lesson, you will cover some exercises to help you improve your Pen tool skills.

Reading the Pen tool cursor

Before starting, note that the Pen tool has a versatile feature that allows you to create new anchor points, add anchor points to existing paths, and remove anchor points from existing paths. The tool's appearance changes based on the item that the cursor is hovering over on the art board. Pay attention to the appearance of the tool cursor, since it will assist you in using all the Pen tool's functions.

PEN TOOL VARIATION	DESCRIPTION
	Indicates that the Pen tool will create a new line.
	Only appears when you are in the process of creating a line; it signals that the next anchor point created will continue that line.
	Indicates that the Pen tool can be used to convert the anchor point it is currently hovering over. This icon only appears when the Pen tool is hovering over the last anchor point that was created in a selected path.
	Indicates that the Pen tool will pick up a path and continue from the end point you are hovering over. This icon only appears next to the Pen tool when it is hovering over the endpoint of a path that you are not currently creating.
	Indicates that the Pen tool will connect the path that is currently being created to the end point of a different path.
	Indicates that the Pen tool will close the path that you are currently creating.
	Indicates that the Pen tool will remove the anchor point that it is currently hovering over. This icon only appears when the Pen tool is hovering over an anchor point on a selected path.
	Indicates that the Pen tool will add an anchor point to the line segment that it is currently hovering over. This icon only appears when the Pen tool is hovering over a line segment on a selected path.

Uses of the Pen tool in Photoshop

Before using the Pen tool, you should understand the reason this is an important tool to know.

Even though there is a shape component to the Pen tool, it is predominantly used for very precise and clean selections. These selections can allow your image to be silhouetted or masked to take advantage of any number of image editing features. In the examples below, you see how the Pen tool was used to silhouette a building and then to change the zigzag stroke on the building.

The Pen tool used to silhouette the building.

The Pen tool used to change the color of a selection.

At first, you might find using the Pen tool awkward, but the more you use it and understand the fundamental concepts, the easier it will become for you to make it your primary go-to tool for making complex selections.

Creating your first path

You will start with a blank document to get some practice.

1   Launch Adobe Photoshop CC, and then choose File > New.

2   From the Preset drop-down menu, choose Default Photoshop Size, leave all other defaults as they are and click OK. A blank canvas appears.

3   Select the Pen tool (✐) and position it anywhere in the image area; note that the Pen cursor has an asterisk in the lower-right area. This indicates that you are just starting a new path.

4   Click anywhere in your image area; notice that an anchor point appears and the asterisk disappears.

5   Position your cursor anywhere else in the image area and click again; notice that the second anchor point appears and it is connected by a path to the first anchor point.

Unlike Illustrator, this path is not a visible stroke, it is simply a path that has no attributes and would not be visible if you printed the image.

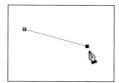

Click to create anchor points.

6   You will now create a closed shape by clicking anchor points until you can come around and close your path by clicking the initial anchor point. You can add as many anchor points as you need, but before clicking the original anchor point, note that a close circle appears indicating that you are closing this path.

Close the path.

7   Keep this file open for the next part of this lesson.

Using the Selection tools

One of the main benefits of using the Pen tool for masks and selections is the ability to edit the path, even after it has been created.

1 Select the Path Selection tool from the Tools panel and click anywhere on the path that you made.

2 Click and drag the path to another location on the page. Notice that the Path retains its original shape.

3 Now click and hold the Path Selection tool to select the hidden Direct Selection tool.

4 Click anywhere on the image area, but off the path to deselect the path.

5 Click any anchor point to activate it, and then click and drag. Note that when you use the Direct Selection tool, you can edit the path.

6 Click off the path to deselect it again, and then click a path segment between two anchor points. Click and drag; note that you are editing both anchor points.

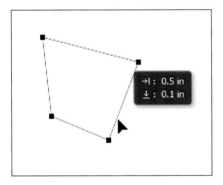

The path selected with the Path Selection tool.   An anchor point selected with the Direct Selection tool.

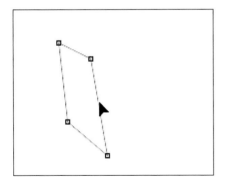

A path segment selected with the Direct Selection tool.

Adding and deleting anchor points

Once you create a path, you might need additional anchor points to complete your shape, or you might need to delete some anchor points.

1 Select the Pen tool and cross over the selected path in an area between two anchor points. Notice that the Pen icon appears with a plus (+) sign, indicating that if you click, an anchor point will be added to the path.

2 Click to add the anchor point.

3 Now, hover over the anchor point that you just added and note that the Pen cursor has a minus (-) sign. This indicates that if you click this anchor point, it will go away.

4 Click the anchor point to make it go away. Notice that the path still remains closed, but the anchor point is no longer there.

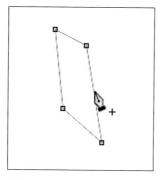 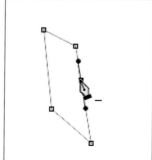

Click the path to add an anchor point.   *Click an anchor point to delete it.*

Working with curved paths

So far, you have been working with straight paths, which you can make by clicking from one anchor point to another. Curved paths are created by clicking and dragging and adjusting the directional point that appears as you drag. In this part of the lesson, you will practice creating curved paths.

1   Find a blank location on your image file and click.

2   Go to another blank location and click and drag. Note the path curves and a directional line appears. If you don't release right away, you can move the directional line up and down to control the path. Release the anchor point to create the curved path.

The directional line is not part of the path. It is used to help you control the curve of the path, and will not be visible when the anchor point is released.

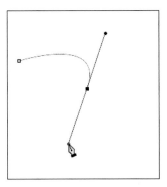

Click and drag to create a curved path.

3   Move your cursor to another blank location in your image and click and drag again, creating another curved segment.

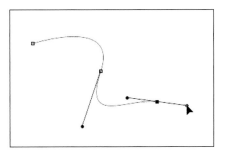

Click and drag to create another curved path segment.

What are direction handles?

When you select or create a smooth point, you can see the direction handles of that point. Direction handles control the angle and length of curves, and they are composed of two parts: direction lines and the direction points at the ends of the lines. An anchor point can have zero, one, or two direction handles, depending on the kind of point it is. Direction handles serve as a road map for the line, controlling how the lines approach and leave each anchor point. If the exiting handle is downward-facing, the line leaves the anchor point and goes down. Similarly, the line faces upward if the direction handle is pointing upward.

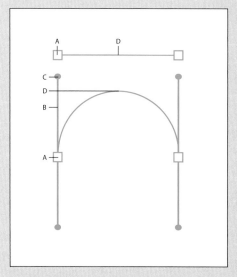

A. Anchor point. B. Direction Line. C. Direction Handle.
D. Line Segment.

 The anchor points you created are called smooth anchor points. Later in this lesson, you will discover how to control the directional line to create precise selections. The anchor points you created with clicking (not dragging) are called corner points.

4   Keep this file open for the next part of the lesson.

Changing anchor points

You can easily change a smooth anchor point into a corner anchor point using the Pen tool. You might use this feature when you have straight edges that you want to smooth out, or when you are creating shapes that have very tight curves.

1 With the Path Selection tool, make sure that you have an active path selected.

2 Select the Pen tool and hover over any of the anchor points.

3 Press and hold the Alt key (Windows) or Option key (Mac OS) while hovering over the anchor point; notice that a convert point icon appears (↖).

4 When the Convert Point icon appears, click one of the anchor points. If it is a corner point, click and drag it to make it a smooth point. If it is a smooth point, it snaps into a corner point.

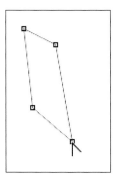

A corner point is selected.

Changed to a smooth point.

5 You will not save this file, so experiment with switching corner points to smooth and back again.

Selecting your path

Here is a helpful tip: you can keep the Pen tool active, and temporarily access the Move tool. This makes it easy for you to make quick edits and then get back to work.

1 Select the Pen tool.

2 Press and hold the Ctrl key (Windows) or Command key (Mac OS) to change your cursor into the Move cursor. As soon as you release the Ctrl/Command key, the Pen tool cursor returns.

3 With the Pen tool still active, press and hold the Ctrl/Command key, and then click any anchor point.

4 Click and drag to move the anchor point, then release the Ctrl/Command key.

5 Now practice by creating a new path. While creating the path, press and hold the Ctrl/Command key and drag your last anchor point to another location. Release the Ctrl/Command key and continue making your path.

If you make a mistake while creating a path, press Ctrl+Z (Windows) or Command+Z (Mac OS) to keep your last anchor point active so you can easily continue the path you started.

6 Choose File > Close to close this file; choose Don't Save,

When creating corner points, you can Shift+click to constrain the angle of your path segments to multiples of 45 degrees. You can also Shift+drag to constrain your directional lines.

Path exercises

In this next section, you will use an exercise file to follow paths and learn how to control the Pen tool. The Photoshop file that you will work with has a locked layer that displays anchor points and paths that you will replicate.

1 Return to Adobe Bridge by choosing File > Browse in Bridge.

2 Navigate to the pslessons folder you copied onto your system, and open the ps11lessons folder.

3 From the ps11lessons folder, select the file called **ps1101.psd**. An image that contains some paths opens in Photoshop.

4 Choose File > Save As and type **ps1101_work** into the Name text field. Leave the format at Photoshop, navigate to ps11lessons folder, and then click Save.

5 Select your Zoom tool from your tools pane and uncheck Scrubby Zoom in the Options at the top.

6   Click and drag with the Zoom tool so that you encompass the entire Exercise 1 path.

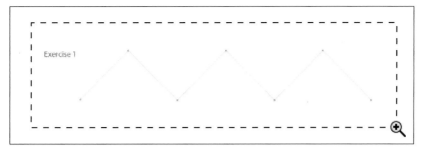

Click and drag with the Zoom tool over Exercise 1.

7   Press Shift+Tab; this is the keyboard shortcut that hides the panels to the right. You can press Shift+Tab at any time to make them visible again.

8   Select the Pen tool, and then click the first square (indicating the placement of an anchor point) in the lower-left area of Exercise 1.

9   Continue clicking from one square to the next until you have completed Exercise 1. The path is now complete, but not closed; deactivate it now before moving on to the next exercise.

10   Keep your Pen tool active, and then press and hold the Ctrl key (Windows) or Command key (Mac OS) and click anywhere on the art board where there is no path. Your path is no longer active.

Creating straight lines

In this next exercise, you will create straight lines and constrain them to 45 degree angles.

1   If you cannot see Exercise 2, keep your Pen tool active while you press and hold the spacebar to turn your cursor into the Hand tool (🖑). Using the Hand tool, click in the image area and drag upwards. This is essentially the same as using the scrollbars, but much quicker. When you release the spacebar, the Pen tool cursor is ready to use.

2   Using the Pen tool, click the first square in the path; an anchor point is created.

3   Press and hold the Shift key and then click the next square; a straight path is created between the anchor points.

4   Continue pressing and holding the Shift key and clicking the squares to create your own corner anchor points to follow the path.

If you want to edit your path, switch to the Direct Selection tool and click and drag the paths or anchor points to adjust their position.

5   When you have reached the last point, press and hold the Ctrl key (Windows) or Command key (Mac OS), and then click off the path to deactivate it.

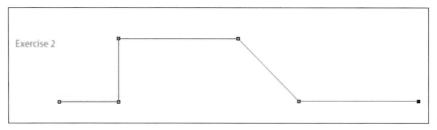

Create art with constrained paths.

Creating the curved path

In this next part of the exercise, you will follow a curved path. Follow the steps carefully.

1   If necessary, press and hold the spacebar and push up the image so you can see Exercise 3.

2   Make sure the Pen tool is active; then click and drag upwards from the first square. Typically, you want the directional line to go in the direction of the curve; for this exercise, the direction of the curve is up. Release your mouse when you have reached the top of the arch you are creating.

You have not yet created a path; you have created a smooth anchor point that will help you complete the curve in the next step.

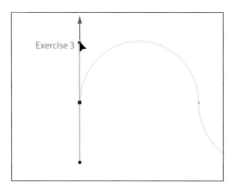

Click and drag upwards to start the path.

When creating perfect arches, you can press and hold the Shift key while dragging to constrain the directional line.

3   Locate the next square and click and drag down; do not release until you have pulled down enough that the path you are creating approximates the path you are tracing over. You don't need to make an exact match, just get the anchor points in the right place. You can edit the anchor points and the directional lines when you are finished with the path.

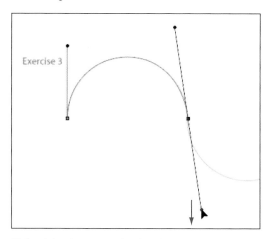

Click and drag down to complete the arch.

4   Click and drag up on the next square to create the next arch, which is upside down.

5   Continue this process by clicking and dragging down on the last path.

6   This time switch to the Direct Selection tool, and then click off the path to deactivate it.

7   Using the Direct Selection tool, make any adjustments to your path or anchor points. Notice that when you click an anchor point, the directional lines reappear so you can edit the size and direction of the curved path.

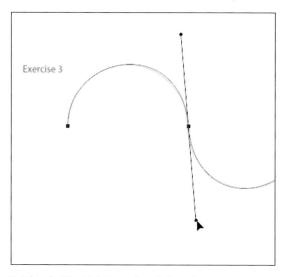

Switch to the Direct Selection tool to edit the path.

Drawing hinged curves

In the previous exercise, you created S-curves; that is, lines curved in the opposite direction from the previous one. In this exercise, you will create hinged curves, which are lines that curve in the same direction; in this case, they will all curve up like a scallop.

1   If necessary, use the spacebar to access the Hand tool and push up the image area so you can see Exercise 4.

2   Select the Pen tool and position your cursor over the first square in the path in Exercise 4. As you did in the previous exercise, click and drag your cursor up slightly above the arch to create your first anchor point.

3   Place your cursor over the second square and click and drag straight down to create the second anchor point. Continue to drag the mouse until you form the curve that you are copying.

4   Press and hold the Alt key (Windows) or Option key (Mac OS). This temporarily changes the Pen tool into the Convert Point tool (⌐), which is a separate tool in the Pen tool grouping. Among other things (covered later in this chapter), this tool is used to edit direction handles. Position the Convert Point tool over the direction handle for the exiting direction line, and click and drag this point so that it points upward. The two direction lines now form a V.

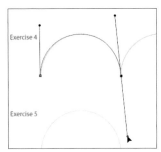
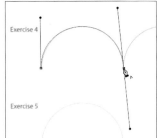
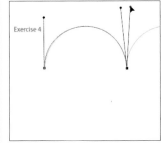

Create your first path.	*Press and hold the Alt/Option key and hover over anchor.*	*Click and drag upwards.*

Direction handles control the curvature of the lines in a path. Because the exiting direction handle created in step 3 is pointing down, the line will want to go down. To draw the hinged curve, you must change the angle of this direction handle so it points upwards.

5   Make sure you release the Alt/Option key; then place your cursor over the next square, located at the end of the second curve. Click and drag straight down to create the third anchor point. Continue to drag the mouse until you form the curve in the template.

6   Again, press and hold Alt (Windows) or Option (Mac OS) to temporarily switch the Pen tool to the Convert Point tool. Once again, position the Convert Point tool over the direction handle for the exiting direction line, and click and drag this point so that it points upward and the direction lines form a V.

7   Repeat step 4 for the final curve at label 4. After you have created this final anchor point, press and hold the Ctrl key (Windows) or Command key (Mac OS) and click the art board.

8   Choose File > Save to save your work, and then choose File > Close.

Creating a selection with the Pen tool

In this section, you will have the opportunity to practice what you have learned. You will use an image to make a pen path around an item, create a selection and a silhouette from your Pen path, and then use your pen path to create an adjustment layer that will change the hue of the selected item.

1   From Photoshop, choose File > Browse in Bridge and locate the ps11lessons folder (if it is not already open).

2   From the ps11lessons folder, select the file called **ps1102.psd**. An image that contains some flowers opens in Photoshop.

3   Choose File > Save As. In the File name text field, type **ps1102_work**, choose Photoshop from the format drop-down menu, and then navigate to the ps11lessons folder. Click Save.

4   Select your Zoom tool from your tools pane and make sure that Scrubby Zoom is unchecked in the Options bar at the top.

5 Click and drag with the Zoom tool so you encompass the center of the flower in the lower-right area of the image. This is the flower that you will build a path around.

Click and drag with the Zoom tool to zoom into the center of the flower.   *The result.*

A very important tip to remember when using the Pen tool is to zoom in closely to the item you want to create a path around. If you are too far out, you will not follow the path as tightly as you should.

Starting your path

You will now start the path that will silhouette the flower. In this exercise, you will be provided with precise instructions to start your path. You will then take the techniques that we covered and complete the path on your own.

1 Using the Pen tool, click and drag a short bit to the left on the base of the petal on the left side of the flower. You should keep the directional line that you are creating parallel to the side of the petal; the directional line is resting on the petal.

Start your path from the base of the left petal.

2   Move the cursor approximately halfway up the petal and click and drag again. Keep the directional lines parallel to the side of the petal again. Repeat this clicking and dragging until you reach the edge of the petal.

Keep the directional lines parallel with the petal.

3   Click and drag from one anchor point to another, keeping the directional lines resting on the side of the petal.

When you reach the top of the petal, you will need to curve back around to go down the other side.

4   Click the other underside of the petal, almost exactly in line where your last anchor point was placed and click and drag down to form the arch in the petal.

Continue adding additional anchor points while clicking and dragging.

5   Click and drag down; again, keep the directional lines along the side of the petal. Stop when you reach the part of the petal that touches the next petal.

If you need to shorten one of the directional lines to achieve the small curve on the underside of the petal, press and hold the Alt key (Windows) or Option key (Mac OS) and push it into the anchor point. Try to keep it on the same angle.

For this next path, you need to change the smooth anchor point you just created to a corner point.

6   Press and hold the Alt key (Windows) or Option key (Mac OS) and click the last anchor point you created. Pull the directional line so it follows the side of the next petal.

Press and hold the Alt/Option key to change the last anchor point to a corner point.

7   Now that you have seen how to follow the basic path, continue using these techniques to complete your path around the rest of the flower. You don't need to follow the path exactly; using the Pen tool takes a lot of practice.

The completed path.

8   Choose File > Save; keep the file open for the next part of this lesson.

Saving the path

While you were creating your path, a work path was created in the Paths panel. You will now save that path.

1   Note that after you create a path, you can see a line that indicates that the path is active. Choose Window > Paths to open the Paths panel; notice that you created a Work Path and that it is highlighted.

You can deactivate a path by clicking in any blank area in the Paths panel. You should deactivate paths when transforming layers, since the Path will be transformed, rather than the layer content, if it is active.

2   Make sure that your Work Path is still highlighted; then, from the Paths panel menu, choose Save Path. In the Save Path dialog box, type **flower**, and then click OK.

Choose to save your Work Path.

3   Choose File > Save; keep the file open for the next part of this lesson.

Turning the path into a selection

Now that you have created and saved a path, you can use it in many ways; for example, you can use it as a selection, a mask, or leave it as path. In this next part of the lesson, you will activate your path as a marquee selection.

1   Make sure that your Paths panel is visible; if it is not, choose Window > Paths.

2   Press and hold the Ctrl key (Windows) or Command key (Mac OS) and hover over the flower path thumbnail in the Paths panel. Click the thumbnail when a dashed marquee appears. Your path is now converted into a marquee selection.

*Press and hold the Ctrl/Command key
and click a path to create a selection.*

3   Choose Edit > Copy to copy your selection.

4   Choose File > New. When you copy a selection, the new document is automatically sized to fit the copied item in the clipboard, so you can just click OK in the New dialog box.

5   Choose Edit > Paste to paste just the flower selection on the new file.

6   You don't need to keep this new file; choose File > Close and choose to not save the file.

Turning the path into a vector mask

You will now return to your **ps1102_work** file and convert your path into a vector mask.

1   If the **ps1102_work** file is not forward, make sure it is the active image file in Photoshop.

2   Make sure there are no active selections by pressing Ctrl+D (Windows) or Command+D (Mac OS)

3   If you do not see the Layers panel, choose Window > Layers.

4   Press and hold the Ctrl key (Windows) or Command key (Mac OS) and hover over the mask icon at the bottom of the Layers panel. When the tool tip shows Add a vector mask, click to create a vector mask using your pen path. Your flower is now silhouetted, and all the other content is masked or covered by the vector mask.

Press and hold the Ctrl/Command key to add a vector mask.   *The result.*

Keep in mind that you must have a layer, not a background, in order to use this shortcut to creating a vector mask.

You now see a mask off to the right of the Layer 0 thumbnail. (Learn more about masks and what you can do with them in Lesson 4, "Making Selective Changes in Photoshop CC.")

5   Choose File > Save and keep this file open for the next part of this lesson.

Using the path to adjust color

In this final part of this lesson, you will use the pen path that you created to apply a color change to the flower.

1   In the Paths panel, click the flower path to highlight it. Notice that a new path was automatically added when you created a vector mask in the previous exercise.

2   In the Layers panel, click the Create new fill or adjustment layer icon (●) at the bottom of the Layers panel and select Hue/Saturation. A new adjustment layer is added to your Layers panel and the Properties panel appears.

3   In the Properties panel, click and drag the Hue slider to change the color (choose any color you want). Notice that hue changes the color; Saturation affects how grey (washed out) or vibrant a color is; and Lightness controls how light the values in the image are.

4   Choose File > Save. You can now close the file.

Self study

Using the **ps1102.psd** file, select another flower and change its color using a new adjustment layer.

Open the image called **ps1103.psd** and save it as **ps1103_work.psd**. Use the Pen tool to make a selection and then change the color of one or more of the crayons, using the techniques covered in this lesson.

Review

Questions

1   What is the benefit of using the Pen tool to create selections and masks rather than one of the marquee tools?

2   When drawing with the Pen tool, how does creating the first point of a straight line differ from creating the first point of a curved line?

3   What steps do you take to turn a path into a mask?

Answers

1   There are many benefits to using the Pen tool to create selections and masks, for example:

   • More precise controls;

   • Cleaner and smoother selections;

   • The vector path created with the Pen tool can be edited;

   • Path can be used as vector mask or adjustment layer.

2   To create the first point for a straight line, you must click and release the Pen tool. When creating a curved line, you should click and drag the Pen tool in the direction of the curve you want to create.

3   To turn a path into a mask, you must follow these steps:

   a. Make sure the path is active by highlighting the path in the Paths panel.

   b. Press and hold the Ctrl/Command key and click the Add vector mask button at the bottom of the Layers panel.

What you'll learn in this lesson:

- Opening an image as a Smart Object

- Converting a layer to a Smart Object

- Placing and editing a Smart Object

- Replacing the contents of a Smart Object layer

Using Smart Objects in Photoshop

Using Smart Objects adds more capabilities to Photoshop's non-destructive workflow. In the simplest form, you can use them to retain an image's original information, even after a filter has been applied. You can also place graphics as Smart Objects, convert them to Smart Objects right in Photoshop, and even combine Smart Objects for greater flexibility and creativity.

Starting up

Before starting, make sure that your tools and panels are consistent by resetting your preferences. See "Resetting Adobe Photoshop CC preferences" in the Starting up section of this book.

You will work with several files from the ps12lessons folder in this lesson. Make sure that you have loaded the pslessons folder onto your hard drive from the supplied DVD. See "Loading lesson files" in the Starting up section of this book.

See Lesson 12 in action!

Use the accompanying video to gain a better understanding of how to use some of the features shown in this lesson. You can find the video tutorial for this lesson on the included DVD.

Smart Objects allow you to transform pixel-based layers in new ways: you can scale, transform, and warp images without permanently destroying the original image data. In addition, Smart Objects create a link to their source files, which means that when you make changes to the source files, the Smart Objects are automatically updated with those changes.

Knowledge of Smart Objects will change the way you work with layers. In this lesson, you will find out how to open new images as Smart Objects, in addition to how to convert existing layers into Smart Objects. Throughout this lesson, you will have the opportunity to place and edit Smart Objects.

Creating a composition using Smart Objects

1   Choose File > Browse in Bridge to open Adobe Bridge. Navigate to the ps12lessons folder, and then double-click the image named **ps1201.psd** to open it in Photoshop. Alternatively, you can choose to right-click (Windows) or Ctrl+click (Mac OS) and select Open with Photoshop CC.

2   Choose File > Save As; the Save As dialog box appears. Navigate to the ps12lessons folder. In the File name text field, type **ps1201_work**, leave the format as Photoshop, and select Save. Keep the image open for the next section.

3   Open **ps1201_done.psd** to view the compilation you will create. You can keep this file open for reference, or choose File > Close. If asked, don't save changes.

The completed version of the lesson file.

Opening an image as a Smart Object

In this lesson, you'll compile many images of rainforest animals to create a photo illustration that could be used for a travel advertisement.

One of the defining characteristics of Smart Objects is the ability for layers to be transformed multiple times without the traditional resampling that occurs by default with Photoshop. In this section, you will go through an exercise to help you understand the main difference between a standard Photoshop layer and a Smart Object.

1 Click the Visibility icon (👁) to the left of the type layer named Visit the Rainforests of Palenque. This layer has been locked so you can't accidentally move it, and it will remain hidden for most of this lesson.

2 Select the Butterfly layer, and then select the Move tool (⊹). Choose Edit > Free Transform to scale this layer. Alternatively, you can use the keyboard shortcut Ctrl+T (Windows) or Command+T (Mac OS).

3 Press and hold the Shift key, and then click and hold the bottom-right corner of the transform box. Drag toward the center of the box to make the box smaller. Pressing and holding the Shift key ensures that the width and height are constrained proportionally. In the Options bar at the top of the screen, note that as you scale down, the percentage values begin to decrease. Scale the butterfly until the horizontal values are approximately 25 percent. Press Enter (Windows) or Return (Mac OS) to commit the transformation (you can also press the Commit check mark (✔) on the right side of the Options bar).

You can view the scale percentage in the Options bar.

You have reduced the width and height of this layer by 75 percent. This also means that the original pixel data has been lost through the scaling process (also called downsampling). This creates problems if you decide at some point to make the image on this layer larger.

You can type 25 into the Width text field in the Options bar and click the Maintain aspect ratio icon (⦚) to reflect the exact percentage in the Height text field.

4   Choose Edit > Free Transform, or use the keyboard shortcut Ctrl+T (Windows) or Command+T (Mac OS), to turn the transform bounding box on again. Press the Shift key, and then click and drag the bottom-right corner of the transform box diagonally downward and to the right to scale the image to approximately 400 percent. Remember to watch the percentage as it changes in the options W (Width) and H (Height) text fields. Press Enter (Windows) or Return (Mac OS) to commit the scale transform.

The butterfly layer after rescaling.

The image is fuzzy and pixelated because you forced Photoshop to fill in pixel information. This is called destructive editing because the original layer lost its detail through the resampling process.

You will now open the same image as a Smart Object so you can see the benefit of non-destructive editing.

5   Click the Visibility icon (👁) next to the Butterfly layer to turn the layer's visibility off. You will turn it back on shortly so you can compare the two layers.

6 Choose File > Open As a Smart Object. Navigate to the ps12lessons folder and choose the **ps1202.psd** file. Click Open to open the image in a new document window. In the Layers panel, note that the thumbnail for the layer is now a Smart Object thumbnail. All Smart Objects have a Smart Object icon in the lower-right corner of the layer thumbnail to help you distinguish them from standard layers.

The image is opened as a Smart Object.   *Smart Object icon.*

7 Select the Move tool (✦). Click and drag the butterfly image onto the tab labeled **ps1201_work.psd**. Wait for a moment until this image toggles into view, and then drop the butterfly image onto the image. Using the Move tool, reposition the new layer at the bottom of the screen. The bottom of the butterfly wings should be touching the bottom of the image.

8 In the Layers panel, double-click directly on the layer name, ps1202. When the layer name becomes highlighted, type **Butterfly 2** and press Enter (Windows) or Return (Mac OS) to commit the change.

9 Click the tab for the **ps1202.psd** image to make it active, and choose File > Close. When prompted to save, choose to not save the file.

You'll now perform the same scaling on the new Smart Object that you performed earlier on the first butterfly.

10 In the **ps1201_work** file, choose Edit > Free Transform or use the keyboard shortcut Ctrl+T (Windows) or Command+T (Mac OS).

11 Press the Shift key, click and hold the top-right corner of the transform box, and drag toward the center of the box. Scale the butterfly down in size until the horizontal value is approximately 25 percent. Press Enter (Windows) or Return (Mac OS) to commit the transformation.

12 Use the keyboard shortcut Ctrl+T (Windows) or Command+T (Mac OS). Press the Shift key, and then click and drag the top-right corner of the transform box away from the center to scale the image up to 100 percent. Press Enter (Windows) or Return (Mac OS) to commit the change.

When scaling Smart Objects, they "remember" their original size in the scale text boxes for Width and Height in the Options bar. This makes it easy for you to control the sizing and not dramatically stretch the image beyond its original size.

13 In the Layers panel, click the Visibility icon (👁) to the left of the Butterfly thumbnail. Readjust the layers as needed to compare the two images. Notice that the detail has not been lost, because Smart Objects maintain their original pixel data even if they are scaled and resized.

A. Standard layer, scaled and resized. B. Smart Object layer, scaled and resized.

Converting a layer to a Smart Object

In the last exercise, you created a Smart Object by using the Open as Smart Object feature. However, this is not always ideal. For example, perhaps you have a document in which you have already added several layers, and then you realize that you will be performing operations that require the use of Smart Objects. Rather than opening the original images again as Smart Objects, you can convert existing layers to Smart Objects.

1 Drag the Butterfly layer to the Delete button (🗑) at the bottom of the Layers panel. The Butterfly layer is deleted.

2 Select the Butterfly 2 layer in the Layers panel. Choose Edit > Free Transform, or press Ctrl+T (Windows) or Command+T (Mac OS).

3 You will now enter an exact value into the Width and Height text fields in the Options bar. Type **35** into the W (width) text field, and press the Maintain aspect ratio icon (∞) in between the W and H text fields. Press Enter (Windows) or Return (Mac OS) to commit the transformation. The layer is scaled to 35 percent. Reposition the butterfly to the upper-left corner.

4 In the Layers panel, select the Toucan layer and then click the Visibility icon (👁) next to the left of the Toucan layer thumbnail; the layer is now visible. You will now convert this layer to a Smart Object.

5 Choose Layer > Smart Objects > Convert to Smart Object.

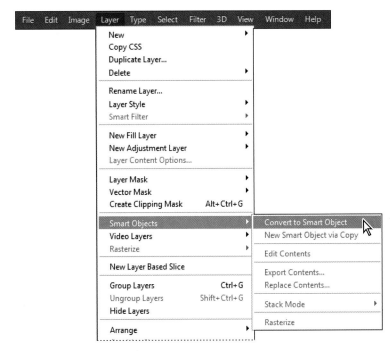

Changing a layer to a Smart Object.

There is no visible change in the image, but the Smart Object icon (🔳) in the Toucan layer now appears in the lower-right corner, indicating that it is now a Smart Object.

6 Choose Edit > Free Transform, or use the keyboard shortcut Ctrl+T (Windows) or Command+T (Mac OS) to transform the toucan image. Grab the top-right corner of the bounding box, and while holding the Shift key, click and drag a corner point to scale it to about three-quarters its current size (75 percent). If necessary, reposition the image in the lower-left corner. Press Enter (Windows) or Return (Mac OS) to commit the change.

Placing a Smart Object

In addition to opening new documents as Smart Objects and converting existing layers to Smart Objects, you can use the Place feature to import an image as a Smart Object.

1   Choose File > Place; the Place dialog box appears. Navigate to the ps12lessons folder, select the **ps1204.psd** file, and click Place. This places the parrot image into your **ps1201_work.psd** file.

When documents are placed, they become Smart Objects by default. Note the large X on the layer; this is a bounding box that allows you to transform the Smart Object before confirming the placement.

2   Click and drag the parrot image until the bottom-right corner snaps against the bottom-right corner of your work file. Press and hold the Shift key, and then click the top-left anchor point of the transform bounding box. With the Shift key still pressed, click and drag toward the center to scale the image down in size. Scale the parrot about 50% until it is just slightly smaller and the two images are not overlapping.

Scale the parrot so that it is approximately the same size as the toucan.

3   Select the Commit check mark (✔) in the Options bar, or press Enter (Windows) or Return (Mac OS) to commit the change. Remember that because this is a Smart Object by default, you can scale it back to its original size and still retain the original detail.

4   In the Layers panel, double-click the layer name, ps1204. When the layer name becomes highlighted, type the name **Parrot**.

Editing a Smart Object

There are additional benefits to Smart Objects besides their ability to be resized without loss of detail. To fully understand these benefits, you should know a little bit about how Smart Objects work. When a layer is a Smart Object, Photoshop preserves the original content of the source file by embedding it into the current file. In this exercise, you will learn how to edit the contents of Smart Objects. You will also find out how multiple Smart Object layers can be modified at the same time, how to replace the source for Smart Objects, and how to export the contents of a Smart Object.

1   Choose File > Open As Smart Object. Navigate to the ps12lessons folder, select the **ps1205.psd** file, and click Open to open the image in a new window. Notice that the title bar of the window reads ps1205 as Smart Object-1. This is not the original file, but rather a copy of the original file.

An image opened as a Smart Object.

2   Select the Move tool (✛), then click and drag the butterfly image onto the tab labeled **ps1201_work.psd**. Wait for a moment until the image toggles into view, and then drop the new layer onto your image. Note that the layer is named ps1205 and has the Smart Object thumbnail.

3   In the Layers panel, double-click the layer name ps1205. When the text becomes highlighted, type **Butterfly 3**. Press Enter (Windows) or Return (Mac OS).

4   Select the **ps1205.psd** image, and choose File > Close, or select the Close button in the document window. When prompted to save, choose to not save the file. The Smart Object file is separate from the original and is essentially embedded inside the **ps1201_work.psd** file.

5   In your **ps1201_work.psd** file, select the Butterfly 3 layer, and using the Move tool (✛), drag it to the center of the image window. Choose Edit > Free Transform, or use the keyboard shortcut Ctrl+T (Windows) or Command+T (Mac OS). Press and hold the Shift key while dragging any corner anchor point. Scale the butterfly to approximately 20 percent. Press Enter (Windows) or Return (Mac OS) to commit the change. Reposition the butterfly to the upper-right corner.

*This is a large image. If you cannot see the edges of the Butterfly 3 smart object, type **20** into the W and H text boxes in the Options bar at the top of the workspace.*

6   Choose Image > Adjustments. Note that virtually all the options are grayed out. This is because image adjustments, such as Levels and Curves, are destructive by nature and cannot be applied to Smart Objects. Release the mouse without making a choice. In a few steps, you will look at an alternative method for adjusting the appearance of this layer.

7   Click the Brush tool (✏). Position your cursor over the image. Don't click, but notice that the Non-editable icon (⊘) appears. You cannot paint on this layer because that would be destructive.

So, what if you need to modify the layer? Perhaps you want to selectively dodge and burn parts of the image or use image adjustment commands. You have two choices when working with Smart Objects:

• Edit the original in its own separate window.

• Rasterize the Smart Object layer before using common editing tools.

For this example, you will rasterize the Smart Object. Using the term *rasterize* is a bit confusing in this instance. The image is already a raster image (composed of pixels), but the term refers to the step of *unsmarting* your image and putting the original pixels back into the **ps1201_work.psd** image.

8   Select the Blur tool (⬤) from the Tools panel. Click anywhere on the butterfly; a warning dialog box appears, informing you that the layer will be rasterized. Click OK to rasterize the image.

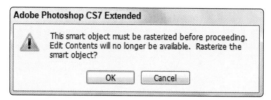

Click OK to rasterize the layer.

9   Using the Zoom tool (🔍), zoom in closer to the butterfly, and click and drag the Blur tool several times over the edges of the butterfly to see the blur effect. You are now able to edit the image because it has been converted to pixels. However, it has also lost its Smart Object status.

All the editing tools, such as Dodge, Burn, Clone Stamp, and Eraser, are destructive and therefore not usable when a Smart Object layer is active.

Ideally, everything in Photoshop should be as non-destructive as possible. Depending on your objectives, you will need to determine when you can accept the consequences of rasterizing a Smart Object. However, you should also know the alternatives.

10   Drag the Butterfly 3 layer to the Delete icon (🗑) in the Layers panel. You will add the layer again in the next exercise and learn how to access the contents of a Smart Object. Later in the lesson, you will return to the issue of adding a blur non-destructively.

Editing the contents of a Smart Object

In the last exercise, you saw how you could modify a Smart Object by rasterizing the layer. The problem with this method is that rasterizing the layer removes the unique characteristics of the Smart Object layer. Using the following method, you will edit the contents of the embedded Smart Object without changing its Smart Object status.

1   Choose File > Place, and navigate to the ps12lessons folder. Select the **ps1205.psd** file and click Place. The butterfly image appears in your screen.

2   Pressing and holding the Shift key, click and drag any corner anchor point toward the center until you see an amount close to 25 percent in the W and H text fields in the Options bar, or type **25** into the W and H text fields. Reposition the butterfly to the upper-right corner of the image. Press Enter (Windows) or Return (Mac OS) to commit the change.

3   In the Layers panel, double-click the layer name ps1205, to highlight the text name. Type **Butterfly 4** and press Enter (Windows) or Return (Mac OS).

4   Now, double-click the Butterfly 4 layer thumbnail in the Layers panel (do not click the layer name or the layer itself, but specifically the Smart Object thumbnail). A dialog box appears, reminding you that you need to save the document after you edit the contents. Click OK. The **ps1205.psd** file is now open on your screen.

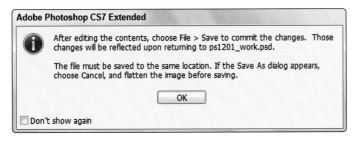

A warning dialog box appears when you edit a Smart Object.

By double-clicking the Smart Object layer, you open the original file as a separate document. You'll now make some adjustments to the original image. In this case, you will be adjusting the hue and saturation.

5   In the Adjustments panel immediately above your layers, click the Hue/Saturation icon to open the Properties panel.

Click the Hue/Saturation icon.

The Properties panel for the Hue/Saturation settings appears. Using an adjustment layer ensures that your original pixel data remains untouched.

6   Drag the Hue slider to the left to approximately the -180 mark, or type **-180** in the Hue text field. This adjusts the color of the butterfly to blue. Click the Properties tab to close the panel.

7   Choose File > Save. This is the crucial step. As noted in the dialog box in step 4, you must save the current document without renaming it. Choose File > Close to close the image.

8   In the **ps1201_work.psd** file, notice that the blue butterfly has been updated. This is because Butterfly 4 is a Smart Object layer connected, or linked, to the original file, which is now embedded inside the **ps1201_work.psd** file.

Suppose you need to adjust the settings of the hue/saturation layer again; you can return to the adjustment layer to make any necessary changes.

9   Double-click the Butterfly 4 layer thumbnail to reopen the source file. The warning dialog box you saw previously appears. Click OK.

This dialog box can be turned off by clicking the Don't Show Again *check box in the lower-left corner.*

10 In your layers panel, double-click the Layer thumbnail icon on the Hue/Saturation layer to reopen the Properties panel with the Hue/Saturation options visible.

Double-click the Layer thumbnail icon to reopen the properties panel for Hue/Saturation.

11 In the Properties panel, click and drag the Saturation slider to -60, or type **-60** in the Saturation text field. This tones down the bright blue. Click the Properties tab to close this panel.

12 Choose File > Save, and then File > Close to close the file. As before, the butterfly in your work image has been automatically updated.

Using this combination of adjustment layers and Smart Objects gives you tremendous flexibility with your layers. Adjustment layers and Smart Objects encourage you to experiment without fear of destroying the integrity of the original image. As you will see in the next exercise, this ability to edit the contents of a Smart Object has even more power when you have multiple Smart Objects.

Modifying multiple Smart Object layers

Another benefit of Smart Object layers is that multiple layers can be modified at the same time.

1   In the main composition, **ps1201_work.psd**, click and drag the Butterfly 4 layer down and release it on the Create a New Layer button (◁) in the Layers panel to duplicate it. Select the Move tool (+), then click and drag the copy to the far left, next to the yellow butterfly.

Duplicate the Butterfly 4 layer.

You can duplicate layers by choosing Layer > Smart Objects > New Smart Objects Via Copy.

2   In the Layers panel, double-click the layer name, Butterfly 4 Copy. When the layer name becomes highlighted, type **Butterfly 5** to rename the layer.

3   Double-click the Butterfly 5 layer thumbnail in the Layers panel to open the original **ps1205.psd** image. Click OK to dismiss the Save dialog box if necessary. You will now add a Curves adjustment layer to increase the contrast of both butterflies.

4   In the Adjustments panel, click the Curves icon (⌇)—it is the third icon in the first row of icons. The Properties panel for curves opens.

5   Position your cursor in the middle of the curves graph, then click and drag the line upward and to the left to increase the brightness and contrast. If you would like to match the image in this example, type an Input value of **105** and an Output value of **137**. If you cannot see the Input and Output fields, you might need to expand your Properties window slightly. (Additionally, if you are not able to enter these values in, you might need to change your display options for curves. To do so, click the context menu of the Properties panel, choose Curves Display Options and select Light (0–255).)

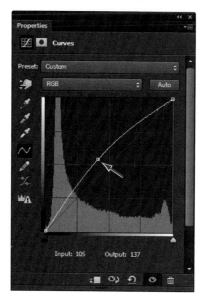

Adjust the curve in the Adjustments panel.

Click the Properties tab for the Curve adjustments to close it.

6   Choose File > Save, and then File > Close to close the file. Both butterflies in your work image are now brighter. Multiple Smart Object layers can be linked to the same source file. When the source file is changed in some way, all the linked files also change.

Replacing the contents of a Smart Object layer

Now that you have seen how multiple Smart Object layers are linked to the source file, you will change the source file for the (now blue) butterfly. To understand the usefulness of this exercise, imagine that you have duplicated several butterfly Smart Object layers and then rotated, resized, or warped them in different ways. Now imagine that you have found a better source file for these layers. Instead of deleting the existing layers and repeating the steps, you can replace the existing butterfly image with a new one, and all the transformations will stay the same.

1   In your **ps1201_work.psd** image, click Butterfly 5 in the Layers panel. Then select Edit > Free Transform, or use the keyboard shortcut Ctrl+T (Windows) or Command+T (Mac OS), to transform the first butterfly in the left corner. Hold the Shift key, click the top-left anchor point of the transform bounding box, and drag downward and to the right, scaling the image down to approximately 15 percent.

2   Position your cursor slightly above and to the right of the top-right corner anchor point. A cursor with a rounded arrow appears. Click and drag to the left to rotate the image approximately –45 degrees. Reposition the image slightly to the right of the yellow butterfly. Press Enter (Windows) or Return (Mac OS) to commit the transformation.

Both the scaling and rotating are tracked in the Options bar.

3   Select the Butterfly 4 layer in the Layers panel. Press Ctrl+T (Windows) or Command+T (Mac OS) to transform the layer. You will now use Photoshop's Warp feature to simulate the butterfly moving through the air.

4   Choose Edit > Transform > Warp. Feel free to create your own warping effect; for this effect, you would click and drag the left wing upward and the right wing downward.

Clicking and dragging the warp handles to warp the image.

5   Press Enter (Windows) or Return (Mac OS) when you are satisfied with the effect.

Now you will replace the two butterflies with a new image, while maintaining the transformations you created.

6 With the Butterfly 4 layer still selected, choose Layer > Smart Objects > Replace Contents. Locate the ps12lessons folder, select **ps1206.psd**, and click Place. Both images update automatically while retaining their individual transformations.

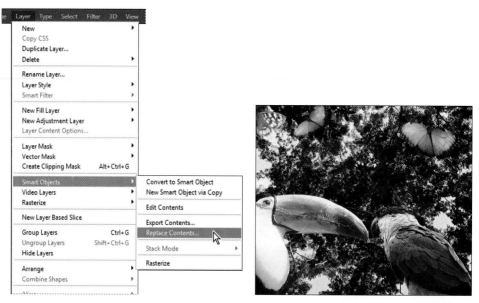

Chose to replace your smart object.   *The result.*

This technique can be extremely helpful, because it saves you from having to repeat similar steps.

Working with Smart Filters

Now that you have a good foundation for Smart Objects, the concept of Smart Filters shouldn't be too hard to follow. A Smart Filter is simply one of the Photoshop filters applied to a Smart Object layer. Filters are usually destructive—that is, any effect applied to a layer becomes more difficult to remove. When you use a Smart Filter, any filter you apply is not permanent. Effects can be toggled off and on, combined, or deleted. As you will see in this exercise, you can work with the built-in mask of a filter effect to customize your filter effects in ways that were previously not possible in Photoshop.

In this exercise, you will be applying a combination of two filters to create an effect of motion, then you will use the layer mask to refine the effect with the Brush tool.

1 Select the Butterfly 4 layer, and choose Filter > Sharpen > Smart Sharpen. The Smart Sharpen dialog box appears. Change the Amount value to **200** percent and the Radius to **1.0**, and then click OK. A dramatic sharpen effect is applied; the butterfly should now show more detail.

2   In the Layers panel, below the Butterfly 4 layer, there is a Smart Filter listed with a white thumbnail to the left. Immediately below that is the Smart Sharpen filter effect. These two lines were automatically added when you applied the filter. You will now examine how they work.

3   Click the Visibility icon (👁) next to the Smart Sharpen filter effect. This turns the Smart Sharpen filter off and allows you to view the original image. Click in the now-empty space to toggle the filter back on.

Clicking the Visibility icon toggles a filter effect on and off.

You will now add a Blur filter in addition to the Smart Sharpen filter.

4   Choose Filter > Blur > Motion Blur. You might have to click and drag the Motion Blur dialogue box down and to the left to see the image. In the Motion Blur window, type **50** in the Distance text field. This creates a blur of 50 pixels in both directions. Now you will change the angle of the blur.

5 Click the right side of the angle dial, and then click and drag counter-clockwise until the angle value is approximately -65 degrees, and then click OK. Don't worry about how the effect looks; you will be editing it shortly. The Motion Blur effect is now above the Smart Sharpen effect.

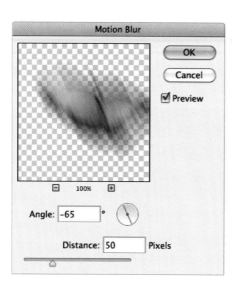

Apply a motion blur to the layer.

Two smart filters are applied to the same layer.

6 Click the Visibility icon to the left of the Motion Blur effect. The Smart Sharpen effect is still active; it is just hidden because you've turned the filter off. Click the Visibility icon in the Motion Blur line to bring the Motion Blur effect back.

This feature of Smart Filters is great, but what if you want only part of the filter to be applied to the layer? In this example, combining Sharpen and Blur filters doesn't make much sense. However, with a bit of masking, you can allow certain areas to remain sharp, while other areas are blurred.

7 Click the white thumbnail to the left of the Smart Filters label, immediately above the two filter effects. This is the default layer mask that is created whenever you add a Smart Filter. It will allow you to mask out the areas where you don't want the filter effects to appear, while leaving the areas you do want filtered alone.

8 Select the Brush tool (✐), and click and hold the arrow to the right of the Brush Preset picker in the Options bar at the top of your screen. Select the Soft Round brush preset, and use the slider to change the Size value to approximately 45. Click the Options bar to make the Brush Preset picker disappear.

Select the Soft Round brush and change the size.

For more information about working with Photoshop brushes, review Lesson 5, "Painting and Retouching."

9 Press **D** on your keyboard to revert the foreground and background colors back to the default of black and white. Press **X** on your keyboard to swap the foreground and background colors. Black is now the foreground color and white is the background color.

10 Place your brush at the top of the butterfly and begin painting from left to right and then downward. As you paint, the filter effects are concealed by the layer mask you are adding.

For a more in-depth look at layer masks, review Lesson 8, "Introduction to Photoshop Layers."

11 Continue painting downward until only the bottom half of the butterfly is blurred. Press the letter **X** on your keyboard to swap the foreground color to white. Now, paint over the top half again, and notice how the effect is revealed again. By toggling between white and black and painting on the Smart Filter mask, you can reveal or conceal the filter effects.

Painting on the mask for the butterfly.

The resulting mask.

12 Press **X** on your keyboard to set black as the foreground color, and then paint the mask to hide virtually all the filter effect at the top part of the image. There are also areas at the bottom right that you will want to hide. You want your Butterfly 4 layer to look approximately the same as the example shown here. The effect is still not exactly what you need, but in the next section, you will fine-tune the motion blur effect.

The Butterfly 4 layer at this point.

Modifying a Smart Filter

Once you add a Smart Filter, you can go back and modify the effect, even if you've added a mask, as in this case.

1   In the Butterfly 4 layer, double-click the Motion Blur effect; the Motion Blur dialog box appears. You might have to click and drag down and to the left inside the filter preview window to see the image. Change the angle to 87 degrees by clicking and dragging the dial to the right. Click OK when done.

Changing the angle of the motion blur now requires you to go back with the paintbrush and modify the mask.

2   Click the layer mask thumbnail to the left of Smart Filters to activate it. Then begin to paint from the top down, leaving just a blur at the bottom of the butterfly. If you mask out too much of the effect, you can press **X** to switch to white as the foreground color to restore the effect in the desired areas.

3   Click the Visibility icon (👁) next to the Smart Filter mask. This turns the mask off completely, and can help identify areas affected by a filter that you might have missed. Click the Visibility icon again to turn the mask back on and clean up any areas where you don't want the filter applied.

Turn off the effects of the mask by selecting the Visibility icon.

4   In the Layers panel, click the Visibility icon to the left of the Visit the Rainforests type layer on the top. (You turned this layer off at the beginning of the exercise). Click the padlock icon in the Lock section of the Layers panel. Select the Move tool, and then click and drag to reposition the layers as needed.

5   Choose File > Save.

The completed lesson file.

Self study

In this section, you can complete some exercises on your own. Use adjustment layers to adjust the brightness, contrast, hue, and saturation of the lesson files.

Currently, the individual butterfly and bird images do not blend as well into the background as they could. Using the techniques laid out in "Editing the contents of a Smart Object," add adjustment layers to the objects in the photo-illustration, and fine-tune the appearance of the individual objects. Try to make the individual layers match each other as much as possible to create a cohesive photo illustration.

Creating multiple Smart Objects

In this lesson, you learned how to work with Smart Objects in their various forms. Create additional copies of the butterfly or bird images, and experiment with creating a collage. Apply filters to your existing Smart Objects. For different effects, try applying a black-to-white gradient on a Smart Filter mask to achieve a smooth transition that would be difficult to achieve using just the Brush tool alone.

Working with Illustrator files

If you have Adobe Illustrator, you can also place .ai files into Photoshop files as Smart Object layers. They work in similar ways. Create an image in Illustrator, and place it into Photoshop. Create multiple copies of the Illustrator layer, and then modify the original .ai file to see the changes applied to the layers in the Photoshop file.

Review

Questions

1   What are three ways that you can create a Smart Object layer?

2   Why would you convert a standard layer to a Smart Object layer?

3   How do you replace the contents of a Smart Object layer? When would you do so?

4   What are Smart Filters, and what are the benefits of using them?

Answers

1   You can bring an image into an existing file as a Smart Object by choosing File > Open as Smart Object and selecting the file; choosing File > Place; or when using Adobe Bridge, selecting the file and choosing File > Place > Into Photoshop. If an image is currently inside a document and you would like to convert it to a Smart Object, select the layer in the Layers panel and choose Layer > Smart Objects > Convert to Smart Objects.

2   You would convert a standard layer to a Smart Object layer because a Smart Object layer can be resized indefinitely without losing resolution due to resampling.

3   You can replace the contents of a Smart Object layer by choosing Layer > Smart Objects > Replace Contents. You might use this technique if you wanted to replace one image with another without losing any scaling, rotating, or warping you had created for the image.

4   Any filter applied to a Smart Object is a Smart Filter. Smart Filters appear in the Layers panel below the Smart Object layer to which they are applied. Because you can adjust, remove, or hide Smart Filters, they are non-destructive.

Creating Images for Web, Video, and Interactive Use

Photoshop's flexibility and range of features have allowed it to gain acceptance in nearly every sector of the creative design industry. A very common use for Photoshop is creating imagery for web, application, and video production.

Starting up

In this lesson, you'll create a group of projects for web and video production. You'll work with still and animated graphics for each medium.

Before starting, make sure that your tools and panels are consistent by resetting your preferences. See "Resetting Adobe Photoshop CC preferences" in the Starting up section of this book.

In this lesson, you will work with several files from the ps13lessons folder. Make sure that you have loaded the pslessons folder from the supplied DVD onto your hard drive. See "Loading lesson files" in the Starting up section of this book.

To work with video in Photoshop, you should have the QuickTime player plug-in installed on your computer. QuickTime is pre-installed with the Mac OS operating system; Windows users can download the QuickTime player for free from the Apple website, *apple.com/quicktime*.

See Lesson 13 in action!

Use the accompanying video to gain a better understanding of how to use some of the features shown in this lesson. You can find the video tutorial for this lesson on the included DVD.

Viewing the completed file

Before starting this lesson, you'll use your browser to view the completed page with navigational links that you will create in this part of the lesson. You should note that creating an entire web page as a graphic (as you will see in this example) has limited use, such as creating a mock-up for a page that will later be converted to HTML, CSS, and images.

1   Open your web browser—you can use any browser for this lesson (Firefox, Safari, Opera, or Internet Explorer, to name a few).

2   Choose File > Open, or Open File. The exact menu selection varies depending on the type and version of your browser, but the menu item for opening a page in your browser should be under the File menu.

3   In the Open dialog box, navigate to the ps13lessons folder on your hard drive and open the file called **ps1301_done.html**. An image created to help viewers navigate a website appears. If you prefer, locate ps1301.html in the ps13lessons folder and double-click it to open the file in your default browser

The completed web page in a web browser.

4   Click the Sales, Service, About, and Contact text links to see that you are directed to generic pages with related titles.

You will create this web page from start to finish, including adding the links, and export the page using CSS technology.

5   You can keep the finished web page open in the browser for reference, or choose to close it now.

6   Return to Photoshop CC.

Determining image size for the Web

This figure represents a typical monitor that is set at a screen resolution of 800×600. Many viewers will use a higher resolution, such as 1024×768, 1280×800, or higher. A common size that many web designers are using at this time is 960 px wide.

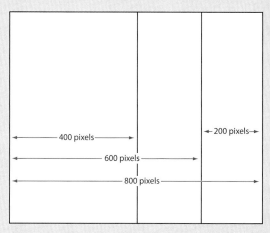

A screen size of 800 pixels broken into quarters.

To determine how wide an on-screen image should be, break down the total number of screen pixels into sections. Instead of thinking about how many pixels wide an image should be, think about what percentage of the screen you want the image to occupy. In other words, if you want the image to occupy half the screen for a 1024×768 monitor, you would type **512** into the Width text field in the Pixel Dimension section of the Image Size dialog box. For one quarter of the screen, type **356**, and so on. It is a different way of thinking, especially for those from the print design environment. It should also be noted that a pixel is a pixel, no matter what the ppi resolution of your image is. So, 200 pixels in a 300 ppi image takes up the same amount of screen and disk space as 200 pixels in a 72 ppi image.

Changing your units of measurement

Before starting the web project, verify that your measurements are set in the pixel unit. Make that change in your Photoshop Preferences.

1   Choose Edit > Preferences > Units & Rulers (Windows) or Photoshop > Preferences > Units & Rulers (Mac OS). The Preferences dialog box appears, with Units & Rulers already selected.

2   From the Units section of the Preferences dialog box, choose Pixels from the Rulers drop-down menu. Leave all the other settings at their default. Click OK.

You can also change your unit of measurement by pressing Ctrl+R (Windows) or Command+R (Mac OS) to show your rulers, and then right-clicking the horizontal ruler at the top to choose Pixels (or any other measurement from the context menu that appears).

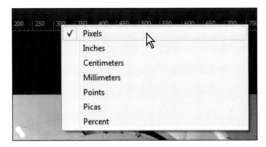

Changing your unit of measurement right on the ruler.

Creating the web page

In this part of the lesson, you will open the start file and get right to work adding content, links, and slices.

1   From Photoshop, choose File > Browse in Bridge. When Adobe Bridge appears, navigate to the ps13lessons folder and double-click to open the file called **ps1301.psd**. An image of a man with a kite on a beach appears.

The ps1301.psd image.

The first step you will take with this file is to save it as a work file, then flip the image so the man is on the left rather than on the right.

2   Choose File > Save As. When the Save As dialog box appears, navigate to the ps13lessons folder and type **ps1301_work.psd** into the File name text field. Choose Photoshop from the Format drop-down menu and click Save.

3   Choose Image > Image Rotation and select Flip Canvas Horizontal. The image flips so the man is now on the left. Press Ctrl+S (Windows) or Command+S (Mac OS) to save the file.

Adding the Text

You will now add the header text on the upper-left side of the image and the text that will serve as links on the final page.

1 Select the Horizontal Type tool (T) and click anywhere on the upper-left side of the image; the text cursor appears. In the Options bar at the top of your screen, select Myriad Pro from the Font family drop-down menu, Bold from the Font style drop-down menu, and **60** from the Font size drop-down menu.

2 Click the Center text button (≡) in the Options bar, then click once on the Text color swatch in the Options bar and choose white from the Color Picker dialog box that appears. Click OK.

The Options bar as it appears after Steps 1 and 2.

3 Now that the text options are set, type the following with returns:

Go
Fly
a Kite

If you need to reposition your text and do not want to exit the type options, press and hold the Ctrl (Windows) or Command (Mac OS) key, then click and drag to reposition the text layer.

You will now fine-tune the text by adjusting the leading (space between the lines of text) and the kerning (space between the letters).

4 With the text area still active, press Ctrl+A (Windows) or Command+A (Mac OS) to select all the text, then press Alt+Arrow Up key (Windows) or Option+Arrow Up key (Mac OS) to reduce the space (called leading) between the lines of text. If the space is reduced too much, press Alt+Arrow Down key (Windows) or Option+Arrow Down key (Mac OS) to move the lines of text further apart from each other. Try to set the leading so the text is almost on top of the next line.

5 Reduce the spacing between the word *a* and *kite* by clicking to insert the cursor anywhere between those letters, then press and hold the Alt+Left Arrow key (Windows) or Option+Left Arrow key (Mac OS) and press repeatedly until the space is smaller; choose the amount of space you want. In our example, the Alt/Option+Left Arrow key was pressed approximately 15 times.

Alternatively, you could have left no space between the words a and kite; kern out the space between by repeatedly pressing the Alt/Option+Right Arrow key.

6   While the text is still active, click the Create warped text button (ℐ) in the Options
     bar. The Warp Text dialog box appears. You can warp text to create all sorts of effects;
     in this example, the text is distorted to add a little dimension.

7   In the Warp Text dialog box, select Rise from the Style drop-down menu, and make
     sure that the Horizontal option button is selected.

8   Click and drag the Bend slider to the left to change the value to +10, or type **+10** into
     the Bend text field.

9   Verify that the Horizontal Distortion is set to 0 (zero), then click and drag the Vertical
     Distortion slider to the right to about the value of 25, or type **25** into the Vertical
     Distortion text field. Click OK. The warp is applied to the text.

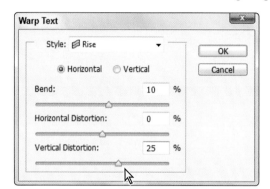

Applying the Rise warp.

The result after warping the text.

10   Click the Commit check mark (✔) on the right side of the Options bar to confirm
     your text edits. If necessary, choose the Move tool (▸⊹) and click and drag to reposition
     the text so it is visible in the upper-left corner of the image.

Adding Style to the text

Now that you have your header text created, you will add a layer style to it.

1   With the Go Fly a Kite text layer still selected, click the Add a layer style button (*fx*)
     at the bottom of the Layers panel. Select Outer Glow from the layer style drop-down
     menu. The Layer Style dialog box appears with Outer Glow settings visible.

2   From the Blend Mode drop-down menu, choose Normal.

3   In the Structure section, click once on the Set color of glow swatch; the Color Picker
     appears. Click and drag the slider, on the right of the color pane, until you see blue
     colors in the color pane. Choose a navy blue and click OK.

4   In the Elements section, click and drag the Size slider to the right until you reach the value of 25 px, or enter **25** into the Size text field. Click OK to close the dialog box.

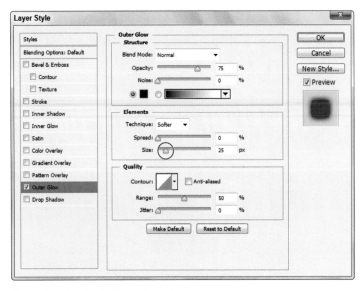

Change the options for the Outer Glow style.

Result after applying outer glow.

Creating text for the links

Now that you have the header text completed, you will create the individual text layers that will serve as links.

1   Select the Type tool (T) and click somewhere on the top right of the large kite the man is holding in the image. The blinking insert text cursor appears.

The Type tool remembers the last settings, such as font and size. Before typing, you need to change the text size and orientation.

2   Choose 30 from the Font size drop-down menu, then click the Left align text button (≡) in the Options bar.

3   Type **Sales**, then press Ctrl+Enter (Windows) or Command+Return (Mac OS) to commit the text entry and exit the type options.

Pressing Ctrl/Command+Enter or Return is the same as clicking the Commit (✔) check mark in the Options bar.

4 Position your cursor under the Sales text and click to create a new text entry. Exact position is not important, since you will reposition the text later. Type **Service**, then press Ctrl+Enter (Windows) or Command+Return (Mac OS) to commit the text entry and exit the type options.

5 Position your cursor under the word Service and click and type **About**, then press Ctrl+Enter (Windows) or Command+Return (Mac OS) to commit the text entry and exit the type options.

6 Position your cursor under the word About to make the last text entry, and click. Type the word **Contact**, then press Ctrl+Enter (Windows) or Command+Return (Mac OS) to commit the text entry and exit the type options.

7 Choose File > Save, or press Ctrl+S (Windows) or Command+S (Mac OS) to save the file. Keep this file open for the next part of this lesson. (If the Photoshop Format Options window appeared when you saved, click OK.)

Positioning and distribution of text

In this part of the lesson, you will use the Move tool to reposition the text and then distribute the vertical space between them evenly.

1 Select the Move tool (⊕) and Ctrl+Click (Windows) or Command+Click (Mac OS) the word Sales (in the image). By pressing and holding the Ctrl/Command key, you have turned on the auto-select feature. You can easily activate layers without having to go to the Layers panel.

   With the Sales layer selected, click and drag the text so it is off to the right of the curved edge of the kite.

2 Press and hold the Ctrl/Command key, click the other three text layers, and position them off to the right of the kite, following the curve of the kite image.

3 Make sure that the Layers panel is visible and select the Sales text layer. Then, Ctrl+Shift+click (Windows) or Command+Shift+click (Mac OS) the Service, About, and Contact text layers (in the Layers panel).

   Note that when you select three or more layers, the Align and Distribute options become visible in the Options bar. Align becomes visible with two layers selected.

4 Choose Distribute vertical centers (≛) from the Options bar. The text layers are distributed evenly.

Click the Distribute vertical centers button.

The selected layers now have equal amounts of vertical space between them.

Creating slices

A slice is a part of an image that is cut from a larger image. Think of a slice as a piece of a puzzle that, when placed alongside other related pieces, creates an entire image. An HTML table or CSS holds the pieces together. In this example, you will use Cascading styles to create the final HTML page.

An example of a sliced image.

In the early days of the Web, slicing was used to create the appearance that a page was loading faster; a user could see the different slices loading instead of waiting for the entire image to appear. These days, slices can still be used in this way for web graphics, but it is more likely that you would use slices to precisely choose the area of an image you would like to export. You might then use the slice for a CSS background image or some other element of your web page (such as a button). In this exercise, you will create guides that will determine where the slicing of your image occurs.

1   If rulers are not displayed, choose View > Rulers to show the rulers on the top and left side of the document window.

2   Choose View > Snap to turn off the snapping features for the rest of this lesson. The snapping features sometimes force the cursor to align with elements in your images, such as the edges of the text layers.

Using the rulers, you will create guides on your document that will later define where you want to slice your image.

3   Click directly on the top (horizontal) ruler, and then click and drag to pull a guide from the ruler. Continue dragging the guide; release it when the guide is just above the Sales text layer.

4   Now, click and drag another guide from the top ruler and release it when it is between the word *Sales* and the word *Service* in the image area.

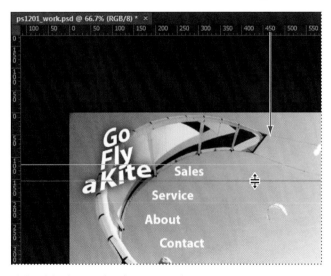

Click and drag horizontal guides to separate the text.

5   Click and drag another guide from the top ruler and release it between the *Service* and *About* text on the image, and another between the *About* and *Contact* text.

6   Finally, click and drag a guide from the top ruler and release it underneath the *Contact* text. You should have a total of five horizontal guides. You will now create the vertical guides.

7   Click the ruler on the left side of the image window and drag out a guide; release the guide when you reach the left side of the *Sales, Service, About, Contact* text on the image.

8   Click again on the ruler on the left and drag out a guide; release it when it is on the right side of the *Sales, Service, About, Contact* text on the image.

The guides are completed; the image with guides should look similar to our example.

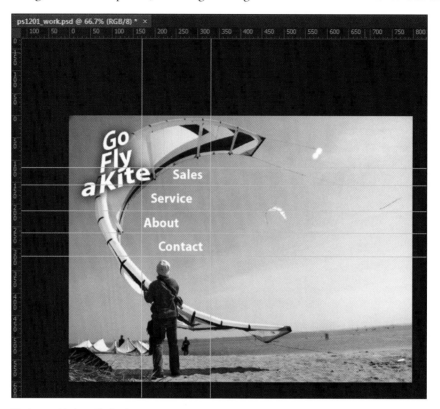

The image with the guides in place.

If necessary, use the Move tool to click and drag existing guides.

Slicing it up

No slicing has occurred at this point. In this part of the lesson, you will use options that are available when using the Slice tool to easily create your slices.

1. Click and hold the Crop tool to select the hidden Slice tool (⌁). Note that the options change in the Options bar.

2. Click the Slices From Guides button in the Options bar. Your image is automatically sliced into several smaller images, based on the location of your guides. The image is not actually sliced in Photoshop, but will be when you save the file in the Save for Web section of this lesson.

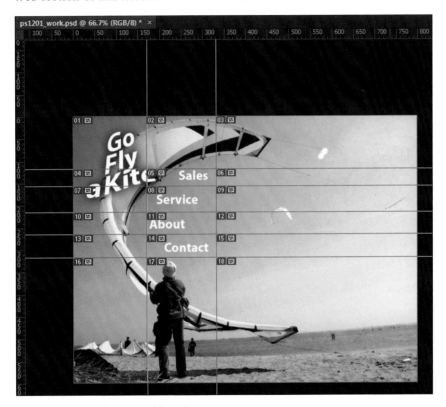

The slices created from the position of the guides.

3. Choose File > Save and keep this file open for the next exercise.

Selecting and combining slices

In this section, you will select several slices and combine them into one slice. You can combine and divide slices easily using context tools in Photoshop. You will first remove the guides, since you no longer need them.

1   Choose View > Clear Guides. The guides are cleared, but the slices remain.

2   Click and hold the Slice tool (✐) to choose the hidden Slice Select tool (✐). Using this tool, you can click to activate and adjust your slices.

    You will now select all the slices that are not going to be hyperlinks and combine them.

3   Using the Slice Select tool, click the large slice in the lower-left corner of the image. Then Shift+click each of the slices above. This adds each slice to the selection.

4   When you have selected all the slices on the left side, right-click (Windows) or Ctrl+click (Mac OS) and select Combine Slices from the menu. The slices are combined into one slice.

Select all slices on the left.   *Combine into one.*

5   Now use the Slice Select tool to select the slice directly above the Sales text slice, then press and hold the Shift key and select the slice to the right. Right-click (Windows) or Ctrl+click (Mac OS) and select Combine Slices from the menu. The slices are combined into one slice.

6   Select the large slice in the lower-right of the image with the Slice Select tool. Shift+click the slices above it, excluding the top slice, which you have already combined. Right-click (Windows) or Ctrl+click (Mac OS) and select Combine Slices from the menu. The slices are combined into one slice.

The task of combining slices is finished.

The slices as they appear after being combined.

In this example, you are combining slices manually, but you can also select slices across columns and rows and let Photoshop determine which slice combination works best.

7   Choose File > Save to save this file. Keep the image open for the next part of this lesson.

Applying attributes to your slices

Now that you have defined your slices, you will apply attributes to them. The attributes that you will apply in this lesson are URL and Alt Tags. By defining a URL, a link is made from that slice to a location or file on the Web. By defining an Alt Tag, you allow viewers to read a text description of an image. This is helpful for visually impaired users and for users who have turned off the option for viewing graphics. An Alt Tag also helps search engines find more relevant content on your page.

1   With the **ps1301_work.psd** file still open and the Slice Select tool (✂) still selected, select the slice containing the Sales text.

2   Click the Set options for the current slice button (▤) in the Options bar (immediately to the right of the "Hide Auto Slices" button). The Slice Options dialog box appears.

You will be supplied with a link to a file in your lessons folder to test your links.

3   Type **sales.html** into the URL text field.

4   Type **Sales** into the Alt Tag text field and click OK.

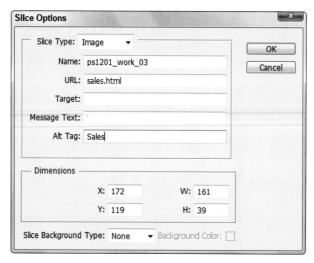

Enter the URL and Alt Tag information.

Your HTML file must be saved inside the ps13lessons folder to have a working link.

5   Now, select the slice containing the text *Service*, and choose the Set options for the current slice button in the Options bar. The Slice Options dialog box appears.

6   Type **service.html** into the URL text field and **Service** in the Alt Tag text field. Click OK.

7   Select the slice containing the text *About*, and choose the Set options for the current slice button in the Options bar. The Slice Options dialog box appears.

8   Type **about.html** into the URL text field and **About Us** in the Alt Tag text field. Click OK.

9   Select the slice containing the text *Contact*, and choose the Set options for the current slice button in the Options bar. The Slice Options dialog box appears.

10   Type **contact.html** into the URL text field and **Contact Us** in the Alt Tag text field. Click OK.

11   Choose File > Save. Keep the document open for the next part of the lesson.

For this lesson, you do not put an Alt tag on each slice, but we recommend that you assign a descriptive Alt tag to each slice when producing images for the Web.

Using Save for Web

The process of making an image look as good as possible at the smallest file size is called optimizing. This is important for all images that will be used on the Web, since most viewers don't want to wait long for information to appear.

In this part of the lesson, you'll use the Save for Web feature to optimize your navigational banner.

1   With the **ps1301_work.psd** file still open, choose File > Save for Web. The Save for Web dialog box appears.

2   Select the 2-up tab to view your original image on the top and your optimized image on the bottom. Note that the window may display the original on the left side and the optimized image on the right.

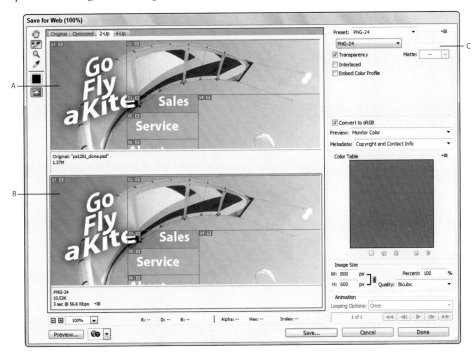

A. *Toolbox.* **B.** *Preview window.* **C.** *Optimization settings.*

3   Select the Hand tool (✋) and click and drag directly on the image in either window to reposition the image so you can see the four slices containing text.

The Save for Web window is broken into three main areas:

Toolbox: the Toolbox provides you with tools for panning and zooming in your image, selecting slices, and sampling color.

Preview window: in addition to having the ability to view both the original and optimized images individually, you can preview the original and optimized images side-by-side in 2-up view or with up to three variations in the 4-up view.

Optimization settings: the Optimization settings allow you to specify the format and settings of your optimized file.

How to choose web image formats

When you want to optimize an image for the Web, what format should you choose? Choose the format best suited to the type of image you are using.

GIF: an acronym for Graphic Interchange File, the GIF format is usually used on the Web to display simple colored logos, motifs, and other limited-tone imagery. The GIF format supports a maximum of 256 colors, as well as transparency. GIF is the only one of the four formats here that supports built-in animation. Keep in mind that, unless you are using animation, you should consider the preferred format of PNG.

JPEG: an acronym for Joint Photographic Experts Group, the JPEG file format has found wide acceptance on the Web as the main format for displaying photographs and other continuous-tone imagery. The JPEG format supports a range of millions of colors, allowing for the accurate display of a wide range of artwork.

PNG: an acronym for Portable Network Graphics. PNG was intended to blend the best of both the GIF and JPEG formats. PNG files come in two different varieties: like GIF, PNG-8 can support up to 256 colors, while PNG-24 can support millions of colors, similar to the JPEG format. Both PNG varieties support transparency, and as an improvement on GIF's all-or-nothing transparency function, a PNG file supports varying amounts of transparency so you can actually see through an image to your web page contents. Older browsers, in particular IE6, do not support PNG transparency, but this is seldom a problem, unless you specifically need to support the older browsers.

4   Click the Slice Select tool (✓), then the Sales slice, then Shift+click the Service, About, and the Contact slices. Now all slices are active.

Make sure you are selecting the text slices in the Optimize preview, not the Original preview window.

Now you will use a preset to optimize this text for the Web. Typically, artwork with lots of solid colors and text are saved as GIF or PNG-8, but images, such as photographs, fare better in size and final appearance when saved in the JPEG or PNG-24 format. In this example, you will save all the slices as PNG-24 to assure a superior optimized copy of the original image.

5   In the Optimize panel, on the right, choose PNG-24 and keep all other settings the same.

You can individually select slices right in the Save for Web window and choose to export them in a different format or quality level.

Note that the file size of the optimized image, based on your current settings, is displayed at the bottom of the optimized image preview.

The file size of the optimized image.

6   Select the Preview in default browser button at the bottom of the Save for Web dialog box. If you have a default browser installed, your image is opened on a browser page. You can also define a browser using the Preview the optimized image drop-down menu in the lower-left corner of the Save for Web dialog box.

Notice that the slices are not apparent and the code is visible in your preview.

Preview the optimized image in a browser.

The slices you created for the navigation will not be working yet because this test page has not been saved into your lesson folder; it is just a temporary page.

7   Close the browser window to return to the Save for Web dialog box.

8   Choose Save; the Save Optimized As dialog box appears. Browse to the ps13lessons folder and choose HTML and Images from the Format drop-down menu. Click Save.

An HTML page, along with the sliced images, is saved in your ps13lessons folder. You can now open the file in Dreamweaver, or any other web editing program, and continue building the page, or copy and paste the table to another page.

9   Choose File > Save to save your original image. Choose File > Close to close the file.

Saving files for video

Photoshop can be a very useful tool for preparing images for use in video programs such as Adobe Premiere, After Effects, or other video editing programs such as Final Cut Pro. You might use Photoshop to create a still image to be used as a title or some other element within a video. In general, most Adobe programs work extremely well with the native PSD format and require no conversion.

When importing into a non-Adobe video application, you might need to consider the support for the PSD file format and for other properties, such as transparency. Each video application has its own set of rules, and you should check with the software manufacturer for details. For this lesson, you will open a pre-built file and save it as a TIFF with an alpha channel. Most video editing applications recognize alpha channels when defining transparent areas on an image.

1   Open the file **ps1302.psd**. The image that appears will be used as a transparent overlay in a video.

An image with a largely transparent bottom half.

2   If the Layers panel is not visible, choose Window > Layers to open the Layers panel.

3   Position your cursor over the layer thumbnail for the Shape 1 layer. Press and hold the Ctrl (Windows) or Command (Mac OS) key and click; this makes an active selection of the shape.

4   Press and hold the Ctrl+Shift (Windows) or Command+Shift (Mac OS) keys, and click the layer thumbnail for the layer called balloon. This adds the balloon layer to the selection.

Ctrl/Command+click the Shape 1 thumbnail to make a selection from a layer's contents.

5 If the Channels panel is not visible, choose Window > Channels to open the Channels panel.

6 Click the Save Selection as channel button () at the bottom of the Channels panel. This creates an alpha channel from the active selection.

Create an alpha channel from the selection.

In your alpha channel, the areas that are black are fully transparent, the areas that are white are fully opaque, and any areas that are gray will be varying degrees of transparency. This is the standard way that video editing applications treat alpha channels.

7 Choose File > Save As. When the Save As dialog box appears, navigate to the ps13lessons folder and type **ps1302_work** into the File name text field. Select TIFF from the Format drop-down menu.

8 In the Save Options section, make sure that Layers is deselected and Alpha Channels is selected. A warning stating that this image needs to be saved as a copy appears, which means that your original file will keep layers intact. Click Save. The TIFF Options dialog box appears.

9 In the TIFF Options dialog box, make sure that None is selected in the Image Compression section and select the Save Transparency check box If you see a warning about transparency support, click Yes. Click OK in the TIFF Options window. You have saved a TIFF file with an area that will appear transparent in your video editing application.

10 Close the original Photoshop document by choosing File > Close. If asked whether you would like to save the changes, choose not to save the file.

Creating animation

In this lesson, you will create an animation using the default animation panel. Photoshop CC has two modes for animation: the Frame mode and the Video timeline mode. Typically, you would use Frame mode to create animated gifs for use on the Web. The video timeline mode allows you more control and export options for video formats. You'll start with the simpler Frame mode first, and then work with the Video timeline.

Working in Frame mode

Working in the Frame mode of the animation panel is much like creating an animation using a flip book. When played, each frame is converted into a final animation. Using the Frame animation panel, you can build individual frames and then have Photoshop automatically create transitions between the frames for you. This process is called tweening. For this part of the lesson, you will add a floating hot air balloon to the image of the lake.

1   Choose File > Browse in Bridge and navigate to the ps13lessons folder. Select the images called **ps1303.psd** and **ps1304.psd**, then right-click (Windows) or Ctrl+click (Mac OS) and select Open from the context menu. An image of a lake and an image of a red hot air balloon open in separate document window tabs.

2   Select the Move tool (✛) and then click and drag the balloon image (ps1304.psd) to the tab for ps1303.psd. Keep holding the mouse until the image of the lake toggles into view. Drag the mouse down to make sure your cursor is over the lake image and then release the mouse to add the balloon layer to this document.

The balloon layer is added to the image of the lake.

3   Click the ps1304.psd image to make it active, and choose File > Close.

4 Choose Window > Timeline to open the Photoshop Timeline panel. Initially, a dialog box might appear in the middle of the timeline panel asking if you would like to Create a Video Timeline. Click and hold the arrow to the right and select Create Frame Animation.

Initially, you might be asked which timeline you want to use.

If you are already in the Video Timeline, click Convert to frame animation (□□□) control in the lower-left of the Timeline pane. If you see the Convert to video (⊟) timeline in the lower-right corner, you are already in the Frame timeline.

You will now create an animation by adding another frame, changing the position of the balloon, and then allowing Photoshop to build the intermediate frames automatically.

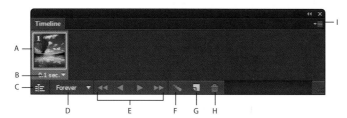

A. Key frame. B. Select frame delay time. C. Convert to video timeline.
D. Select looping options. E. Player controls. F. Tween animation frames.
G. Duplicate selected frames. H. Delete selected frames. I. Panel menu.

5   If the Layers panel is not visible, choose Window > Layers. Select the balloon layer to make sure it is the active layer. Then, using the Move tool, click and drag the balloon so it is in the lower-left corner of the lake image.

Position the balloon to be in the lower-left corner.

6   Type **15** to change the layer to a 15% opacity. You do not have to activate the Opacity text field to change an active layer's opacity when you have the Move tool selected.

7   Click the Duplicate selected frames button (⬚) at the bottom of the Animation panel. A second frame is added to the right of the original.

8   Verify that you still have the balloon layer selected. Then, using the Move tool, click and drag the balloon to the upper-right corner of the lake image. Type **0** (zero) to set the layer opacity at 100%.

9   Click the Add a layer style button (*fx*) at the bottom of the Layers panel, and choose Outer Glow from the list of styles. The Layer Style dialog box appears with Outer Glow selected.

10   In the Elements section of the Layer Style dialog box, click and drag the Size slider to the right until you reach approximately 70, or type **70** into the Size text field. Click OK. A glow has been applied to the balloon layer.

11   From the Animation panel menu, select Tween or click the Tween button (⬚) at the bottom of the Animation panel.

12 On the Tween menu, confirm that tweening is set to the Previous Frame and the Frames to Add is 5.

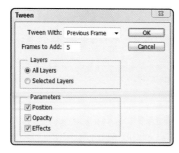

Choose to insert five frames in between the frames.

13 Click OK to add five frames to your animation. Photoshop interpolates the starting position, opacity, and layer style between the first frame and the 7th frame, thus creating an animation in which the balloon starts in the bottom-left and rises to the top-right.

In addition to the number of frames to add to the animation, the Tween menu gives you the ability to choose which layers to include in your frames and which parameters to animate. As the default, all layers and parameters are included.

14 Select all the frames of your animation by clicking the first frame, pressing and holding the Shift key, and clicking the last frame.

15 With all your frames selected, click the value for Selects frame delay at the bottom of any frame and select 0.5. Because all the frames are highlighted, the delay time of all your frames is adjusted.

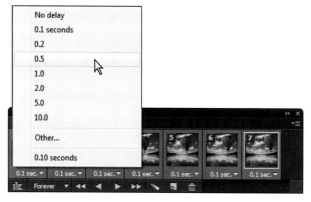

Select 0.5 as the frame delay time.

16 Click the Play button (▶) at the bottom of the Animation panel to preview your animation. If your animation continues to loop, press the Stop animation button (■) (same location as the Play button) to stop the animation.

As a default, your animation is set to replay over and over again. If you prefer to set the number of times your animation plays, click and hold the text Forever that appears in the lower-left corner of the animation panel and select Once, or choose Other to input a custom value.

17 Choose File > Save As. The Save As dialog box appears. Navigate to the ps13lessons folder and type **animation_done** in the File name text field. Choose Photoshop from the Format drop-down menu and click Save. Keep the file open for the next part of this lesson.

Saving an animated GIF

Now you will save the animation in a format that will recognize the frames and can be posted to the Web.

1 Choose File > Save for Web.

2 In the Save for Web dialog box, choose 2-up from the display tabs at the top of the dialog box. This allows you to see the original image next to a preview of the optimized image.

3 Choose GIF 128 Dithered from the Preset drop-down menu. This is a good preset to use for an animation with multiple colors. It creates a good balance between file size and image quality.

4 Click the Preview button in the lower left to see a preview of the animated GIF. In your own projects, this would be a good way to test your animation and then return to the Save for Web interface and make adjustments. For now, just close the browser.

5 Click the Save button to save your file as a GIF animation. Navigate to the ps13lesson folder and type **animation_done.gif** in the File name text field.

6 In the Format drop-down menu, choose Images Only and click Save.

7 Choose File > Save to save your file, then choose File > Close to close your Photoshop document.

8 To test your file, open any browser application and choose File > Open File, browse to locate your GIF, and then open it directly into your browser window.

Creating animation for HD video

For this part of the lesson, you will create a type of on-screen graphic called a lower third. Usually seen on television and in documentary-style films, a lower third is the text and graphics that usually appear on screen to introduce a speaker. The name comes from the fact that the text and graphic take up the lower third of the frame. To create the lower third, you'll bring a graphic into a blank document and animate its opacity parameter so it fades in. Then you'll render the video file so it can be imported into a high-definition video project.

Working in Timeline mode

The Timeline mode of the Animation panel functions differently from the Frame mode. In the Timeline mode, each layer has parameters for position, opacity, and effects that can have key frames assigned to them individually.

1   Choose File > New and choose Film & Video from the Preset drop-down menu. Click the size menu and choose the HDTV 1080p/29.97 option. This setting refers to the pixel resolution of most high-definition projects (1920 × 1080). Choose Transparent from the Background Contents drop-down menu. Click OK.

A warning dialog box might appear telling you that the pixel aspect ratio is for previewing purposes only. Click OK.

2   Choose View > New Guide. While the presets include guidelines to define the Action and Title safe areas of the video frame, there is nothing to indicate where your lower third should end.

3   In the New Guide dialog box, select the Horizontal radio button, type **66%** in the Position text field, and click OK. This creates a new guideline 66% from the top of your document and marks the lower third of the video frame.

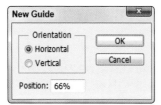

Create a guide indicating the lower third.

4   Choose File > Open and open **ps1305.psd** from the ps13lessons folder.

5   Select the Move tool (✛) and then click and drag the image (ps1305.psd) to the tab for your untitled document. Keep holding the mouse until the empty page toggles into view; make sure your cursor is over the image, and then release the mouse to add the lower third layer to this document. If an Aspect Ratio warning dialog box appears, click OK.

If you hold the Shift key down when moving images from one file to another, the content will automatically center on the canvas.

6   You can close the **ps1305.psd** file after you drag over the contents.

7   Position the graphic so it is below the lower third guide.

Position the graphic so it is below the lower third.

8   If the Layers panel is not open, choose Window > Layers. Layer 1 was created automatically when you created your document and you don't need it, so delete it by highlighting it in the Layers panel and dragging it to the Delete layer button (🗑) at the bottom of the panel.

9   If the Timeline panel is not open, choose Window > Timeline. Click the button labeled Create Video Timeline located in the middle of the Timeline panel; the video timeline appears. The video timeline in Photoshop CC supports basic editing, transitions, and the ability to add a music track.

10 Turn down the arrow to the left of the Wonderland video track layer in the Timeline panel to expose its properties.

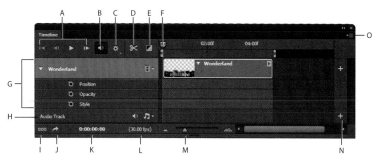

A. Player Controls. B. Mute Audio Playback. C. Set playback options. D. Split at Playhead.
E. Select a transition. F. Scrub to set time. G. Video Track Layers. H. Audio Track.
I. Convert to frame animation. J. Render Video. K. Scrub to set time. L. Frame Rate.
M. Control timeline magnification. N. Add Media to Track. O. Panel Menu.

What are properties?

When using the video timeline, every layer has a set of default properties for Position, Opacity, and Style. In Adobe Photoshop, animation information is stored in keyframes, which represent a change in at least one property over time. For example, if you want to have a circle move from left to right, the first keyframe would have a position property for the circle on the left and the second keyframe would have a position property for the circle on the right. Over a certain period of time, Photoshop moves the circle from one position to the other.

11 Click the Enable keyframe animation icon (⏱) next to the Opacity parameter to enable animation. A keyframe is created at the beginning of the Timeline.

Select the Enable keyframe animation to the left of Opacity to define an opacity keyframe.

If Enable keyframe animation is clicked off, it disables animation. A by-product of disabling the animation of a property is that all the keyframes for that property are deleted.

12 In the Layers panel, type **0** in the Opacity text field and press the Enter or Return key.

Adjust the opacity so the layer is not visible.

13 Double-click the Scrub to set time field (bottom left of Timeline panel). The Set Current Time dialog box appears. Type **3:00** and click OK. This moves your Current Time Indicator to the three-second mark on the Timeline. The Current Time Indicator (the blue wedge at the top of the Timeline) indicates your animation's current time. You can also drag the Current Time Indicator, but setting the time manually is more precise.

Double-click Scrub to set time and enter 3:00.

14 In the Layers panel, type **100** in the Opacity text field, and press Enter/Return. This creates a new keyframe where your Current Time Indicator is located.

This is the nature of timeline-based animation in Photoshop. If animation is enabled for a parameter, any change made to that parameter will create a new keyframe at the location of the Current Time Indicator.

15 Return the Current Time Indicator back to the starting point by clicking 0.0 at the beginning of the Timeline.

16 Press the Play button (▶) at the bottom of the Animation panel to preview the animation. The text fades in over three seconds. You can press the Stop button (■) when you are finished viewing the animation.

17 Choose File > Save As. The Save As dialog box appears. Navigate to the ps13lessons folder and type **ps1305_animation.psd** into the File name text field. Select Photoshop from the Format drop-down menu and click Save. Keep the file open for the next part of this lesson.

Rendering a video file

1 In the lower-left corner of the Timeline panel, click the arrow icon. This is the Render Video button and it will open the Render Video window. (You can also choose File > Export > Render Video.)

Note that the Render Video Window is divided into four areas: Location, File Options, Range, and Render Options.

Location: allows you to specify a name for the file that you are going to export and a location to save that file.

File Options: controls the type of file you want to create from your animation. Adobe Media Encoder is the default option here and gives you numerous options for choosing the format, size, and other parameters of the video file that you will export. The other option in this section is a Photoshop Image Sequence, which is a relatively specialized format that exports each frame of your video as an individual image file.

Range: controls the amount of the animation to export. By default, it will export the entire animation timeline, but you can limit the export range to lesser parts of the Timeline.

Render Options: controls whether an alpha channel is included in the output file along with the file's frame rate. Some exportable formats will not allow you to include an alpha channel.

2 In the Location name section, type **ps1305** into the Name text field. Click the Select Folder button, and navigate to the ps13lessons folder, then click OK or Choose.

3 In the File Options section, note that the Format is set to H.264. This format is the type of compression used, but there are a number of different Presets that determine the size and frame rate as well.

4 Click the Preset menu and choose Apple iPhone, iPod - 320x240 24. This will allow for quick rendering time.

5   In the Range section, make sure that the option button next to All Frames is selected.

Change the settings to render a small video.

6   Click the Render button to create your video file. The rendering time will vary, depending on your computer hardware.

7   Choose File > Close. You can return to the native Photoshop file to make edits at a later point, if necessary. You can test your file by navigating to the ps13lessons folder and selecting your **ps1305** file. It should open the QuickTime Player, and you can view your work in action.

Self study

1 Using the Frame mode in the Timeline panel, create a text layer and experiment with animating its position so it moves around your document.

2 Using the Timeline mode in the Timeline panel, experiment with animating the effects on a layer. Animate a drop-shadow so it moves over time.

Review

Questions

1 What is more important to note in an image size to be used on a web page, pixel dimensions or resolution?

2 When would you need to save a video file with an alpha channel?

3 Name four web image formats and provide an example of when to use each one.

Answers

1 It is more important to have the pixel dimensions of an image accurate, rather than the resolution. As a web and video creator, you would only use the top section of the Image Size dialog box.

2 An alpha channel is a way for applications to understand which parts of your video are transparent and which are opaque.

3 Four web image formats are:

   a. The JPEG format is used for saving photographs and other continuous-tone imagery.

   b. The GIF format is used for saving limited-tone imagery (images with lots of solid color) such as logos and other graphics. GIF supports transparency and animation.

   c. The PNG format is used for saving either photographic imagery or images with a lot of solid color. It can also support transparency in varying amounts.

   d. The WMBP format is used for saving images for mobile content devices, such as cell phones.

What you'll learn in this lesson:

- Isolating your layers
- Shake Reduction
- Live Shape Properties
- Scaling improvements

New Features in Photoshop CC

Photoshop has added many exciting new features in this version, such as the Shake Reduction filter, the ability to more easily isolate layers, use Camera Raw as a filter, edit your shape layers, and more. In this lesson, you get a quick review of what's new in Photoshop CC.

Starting up

If you are a new user, calling out the new Photoshop features may not be important to you, but this lesson is still helpful for you to review. If you have been using Photoshop for years, you will want to investigate the new features covered in this lesson to see if there are new, better ways for you to work in Photoshop.

In this lesson, you have the opportunity to try some of the new features in mini-exercises. This lesson covers some of the many new features, but keep in mind that each lesson in this book has also incorporated additional new features in the lessons as they apply to the task at hand. This lesson does not include questions and answers at the end.

Before starting, make sure your tools and panels are consistent by resetting your preferences. For more information, see "Resetting Adobe Photoshop CC preferences" in the Starting up section of this book.

You will work with several files from the ps14lessons folder in this lesson. Make sure that you have loaded the pslessons folder onto your hard drive from the supplied DVD. For more information, see "Loading lesson files" in the Starting up section of this book.

See Lesson 14 in action!

Use the accompanying video to gain a better understanding of how to use some of the features shown in this lesson. You can find the video tutorial for this lesson on the included DVD.

In this lesson, we will start with an image that was taken without the use of a tripod, so it is a little shaky. In addition to the shaky detail, it has a strong cast produced by the incandescent lighting that was used. In this first part of the lesson, you will select and isolate the layer that needs to be addressed, use the Camera Raw filter to correct it, and then use the new Shake Reduction filter in Photoshop CC (you'll find a new Sharpen Filter to address shake problems). You will then complete a composite image by masking your updated image.

Viewing the finished file

Before starting, you will look at the project in its finished form.

1   From Photoshop CC, choose File > Browse in Bridge and navigate to the ps14lessons folder. Select the image named **ps1401_done** and double-click it to open. An image of an old Land camera appears in a composited illustrative file.

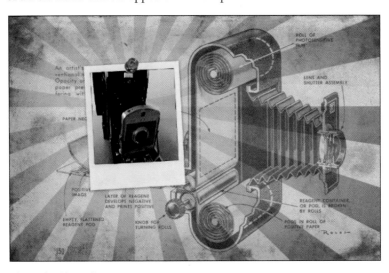

The completed lesson file.

2   You can leave this finished file open for reference, or you can close it by selecting File > Close.

3   Now you will open up the file that you will start with. Choose File > Browse in Bridge, locate the file named **ps1401.psd** and double-click it to open it in Photoshop. You see the start file that contains four layers.

4   Choose File > Save As; in the File name text field type **ps1401_work**. Make sure that you are saving into the ps14lessons folder, and then choose Save, leaving all other options the same. Keep this file open for the next part of this lesson.

Easier methods to manage your layers

By isolating a layer, you can focus on the active layer without sorting through all the other layers to make sure you are on the correct one. In Photoshop CC, you can now isolate a layer or group of layers using the Select menu. This isolate layer feature is essentially an extension of the Layer filter feature that was introduced in Photoshop CS6, and allows users to organize and find layers more easily.

1   Make sure that the layer named Camera is selected in the Layers panel, and then choose Select > Isolate Layers. Note that the other three layers disappear from the Layers panel.

2   To show the other layers, choose Select > Isolate layers again, since it is a toggle control.

In the Layers panel, you'll find a drop-down menu with the default of Selected.

3   Select Kind from the Pick a filter type drop-down menu. This filter allows you to choose the type of layer you want to isolate in the Layers panel. From the filters on the right, you can choose the following types of layers: Pixel layers, Adjustment layers, Type layers, Shape layers, and Smart Objects.

4   Make sure that you have the ability to turn on the layer filtering by verifying the Turn layer filtering toggle is turned on. The switch is in the up position when this filtering is turned on.

You can filter layers in the Layers panel.
A. Pixel. **B.** Adjustment. **C.** Type.
D. Shape. **E.** Smart Objects.
F. Turn layer filtering on.

5   You will now filter using the layer name. From the Pick a filter type drop-down menu in the layers panel, select Name; a text field appears to the right of the drop-down menu.

Select Name from the Pick a filter type drop-down menu.

6   Type **Print** to see that the layer with the name Blank Print appears.

7   Select Kind from the Pick a filter type drop-down menu to see all the layers again.

8   Keep this file open for the next part of this lesson.

You can also right-click (Windows) or Ctrl+click (Mac OS) when on the Move tool (✛) to access Isolate Layers.

Also, if you choose to isolate a collapsed layer group, you will not see the children in the Layers panel in the isolation mode. If you expand the layer group to show the children, and then choose Select > Isolate, you will see the children layers in the isolation mode.

Using Camera Raw as a filter

Previous versions of Photoshop included the Camera Raw component; now, Photoshop has added the Camera Raw filter in Photoshop CC. This filter allows you to access many of the helpful correction tools that were previously available only in the Camera Plug-in. Using the Camera Raw filter, you have many of the same options as the plug-in, though some have been removed because they don't apply to the filter workflow. The features that are removed from the Camera Raw Filter dialog box are Rotate, Crop, Save, Lens, and Camera profile to name a few. In this part of the lesson, you'll try out the filter to make two simple corrections. For more details about working in the Camera Raw, see Lesson 6, "Color Correcting an Image."

1   With **ps1401_work.psd** still open, select the Camera layer and then choose Filter > Convert for Smart Filters. This turns this layer into a Smart Object, thus allowing you to edit it again for a future use. For more details about Smart Objects, see Lesson 12, "Using Smart Objects in Photoshop."

   If a dialog box appears informing you that to enable re-editable smart filters the selected object with be converted to a Smart Object, click OK.

   The Camera layer is a low-quality image that you will use to try out some of the new tools in Photoshop CC.

2   Choose Filter > Camera Raw Filter. The Camera Raw dialog box appears. In this dialog box, you will adjust two items: the white point to balance the color, and the exposure to lighten the image a bit.

3   Select the White Balance tool (🖉) from the toolbar at the top of the Camera Raw dialog box. The White balance tool can be used to click an area in the image that is a shade of grey. By locating a grey or a neutral shade and clicking it with the White Balance tool, you can eliminate casts in the image relatively easy. Keep in mind that this is a quick correction technique; if you need more control, use the Curves panel.

4 With the White Balance tool selected, click the wall behind the camera. The yellowish-orange cast caused by the incandescent lighting is removed. You will now increase the exposure using the Radial filter.

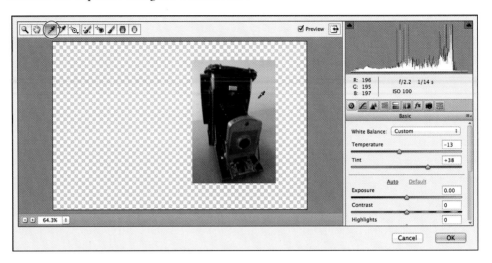

Select the White balance tool and click the wall to remove the color cast.

5 Select the Radial filter tool (0), press and hold Control+Shift (Windows) or Command+Shift (Mac OS), and then drag from the center of the lens of the camera until the edge of the radius reaches the right side of the image. By holding the Control/Command and Shift key, you can make a perfect circular radial filter selection from a center point. The Radial Filter acts as a vignette (or feathered) selection technique in the Camera Raw filter.

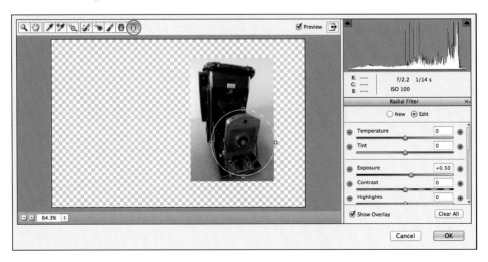

Make a selection in the image with the Radial Filter.

When the Radial Filter is selected, the options on the right change to reflect adjustments that you can make. Changes that you make in the Camera filter are dynamic and easily changed while you are still in this dialog box.

6   Click and drag the Exposure slider to the right until it reaches about +1.15, or type **1.15** into the Exposure text field. Notice that the outside of the selection is affected.

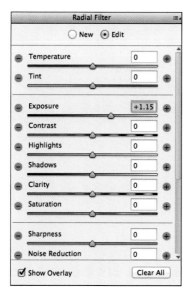

Increase the exposure slightly.

7   Scroll to the bottom of these options to change the results to affect the inside of the selection. Do this by selecting the Inside in the Effect section. This is also where you can change the amount of feathering. For this lesson, keep the feathering at 100.

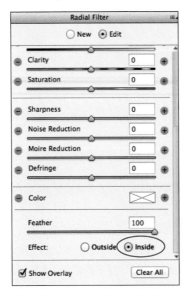

Change the exposure to affect the inside of the radial filter selection.

8   Now that you have made an adjustment, experiment with changing the Radial Filter selection. Make it larger or smaller; change it from a circle to an oblong shape. Work with the filter until you think it improves the exposure in the center part of the camera. No exact settings are necessary for this lesson.

9   Click OK, and choose File > Save. Keep this file open for the next part of this lesson.

Shake Reduction

In this part of the lesson, you'll try out the new Shake Reduction Filter, which is helpful when trying to reduce the effects of camera shake. It works best with images that have the following characteristics:

- Still camera captures

- Low noise or graininess

- Relatively good lighting (not too dark or light)

- Indoor images taken at a slow speed with no flash

- Images captured with long focal length shot both indoor and outdoor

- Forensics; great to use to improve the quality of text in an image

About Shake Reduction

Shake reduction is an incredible new feature available as a filter in Photoshop CC, but while it's a great tool, it does not solve all blurry image problems. Keep the following in mind when selecting images to use with this filter:

- The Shake Reduction filter does not work well with images that have specular highlights. (As discussed in Lesson 6, "Color Correcting an Image," specular highlights are very bright spots caused by shiny material and reflections of light.)

- The Shake reduction will not drastically improve a moving object in your image.

- It is best to use in a portion of your image, rather than apply the filter to the entire image.

1   With the **ps1401_work.psd** image still open, and the Camera layer still active, choose Filter > Sharpen > Shake Reduction. The Shake Reduction dialog box appears.

As soon as the Shake Reduction dialog box opens, the Shake Reduction filter auto-detects a problem area and begins to analyze the shape, size, and shake (motion) of the area. It then determines the best way to address motion, starting from the center of the selected area and moving out.

2   Double-click the center of the camera lens in the image to open the a detail Loupe view right above the area you clicked. Once you open the Loupe view, you can zoom in to enhance the shake reduction in that view (which is referred to as the loupe location).

Click and hold in the Detail view to turn off the preview; release to show the preview again. You can also press Q to dock and undock the Detail view.

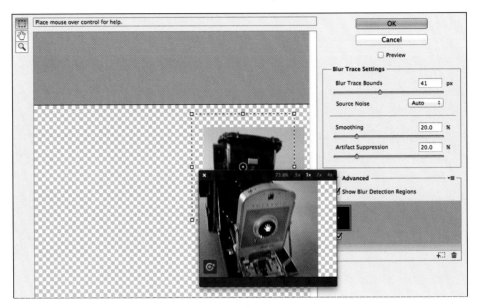

You can enhance just the Loupe view, or use it to zoom in and out of the area.

The shake reduction feature determines and makes automatic adjustments, but you have the ability to tweak them yourself using the Blur Trace Settings area in the Shake Reduction dialog box.

Here are the settings and what each affects:

- **Blur Trace Bounds**: Photoshop automatically figures out the amount of movement in pixels. You can manually adjust that amount when necessary.

- **Source Noise**: You can use this drop-down menu to manually override automatic source image noise detection.

- **Smoothing**: You can use the slider to manually adjust for smaller artifacts that occur with sharpening.

- **Artifact Suppression**: Larger halo like artifacts can be adjusted with this slider.

3   If your loupe preview is open, press **Q** or the "X" in the upper-left corner of the loupe window to re-dock it.

4   Turn the arrow down to the left of Advanced to see the Advanced section and also a selection area on top of the preview.

5   Use the handles on the selected area to center it on the front to the camera.

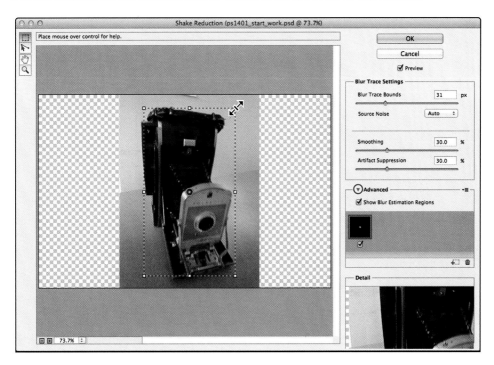

Select the Advanced section to create a selection.

6   You can experiment with the sliders and settings to see the effect they have on the preview. Don't worry about ruining the image; you will reset it in the next step.

7   Press and hold the Alt (Windows) or Option (Mac OS) key; note that OK changes into Reset. Click Reset; you are now at the original default settings.

8   You may have to drag your selection area to re-center it over the lens. Click OK.

9   Choose File > Save, and keep this file open for the next part of the lesson.

Finishing the image composition

You will now put your camera image into the image area of the instant camera border.

1   Turn off the visibility of the Camera layer so you can see the entire Blank Print layer by clicking the visibility icon (👁).

2   Click the Blank Print layer in the Layers panel to make sure it is the active layer.

3   Select the Magic Wand tool (✤); it is the hidden tool for the Quick Selection tool (✎).

4   Using the Magic Wand tool, click in the center of the black area of the blank print. The black area is active.

5   Save this selection for later use. Choose Select > Save Selection. In the Save Selection dialog box, type **Content** into the Name text field, and then click OK, leaving all the other settings at the defaults.

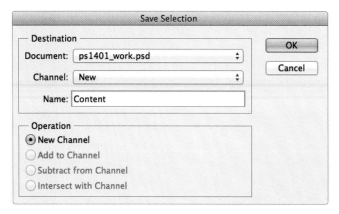

Create a selection for the print area and save it.

6   Choose Select > Deselect, or press Control+D (Windows) or Command+D (Mac OS).

7   Choose File > Save. Keep this file open for the next part of this lesson.

Putting the image into the print frame

In this next section, you will insert the image of the camera that you worked on into the picture frame. To do this, you will reselect your saved Content selection and apply it to your Print layer.

1   With the **ps1401_work** file still open, click the Camera layer to activate it.

2   Click the visibility icon (👁) to turn the visibility of the Camera layer back on.

3   Select the Move tool (✛) and reposition the image of the camera so it is on top of the blank photo frame.

4   Press Control+T (Windows) or Command+T (Mac OS) to transform this image. You might receive an error message alerting you to the fact that Smart filers will be temporarily disabled while you are transforming this layer; click OK.

Since the Smart Filters are disabled, your image might look different. This is fine; the image corrections you made earlier will return after you complete the resize and rotation of the image in the following steps.

5   Using the Transformation handles, press and hold the Shift key and click and drag inward any of the corners to make the camera image smaller. In our example, the image was scaled down to about 75%. You can also type **75** in the Width text field, and then click the Maintain aspect ratio chain icon (⊶) in the Options bar.

You can see the scale percentage in the Options bar at the top of the workspace.

6   Position the cursor outside the lower-right corner transformation handle and click and drag upwards towards the right; this rotates the layer content. In this example, the content was rotated about –2.5 degrees. You can also type **-2.5** in the Rotate text field in the Options bar. Select the Confirm check mark (✔) in the Options bar when you are finished transforming this layer.

You will most likely receive a Shake Reduction warning indicating that the current image size is different than the one you estimated with using the Shake Reduction filter. Click Yes to reset the blur trace for the present size.

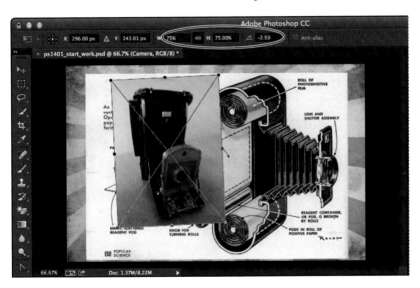

Transform the camera image so that it will fit in the blank picture frame.

7   With the Camera layer still active, choose Select > Load Selection to reload your selection; choose the Content selection. The selection is now active.

8   Stay on the Camera layer, and then click the Add layer mask button (▣) at the bottom of the Layers panel. The camera image is now inside the selection.

9   If you need to reposition the camera image inside the layer mask, unchain the mask from the camera image by clicking the chain icon (⧉) between the mask and the camera image in the Layers panel.

10 Click the Camera thumbnail (left of the mask) to activate only the camera image, not the mask, and then use the Move tool to reposition the image inside the mask.

Unchain the mask from the camera image and select the camera image.   *The image is cropped in the frame.*

11 Choose File > Save; keep this file open for the next part of the lesson.

Changing the Blending mode

Next you will perform the final step: changing the blending mode of the Illustration layer.

1 Select the Illustration layer.

2 From the Set the blending mode drop-down menu, choose Darken. Now only the parts of the Illustration layer that are darker than the underlying image appear.

3 Use the Opacity slider and drag to the left to about 50% or type **50** into the Opacity text field.

Make adjustment to the Illustration layer.   *The final lesson file.*

4 Choose File > Save and then File > Close to close this file.

Additional new features

Here are some other new features you might be interested in.

Live Shape properties

An outstanding new feature that will allow you to create more vector graphics in Photoshop is the new Live Shape Properties feature.

Now, when you create a vector shape, the Properties panel reflects properties that you can change, such as the fill, stroke, stroke width, actual width and height, and more. A favorite will definitely be the ability to change the corner radius of a rounded rectangle, even after you have created it. You can also change the size of each individual corner radius by unchecking the link icon in the corner radius section of the Properties panel.

In the Properties panels, you can more easily access the features that allow you to customize your shape by combining and subtracting shapes.

You can now customize a corner radius.   *The new Live Shape Properties feature.*

Upscaling improvements

As you went through the lessons in this book, you used the Image size window quite frequently. You should know that the Photoshop team has added a new Edge-Preserving Upscaling Algorithm that improves sharpness and preserves detail when enlarging images. This includes a slider for reducing noise that results from detail enhancement. This does not mean that you shouldn't try to use images that do not have to be scaled up in size; it means that if you have to, the results will be much better.

If you are scaling up in size, make sure to choose the resampling method called Preserve Details (enlargement).

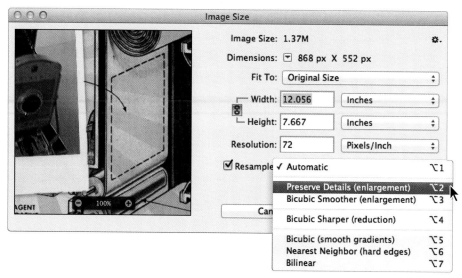

Improvements to help you scale images up in size have been added.

Share on Behance

If you have an online portfolio set up with Behance.com, you can now upload your creative work immediately to this website by selecting File > Share on Behance.

This lesson introduced you to some of the new features; and all of them are included in this book. Many of the new features are built into the lesson files to help you discover how to apply them immediately.

Appendix A

Top Photoshop Keyboard Shortcuts

Time-saving shortcuts that will help you work faster.

Keyboard shortcuts to access tools

TOOL	WINDOWS AND MAC OS
Move tool	V
Rectangular Marquee tool Elliptical Marquee tool	M Shift + M to switch tools
Lasso tool Polygonal Lasso tool Magnetic Lasso tool	L Shift+ L to switch tools
Magic Wand tool Quick Selection tool	W Shift + W to switch tools
Crop tool Slice tool Slice Select tool	C Shift + C to switch tools
Eyedropper tool Color Sampler tool Ruler tool Note tool Count tool*	I Shift + I to switch tools
Spot Healing Brush tool Healing Brush tool Patch tool Red Eye tool	J Shift + J to switch tools
Brush tool Pencil tool Color Replacement tool Mixer Brush tool	B Shift + B to switch tools
Clone Stamp tool Pattern Stamp tool	S Shift + S to switch tools
History Brush tool Art History Brush tool	Y Shift + Y to switch tools
Eraser tool Background Eraser tool Magic Eraser tool	E Shift + E to switch tools

Keyboard shortcuts to access tools

TOOL	WINDOWS AND MAC OS
Gradient tool Paint Bucket tool	G Shift + G to switch tools
Dodge tool Burn tool Sponge tool	O Shift +O to switch tools
Pen tool Freeform Pen tool	P Shift + P to switch tools
Horizontal Type tool Vertical Type tool Horizontal Type mask tool Vertical Type mask tool	T Shift + T to switch tools
Path Selection tool Direct Selection tool	A Shift + A to switch tools
Rectangle tool Rounded Rectangle tool Ellipse tool Polygon tool Line tool Custom Shape tool	U Shift + U to switch tools
3D Object Rotate tool* 3D Object Roll tool* 3D Object Pan tool* 3D Object Slide tool* 3D Object Scale tool*	K Shift + K to switch tools
3D Camera Rotate tool* 3D Camera Roll tool* 3D Camera Pan tool* 3D Camera Walk tool* 3D Camera Zoom*	N Shift + N to switch tools
Hand tool	H
Rotate View tool	R
Zoom tool	Z

Painting and Retouching

FUNCTION	WINDOWS	MAC OS
Return to default Black foreground and white background	D	D
Sample color when painting tool is active	Option (with painting tool selected)	Option (with painting tool selected)
Make brush size larger (next Brush)	Ctrl+] (right bracket)	Command+] (right bracket)
Make brush size smaller (previous brush)	Ctrl+[(right bracket)	Command+[(right bracket)
Make brush harder	Shift+Ctrl+] (right bracket)	Command+] (right bracket)
Make brush softer	Shift+Ctrl+[(left bracket)	Command+[(left bracket)
Switch color ramp (Color pane) color mode	Shift+click on color ramp	Shift+click on color ramp
Erase to History	Alt	Option

Layers

FUNCTION	WINDOWS	MAC OS
Cut selection and put on new layer	Ctrl+J	Command+J
Copy selection to new layer	Shift+Ctrl+J	Shift+Command+J
Turn Background into Layer 0	Alt+double-click on Background thumbnail	Option+double-click on Background thumbnail
Create a new layer	Shift+Ctrl+N	Shift+Ctrl+N
Auto-select layer	Move tool+Ctrl+click on layer content	Move tool+Command+click on layer content
Clone a layer	Move tool+Alt+Drag	Move tool+Option+Drag

Viewing and Navigating

FUNCTION	WINDOWS	MAC OS
Cycle through open documents	Control + Tab	Control + Tab
Switch to previous document	Shift + Control + Tab	Shift + Command + `
Close a file in Photoshop and open Bridge	Shift-Control-W	Shift-Command-W
Toggle between Standard mode and Quick Mask mode	Q	Q
Toggle (forward) between Standard screen mode, Full screen mode with menu bar, and Full screen mode	F	F
Toggle (backward) between Standard screen mode, Full screen mode with menu bar, and Full screen mode	Shift + F	Shift + F
Toggle (forward) canvas color	Space + F (or right-click canvas background and select color)	Space + F (or Control-click canvas background and select color)
Toggle (backward) canvas color	Space + Shift + F	Space + Shift + F
Fit image in window	Double-click Hand tool	Double-click Hand tool
Magnify 100%	Double-click Zoom tool or Ctrl + 1	Double-click Zoom tool or Command + 1
Switch to Hand tool (when not in text-edit mode)	Spacebar	Spacebar
Simultaneously pan multiple documents simultaneously with Hand tool	Shift-drag	Shift-drag
Switch to Zoom In tool	Control + spacebar	Command + spacebar
Switch to Zoom Out tool	Alt + spacebar	Option + spacebar
Move Zoom marquee while dragging with the Zoom tool	Spacebar-drag	Spacebar-drag
Apply zoom percentage, and keep zoom percentage box active	Shift + Enter in Navigator panel zoom percentage box	Shift + Return in Navigator panel zoom percentage box
Zoom in on specified area of an image	Control-drag over preview in Navigator panel	Command-drag over preview in Navigator panel

Viewing and Navigating

FUNCTION	WINDOWS	MAC OS
Temporarily zoom into an image	Hold down H and then click in the image and hold down the mouse button	Hold down H and then click in the image and hold down the mouse button
Scroll image with Hand tool	Spacebar-drag, or drag view area box in Navigator panel	Spacebar-drag, or drag view area box in Navigator panel
Scroll up or down 1 screen	Page Up or Page Down†	Page Up or Page Down†
Scroll up or down 10 units	Shift + Page Up or Page Down†	Shift + Page Up or Page Down†
Move view to upper-left corner or lower right corner	Home or End	Home or End
Toggle layer mask on/off as rubylith (layer mask must be selected)	\ (backslash)	\ (backslash)

Miscellaneous

FUNCTION	WINDOWS	MAC OS
Image Size	Alt+Ctrl+I	Option+Command+I
Change Cancel (in dialog box) to Reset	Alt	Option
Revert to Saved	F12	F12
Step Backward (multiple undo) Alt+Ctrl+Z	Option+Command+Z	
Step forward	Shift+Ctrl+Z	Shift+Command+Z

Keys for blending modes

RESULT	WINDOWS	MAC OS
Cycle through blending modes	Shift + + (plus) or – (minus)	Shift + + (plus) or – (minus)
Normal	Shift + Alt + N	Shift + Option + N
Dissolve	Shift + Alt + I	Shift + Option + I
Behind (Brush tool only)	Shift + Alt + Q	Shift + Option + Q
Clear (Brush tool only)	Shift + Alt + R	Shift + Option + R
Darken	Shift + Alt + K	Shift + Option + K
Multiply	Shift + Alt + M	Shift + Option + M
Color Burn	Shift + Alt + B	Shift + Option + B
Linear Burn	Shift + Alt + A	Shift + Option + A
Lighten	Shift + Alt + G	Shift + Option + G
Screen	Shift + Alt + S	Shift + Option + S
Color Dodge	Shift + Alt + D	Shift + Option + D
Linear Dodge	Shift + Alt + W	Shift + Option + W
Overlay	Shift + Alt + O	Shift + Option + O
Soft Light	Shift + Alt + F	Shift + Option + F
Hard Light	Shift + Alt + H	Shift + Option + H
Vivid Light	Shift + Alt + V	Shift + Option + V
Linear Light	Shift + Alt + J	Shift + Option + J
Pin Light	Shift + Alt + Z	Shift + Option + Z
Hard Mix	Shift + Alt + L	Shift + Option + L
Difference	Shift + Alt + E	Shift + Option + E
Exclusion	Shift + Alt + X	Shift + Option + X
Hue	Shift + Alt + U	Shift + Option + U
Saturation	Shift + Alt + T	Shift + Option + T
Color	Shift + Alt + C	Shift + Option + C
Luminosity	Shift + Alt + Y	Shift + Option + Y
Desaturate	Sponge tool + Shift + Alt + D	Sponge tool + Shift + Option + D

Keys for blending modes

RESULT	WINDOWS	MAC OS
Saturate	Sponge tool + Shift + Alt + S	Sponge tool + Shift + Option + S
Dodge/burn shadows	Dodge tool/Burn tool + Shift + Alt + S	Dodge tool/Burn tool + Shift + Option + S
Dodge/burn midtones	Dodge tool/Burn tool + Shift + Alt + M	Dodge tool/Burn tool + Shift + Option + M
Dodge/burn highlights	Dodge tool/Burn tool + Shift + Alt + H	Dodge tool/Burn tool + Shift + Option + H
Set blending mode to Threshold for bitmap images, Normal for all other images	Shift + Alt + N	Shift + Option + N

Index

layers, 213, 220–222, 266

PSD (Photoshop document), 50

Q

Quick Mask feature, 13, 102–105
Quick Selection tool (W), 13, 99–
    100, 196, 253–254, 259, 385
QuickTime player, 373

R

Radial filter tool, 380
reading histograms, 163–164
Rectangle tool (U), 14
Rectangular Marquee tool, 86–87
Red-Eye Removal feature (E), 182–
    183, 185
redo option, 22
reducing thumbnails, 62
Refine Edge button, 254
Refine Edge dialog box, 100–101,
    254
Refine Edge feature, 97, 100–102,
    253–257
Refine Radius tool, 255–256
Refine Selection dialog box, 118
refining adjustment layer masks,
    271–274
removing
    background, 247
    red eye, 182–183
rendering video files, 372–373
reopening
    Curves panel, 85
    DNG files, 189
    images, 270
repairing fold lines, 147–148
replacing contents of Smart Object
    layers, 330–332

replaying of animation, 367
repositioning text on Web pages, 346
resetting preferences, 3–4
resizing thumbnails, 62
Resources, 8
retouching. *see also* painting
    color settings, 120
    images
        Clone Source panel, 153–155
        Clone Stamp tool, 145–146
        cloning from other sources, 156–
            157
        Healing Brush, 150–151
        History panel, 149
        overview, 145
        Patch tool, 152–153
        repairing fold lines, 147–148
        Spot Healing Brush, 150
    tools, 14
review
    Adobe Bridge, 79
    basics, 56
    images, 191
    layers, 236, 293
    painting, 158
    retouching, 158
    selections, 118
    Smart Objects, 339–340
    Web and video production, 374
    workspaces, 35–36
RGB color mode
    overview, 121
    reasons for using, 162
    working in, 122–123
rotating images, 185
rule of thirds gird, 40–43
ruler, on-screen, 195

S

S (Clone Stamp tool)
  overview, 14, 145–146
  repairing fold lines, 147–148
S (Color Sampler tool), 185
Save Adobe PDF dialog box, 55
Save As dialog box
  applying color, 139
  Black & White adjustment layer, 279
  brushes, 134
  Clone Stamp tool, 145
  Content-Aware Move, 200
  copying and pasting, 107
  creating
    compositions, 220
    Web pages, 345
  Frame mode, 367
  Lasso tool, 93
  Magic Wand tool, 91
  Marquee tools, 83
  opening files, 161
  Pen tool, 111, 113
  Quick Mask, 103
  red eye, 182
  Refine Edge feature, 100
  saving
    DNG files, 189
    files for video, 362
    JPEG files, 51
    Photoshop PDF files, 55
  Smart Objects, 318
  Timeline mode, 372
Save dialog box, 3, 329
Save For Web dialog box, 357, 360, 367
Save For Web feature, 357–360
Save Optimized As dialog box, 360
Save Options dialog box, 189

Save Path dialog box, 112
saving
  animated GIF, 367
  collections, 73–74
  files
    DNG, 188–189
    JPEG, 51
    overview, 49–50
    Photoshop PDF, 55
    for video, 360–362
  layer styles, 291
  for print, 51
  selections, 105–106
  workspace, 25
scaling Background, 197–198
scaling Smart Objects, 322
screen modes, maximizing
    productivity with, 33–35
Scrubby Zoom, 30, 249
searching files, 70–71
selecting
  colors, 126–128
  file formats, 51
  image areas, 111–113
  layers
    overview, 211
    tips for, 211–212
  slices, 354–355
  Web image formats, 358
selection tools, 13, 299
selections
  adding to, 96
  changing
    into layers, 90–91
    paths to selections, 117
  copying and pasting, 107

John Wiley & Sons, Inc.
End-User License Agreement

5. Limited Warranty.

(a) WILEY warrants that the Software and Software Media are free from defects in materials and workmanship under normal use for a period of sixty (60) days from the date of purchase of this Book. If WILEY receives notification within the warranty period of defects in materials or workmanship, WILEY will replace the defective Software Media.

(b) WILEY AND THE AUTHOR(S) OF THE BOOK DISCLAIM ALL OTHER WARRANTIES, EXPRESS OR IMPLIED, INCLUDING WITHOUT LIMITATION IMPLIED WARRANTIES OF MERCHANTABILITY AND FITNESS FOR A PARTICULAR PURPOSE, WITH RESPECT TO THE SOFTWARE, THE PROGRAMS, THE SOURCE CODE CONTAINED THEREIN, AND/OR THE TECHNIQUES DESCRIBED IN THIS BOOK. WILEY DOES NOT WARRANT THAT THE FUNCTIONS CONTAINED IN THE SOFTWARE WILL MEET YOUR REQUIREMENTS OR THAT THE OPERATION OF THE SOFTWARE WILL BE ERROR FREE.

(c) This limited warranty gives you specific legal rights, and you may have other rights that vary from jurisdiction to jurisdiction.

6. Remedies.

(a) WILEY's entire liability and your exclusive remedy for defects in materials and workmanship shall be limited to replacement of the Software Media, which may be returned to WILEY with a copy of your receipt at the following address: Software Media Fulfillment Department, Attn.: *Adobe Photoshop CC Digital Classroom*, John Wiley & Sons, Inc., 10475 Crosspoint Blvd., Indianapolis, IN 46256, or call 1-800-762-2974. Please allow four to six weeks for delivery. This Limited Warranty is void if failure of the Software Media has resulted from accident, abuse, or misapplication. Any replacement Software Media will be warranted for the remainder of the original warranty period or thirty (30) days, whichever is longer.

(b) In no event shall WILEY or the author be liable for any damages whatsoever (including without limitation damages for loss of business profits, business interruption, loss of business information, or any other pecuniary loss) arising from the use of or inability to use the Book or the Software, even if WILEY has been advised of the possibility of such damages.

(c) Because some jurisdictions do not allow the exclusion or limitation of liability for consequential or incidental damages, the above limitation or exclusion may not apply to you.

7. U.S. Government Restricted Rights.
Use, duplication, or disclosure of the Software for or on behalf of the United States of America, its agencies and/or instrumentalities "U.S. Government" is subject to restrictions as stated in paragraph (c)(1)(ii) of the Rights in Technical Data and Computer Software clause of DFARS 252.227-7013, or subparagraphs (c) (1) and (2) of the Commercial Computer Software - Restricted Rights clause at FAR 52.227-19, and in similar clauses in the NASA FAR supplement, as applicable.

8. General.
This Agreement constitutes the entire understanding of the parties and revokes and supersedes all prior agreements, oral or written, between them and may not be modified or amended except in a writing signed by both parties hereto that specifically refers to this Agreement. This Agreement shall take precedence over any other documents that may be in conflict herewith. If any one or more provisions contained in this Agreement are held by any court or tribunal to be invalid, illegal, or otherwise unenforceable, each and every other provision shall remain in full force and effect.

Register your Digital Classroom book for exclusive benefits

Registered owners receive access to:

 The most current lesson files

 Technical resources and customer support

 Notifications of updates

 Online access to video tutorials

 Downloadable lesson files

 Samples from other Digital Classroom books

Register at *DigitalClassroomBooks.com/CC/Photoshop*

DigitalClassroom

Register your book today at
DigitalClassroomBooks.com/CC/Photoshop